F. Nolan   3.95

D1615216

The Northern Music Hall

By the same Author:
POM-POMS AND RUFFLES
PICTURE PIONEERS

FRANK GRAHAM
6 Queen's Terrace, Newcastle upon Tyne, 2

LEONARD SACHS — "AT ENORMOUS EXPENSE!"

THE NORTHERN MUSIC HALL

by
G. J. MELLOR

A Century of Popular Entertainment:
Introduced by KEN DODD *and with a Foreword by*
GEORGE WOOD, O.B.E. (*'Wee Georgie Wood'*).

To All who love Music Hall

Printed By Howe Brothers Limited, Swan Street, Gateshead.

Contents

List of Illustrations

Frontispiece: 'AT ENORMOUS EXPENSE!'—Leonard Sachs introduces the Programme 'THE GOOD OLD DAYS'.

Plate

1 THE OLD TIME HALLS—A look at the old Star at Bolton and the Sheffield Surrey, many years ago.

2 LONDON TOWN—Famous Halls of the Metropolis await your inspection.

3 DANCING GIRLS—The Balmbra Girls show a leg, together with La Pia and Veronica.

4 CAN-CAN!—High kicks by the Gaiety Girls at the Leeds City Varieties.

5 HALLS OF FAME—A look inside the famous Leeds City Varieties and the London Palladium.

6 MORE FAMOUS HALLS—Buildings at Glasgow, Manchester and Hull command your attention.

7 THE FABULOUS POPPLEWELLS—Eric and Leslie show you the Gaiety Theatre, Ayr, with a backward glance at the 'Dandy Militaires'.

8 'LADIES AND GENTLEMEN!'—The Lancashire Lassies and the Yorkshire Pierrots parade for your approval.

9 MUSIC, MUSIC, MUSIC!—Talbot O'Farrell does a bit of song plugging, assisted by Jack Judge, Bert Feldman and Lawrence Wright.

10 DOWN MEMORY LANE—George Burton and his Bohemians take you back to the South Shields of 1909.

11 I SAY! I SAY! I SAY!—Ken Dodd and Freddie Frinton show you how they began in Concert Party.

12 BESIDE THE SEASIDE—Some popular favourites of Yesterday at Blackpool and Scarborough.

13 LAUGHTER MAKERS—George Robey, Albert Whelan and the two George Formby's smile especially for you.

14 FEMININE FAVOURITES—Daisy Dormer, Gertie Gitana, Nellie Wallace and Mona Vivian look their best for the occasion.

15 OUR GRACIE—Gracie Fields, in her Farewell Tour of 1965, looks at a picture of herself, an old play-bill, and hears the fate of the old Theatre Royal at Rochdale.

Foreword

by GEORGE WOOD, O.B.E.

('Wee Georgie Wood')

THE AUTHOR G. J. Mellor is the Yorkshire writer whose book 'Pom-Poms and Ruffles' is acknowledged the best and most readable account of the performers and places of Pierrots and Concert Parties.

Photo: WHITLEY BAY GUARDIAN.

Now, in his latest work, 'The Northern Music Hall', the entertainment once accepted as 'The British Way of Life', he takes us back to 1860 and presents a panorama of those who built what J. B. Priestley calls 'Lost Empires', through the Golden Age of Variety to 1960 when the calls of 'Encore' gave way to the Bingo caller.

With many unique illustrations, this is not just another book on Music Hall, but a 'must' for all those who would wish to know how the North of England, with its showmen and performers, made it possible for the South and the entire British Isles to enjoy the Music Hall.

Introduction

by KEN DODD

Geoff:

Thank you most sincerely for letting me see your most plumpshus and tatty-philarious book—here's to the next one!

—*Ken Dodd*

P.S.—Old comedians never 'die' (or so they tell you!).

Photo: B. FEARNLEY, F.I.I.P., F.R.P.S.

The Stars ... The Halls ... The Memories

'Who is to write the History of the Music Hall? What a splendid theme: and what a lot of material is available ... What a grand evolution could be explained and elaborated ...'

SO WROTE Scots Historian John Robertson many years ago.

It would hardly be true to say that I read that passage and then set about the challenge it contained. But I did feel at the time, with a strange feeling of sentiment and nostalgia, that the gay, robust and slightly vulgar world of Music Hall was dying out and no one seemed to be doing very much about it.

The time was 1950 and I resolved to read everything I could lay my hands on about the Music Hall. It occurred to me that while it would be comparatively easy to concentrate upon the history of one particular theatre, to write about the Music Hall in general was a different matter.

As W. MacQueen Pope had observed:

'Music Hall was not one place, one particular hall; it was hundreds of different centres of amusement scattered all over the British Isles ...

'Certain music halls had personalities of their own, just as theatres have, but by and large they were all much of a pattern. There was never the clear demarcation that exists between the West End and the Provincial Theatres. You would see the identical performers in the music halls of the provincial cities that you saw in the West End ...

'Music Hall had no fixed home, no pivotal centre. That is why its history is so difficult to encompass.'

One thing struck me very forcibly about all the books I read on Music Hall. They were invariably all about London ...

The writers it seemed concentrated upon one aspect only of the subject. Their books contained chapter and chapter again on how

Charles Morton 'The Father of the Halls' founded the Canterbury Music Hall in the Westminster Bridge Road, while the great halls of the Metropolis were described in detail—the Oxford, the Alhambra and the Empire—but I found scarcely a word about the many provincial halls which, I felt sure, must have been equally interesting.

Come to think of it, all the really big names in Music Hall came from the North Country: Moss started in Greenock; Stoll and De Frece in Liverpool; Barrasford in Jarrow; Frank Allen and Richard Thornton in South Shields, and Frank MacNaghten in Sheffield.

Their story had never been told and here I felt *was* a challenge.

Yes, that was it—how the Music Hall magnates from the Industrial North invaded the Metropolis—the Mecca that was their goal . . .

In 1950 what remained of the old places of entertainment seemed to be in danger of dying out (in spite of a post-war revival which I felt would not last) and events proved me right.

Another thing that struck me was that the generation who had lived through the Golden Age of Music Hall were also dying out—and their memories with them.

And so it came about that I resolved to tackle the History of the Music Hall from a new angle. In the course of my interviews and enquiries several interesting facts came to light. Those facets of Music Hall history which always seemed so dear and exclusive to the London area, all had their counterparts in the Provinces.

I found three 'Canterbury Music Halls' in the North—at Middlesbrough, Hull and Sheffield (or rather, that there had been in years gone by)—even an Evans' Song and Supper Room in Liverpool and bless me, if there had not been an old theatre proprietor in Hull called Morton who had lived to be a hundred!

When I started to write this book I wondered if there would be enough material. I need not have worried. In the end it turned out there was too much and the problem was who and what should be left out . . .

Many sources of information have been tapped in the compilation of this work and many interviews conducted. (It is only possible to mention a few of them in the 'Acknowledgments' at the back of this book.)

Of course no one person could have lived through a century of entertainment and have observed everything, but the book is written that way, which seemed to be the best approach to the subject.

As the writer has had no connection with performing in the music halls, this is no collection of personal reminiscences. It is, however, a collection of the memories of many people, most of which are appearing in print for the first time. These memories are supplemented by references to newspaper reports of the day, together with other data, with the object of ensuring accuracy as far as is possible.

But enough of this, read the book for yourself. Read how those ruthless Northern entrepreneurs bull-dozed their way South to the Metropolis—and what happened to their hopes and dreams when they got there . . .

As other bull-dozers grind the grinning cherubs to dust, as super-markets go up on the music hall sites, the auditoriums reverberate to canned nasal accents or the chant of the Bingo caller, read on about the simple, carefree days when a night for entertainment meant a night out. In fact a night at the Music Hall instead of a huddle round a television screen.

Here is a collection of information about the last hundred years of entertainment, from the beginnings to the Golden Age of Music Hall, then, alas, to the decline . . .

Music Hall is dead . . . Long Live Music Hall . . .

1

The Good Old Days

MUSIC HALL—in fact the British Music Hall in general—had its origins in the 'harmonic rooms' or song taverns attached to inns and licensed premises.

Some were modest affairs, just an up-turned box or dais for the artistes, with the customers sitting drinking at small tables round the room. Admission as a rule was by form of Refreshment Check (or 'Wet Money') so-called because it was returnable by drink to the value of the check. Singers, comedians and other entertainers were engaged by the landlords of these inns to entertain and draw clients into the 'singing room'. Many old-time 'stars' began in this way, usually at a very modest salary. Later on, the singing room (or 'music hall') in many cases grew more important than the inn to which it was attached and the latter lapsed into obscurity.

Although the main purpose of this work is to describe the music hall period between 1860 and 1960 (the hundred years in which it can be said to have existed) there were several establishments in being long before that, just as there are a few survivors today.

The Star Music Hall at Bolton, Lancashire (which came into existence in 1832 attached to the Millstones Inn, in Deansgate) was one of, if not *the* first true 'Music Halls' in the country. Other early provincial halls were the Adelphi at Sheffield, which started as a circus in 1837; the Rodney Music Hall in Birmingham, 1840; the Britannia at Huddersfield, dating from 1842, and Thornton's Varieties in Leeds, established by the proprietor of that name in 1857, although there was probably a 'harmonic room' attached to the White Swan Inn long before that.

*   *   *   *

Charles Morton 'The Father of the Halls' is usually credited with the establishment of the first 'Music Hall' in the Metropolis, when he acquired the Canterbury Arms in the Westminster Bridge Road in 1849 and opened there a successful Song and Supper Room. This hall opened in 1852 and was enlarged two years later, as a 'Music Hall'.

17

Prior to that there had been Song and Supper Rooms in the early 1800's at Evans', in Covent Garden. (Evans retired in 1844 when the place was known as 'Evans', late Joys'.) Not far away were two other establishments in the Coal Hole in Fountains Court and the Cyder Cellars in Maiden Lane. Noteworthy is the fact that a branch of Evans' was opened in Liverpool (in Upper Dawson Street) which gained a reputation for succulent steaks as well as good entertainment.

Early in 1859 Wilton's Music Hall opened in Whitechapel. This was in Wellclose Square and also known as 'The Mahogany Bar' on account of its fine furnishings. The proprietor was John Wilton, licensee of the adjacent Prince of Wales' public house. (Incidentally, this music hall building is still in existence.)

In 1860 the original South London Palace opened its doors, in December of that year, with the great E. W. Mackney topping a big bill. Edward Villiers was responsible for the South London Palace, which stood near the Elephant and Castle. The interior resembled a Roman Villa before it was damaged by fire in 1869. Then it was sold to the Poole family, before it finally became one of the 'Syndicate Halls'.

Also in 1860 an energetic Hebrew named Harry Hart established the Raglan at Bloomsbury (later the scene of a big fire) and the following year the original Bedford at Camden Town. This hall was immortalised by Sickert in a series of paintings, before it was replaced by the new Bedford Palace around the turn of the century. Later Harry Hart ran the Star at Bermondsey.

Also going strong at this time was the Surrey Music Hall attached to the Grapes Tavern in the Southwark Bridge Road. This later became the Winchester to avoid confusion with the Surrey Theatre in the Blackfriars Road.

At Islington John Deacon's Music Hall was established in 1861, with Fred Williams as Chairman. Here Arthur Roberts, the comedian, made his first London appearance. Deacon's was swept away in the making of Rosebery Avenue, in 1891.

The original London Pavilion was opened in 1861 by one Loibl as a cafe chantant. It housed waxworks and other amusements before it was enlarged as a music hall in 1885 by Edward Villiers who later sold out to the Syndicate Halls. Later the home of variety and revue under the great Sir Charles B. Cochran, it was again remodelled in 1918, before its final phase as a West End cinema in 1934.

Also in 1861 the Oxford Music Hall opened in Oxford Street, run by Charles Morton of the Canterbury. The Oxford was built

on the site of an old posting house known as the Boar and Castle
and Emily Soldene was one of the first artistes on view. It was
described as 'a magnificent structure in the Italian style' before it
was damaged by fire in 1872, after which it was rebuilt on a larger
scale. In 1892 James Kirk sold it to the 'Syndicate Halls' run by
George Adney Payne, before he went to Glasgow to become
associated with the Gaiety and the Scotia there. The Oxford was
demolished in 1928 to make way for a Lyons' Corner House.

A rival of the Oxford in the early days was Weston's in Holborn.
This had grown out of the Punchbowl Tavern and Edward Weston,
formerly a bar-cellarman, had turned it into Weston's Music Hall.
In 1869 it was rebuilt and enlarged as the Royal. Finally Walter
Gibbons turned it into the Holborn Empire, later run by Moss
Empires, before it was bombed in the 1939–45 War.

The Marylebone Music Hall attached to the Rose of Normandy
Tavern was opened by Sam Vagg (alias Collins) in 1861 and not
far away was the White Lion (or 'Turnham's') in the Edgware
Road. This was reconstructed in 1862 as the Metropolitan Music
Hall and was to last exactly a century, being the last London
music hall outside the West End when it finally closed. In 1892
Henri Gros bought it and, after alterations, it became one of the
Syndicate Halls, running in conjunction with the Oxford, Tivoli,
etc. Finally, it was run by a combine known as Variety Theatres
Consolidated.

The said Sam Vagg, who had been 'discovered' at Morton's
Canterbury Hall, singing 'The Rocky Road to Dublin', and was at
one time a chimney sweep, changed his name to Collins and
acquired the Lansdowne Arms at Islington Green. This was in
1862 and the hall was always known as 'The Chapel on the Green'.
It was remodelled in 1897 and the electric light installed, later
being run by the Barney Richards syndicate, and later still by Lew
Lake who had appeared there with his 'Bloomsbury Burglars'
early in the century. Collins Music Hall was damaged by fire in
1958 and not restored.

Reverting to the old Canterbury; Morton had vacated this place
soon after opening the Oxford, and in 1867 the Westminster Bridge
Road house passed into the hands of William Holland, the self-
styled 'Peoples' Caterer'. Holland, later associated with the Albert
Palace at Battersea and the Winter Gardens in Blackpool, expen-
sively decorated the Canterbury. One of the prize fitments was an
allegedly 1,000-guinea carpet, which the 'Peoples' Caterer' advertised as being for people to spit upon! When Holland went to
Battersea, control passed to the Villiers family, and later still the

Syndicate Halls. The famous old Canterbury, with its unique and noisy sliding roof, was finally destroyed by Hitler's bombs.

Other Metropolitan halls opened in the 1860's included the Royal Standard at Pimlico (1863), rebuilt in 1911 as the Victoria Palace; Carlos Gatti, a restauranteur, opened the The Road Music Hall (Westminster Bridge Road) in 1867, later adding the Hungerford Music Hall which became known as Gatti's Arches, to differentiate it from Gatti's Road; James Mortimer opened the Hoxton Music Hall in 1863 (later known as 'MacDonald's') and quite nearby, the Virgo opened in Pitfield Street, Hoxton during 1867, later nick-named 'The Sod's Opera' as it became a rowdy, low-class place.

More respectable was the Royal Cambridge in Commercial Street, Whitechapel, (where Charlie Chaplin is reputed to have made his first London appearance as a solo artiste) opened in 1864; the St. Leonard's Hall (later the Panorama) opposite Shore-ditch Church in 1867, and in that year the Royal Oriental Theatre at Poplar was being advertised. It was reconstructed as the Apollo Music Hall in 1873 by Maurice Abrahams of the Queens' Arms, which was embodied in the frontage. The Apollo was later known as the Poplar Queens' music hall and functioned until 1956.

In the West End was the Alhambra, a vast Moorish-style build-ing in Leicester Square (where the Odeon now stands). It originated in the Panoptican, a building housing educational novelties, opened by the Bishop of London in 1854. In 1865 it was opened by Fred Strange as the Alhambra Music Hall, with John Hollingshead (who later founded the Gaiety in the Strand) as manager. The proprietor of the Alhambra fell foul of the London County Council in 1870 when the French *Can-Can* (danced there by the Colonna Troupe with 'Wiry Sal') was considered far too naughty and the place closed down for a time.

After a fire in 1882 a new Alhambra arose on the site the follow-ing year. The place had a 'Promenade' frequented by Ladies of the Town and their followers, as was the case at the rival Empire across the way. (The Empire was established in 1884 on the site of the old Walhalla.) Charles Morton was associated with the Alhambra for a time, but its last proprietor was Sir Oswald Stoll who turned it into a 'very respectable' music hall before its demise in 1936.

The 'seventies saw a great expansion of music halls in London and notable places of amusement (in addition to those already mentioned) can be named the Foresters in Cambridge Heath Road; the Sun at Knightsbridge and the Magpie at Battersea. Also note-worthy was the Mogul Tavern (known as 'The Old Mo') enlarged

by J. Laurie Graydon in 1878. This later became the Middlesex
Music Hall when Stoll took a hand in its affairs, and now the
Winter Garden Theatre occupies the site.

By the turn of the century there were over sixty music halls in
the London area alone. Soon after this, most of the halls passed
into the hands of various syndicates, such as the Syndicate Halls;
the De Frece Tour; Walter Gibbons' London Theatres of Variety
and, following the 'invasion' of the Metropolis by the Northern
magnates, the 'Empires' of Moss and Stoll, and the Music Halls
Proprietary Corporation of MacNaghten.

*   *   *   *

The Provinces had their early places of amusement also. Apart
from the Star at Bolton, there was Bianchi's Waxworks in Liverpool, established in Great Charlotte Street at the Parthenon Rooms
in 1845. (This place became the Parthenon Music Hall under the
Stoll family in 1850.) Another waxworks, Springthorpe's, otherwise
the Mechanics' Hall in Grimston Street, Hull became a music hall
in 1851 when the proprietor decided to supplement his dummies
with living entertainers. (This place had a continuous existence
until 1913 when it closed as Bosco and Downs' Empire.)

Other halls of the 1850's included the Surrey Music Hall in
Sheffield (opened as the Casino in 1851); the Peoples' in Man-
chester, 1853 (later still the Casino), and yet another Casino in
Leeds, adapted from a Drill Hall in 1849. Blackburn had the Old
Assembly Rooms in Market Street Lane, built in 1787, and con-
verted to 'The Music Hall' (later 'Papa' Page's Lyceum) in 1851.

All these halls were extant prior to 1860: there were many others
later. To mention only the more interesting, there was the Canterbury at Middlesbrough (where whisky retailed at 16/- a gallon)
of 1860; the Midland Music Hall in Leicester (better known as
'Paul's' after the proprietor) 1865; the Argyle at Birkenhead (1868)
and the Star Palace at Barrow (1871) which became the Tivoli in
later years.

Halls with waxworks, museums or picture galleries (on the same
lines as Morton's Canterbury in London) included the Star at
Bolton (better known as The Museum); the Princess Alexandra at
Burnley (sterio gallery, organ and stuffed birds); the Princess'
Palace in Leeds (waxworks, museum and plaster casts of murderers'
heads!) and the Surrey at Sheffield with its fine collection of pic-
tures. The St. James' Hall in Liverpool, so long the home of Sam
Hague's Minstrels, had waxworks in the basement, while Cox's
Talbot Palace in Nottingham was famed for its nude statuary.

There were spacious promenades at the Star Music Hall in
Bradford and the Princess' Palace in Leeds (on the same lines as
the Alhambra and Empire in London's Leicester Square) frequented
by ladies of a sort until 1896, when they were swept away by the
campaign organised by Mrs. Ormiston Chant, with her 'Prudes on
the Prowl'.

Liverpool had a fine collection of music halls in bygone days.
There was the old Rotunda in the Scotland Road (where Herbert
Campbell made his debut). The roof of this place was laid out like
the deck of a ship and complete with mast! It was burned down
in 1876 but restored. The Teutonic Hall of 1847 became the St.
James' Hall and home of Minstrelsy, before Walter De Frece
erected the Tivoli there (with Vesta Tilley topping the first bill);
then there was the tiny Malakoff in Cleveland Square run by Dan
Lowrey in conjunction with his Star in Dublin. 'Free and Easies'
were the Crystal Palace in Pudsey Street (where the Odeon now
stands) and the Garibaldi in Lime Street (long since swept away).
In Upper Dawson Street stood that home of succulent steaks and
fine cigars—Evans' Song and Supper Rooms—a branch of the
noted Covent Garden establishment.

On the subject of Nottingham and its halls, Emrys Bryson
reports:

'By 1865 the Music Hall proper was in full swing in
Nottingham, moving from the "Free and Easy" to the properly
equipped theatre. Middleton's "Alhambra Palace of Varieties"
was none other than the old Theatre Royal in St. Mary's
Gate "thoroughly cleaned, entirely re-decorated, splendidly
illuminated, and with prices reduced". Admission was 6d. of
which 2d. was returned in refreshment once you were inside.
Some of the refreshment you occasionally offered the Chairman—usually at his request.

'The Chairman was a splendid figure in his white tie and
tails, banging his gavel with white-gloved hands, announcing
the "turns" in a fruity voice, delivering the odd song or monologue, and inviting himself to a drink by singling out the
payee with polite but firm: "The Chairman will take wine
with his friend in the cloth cap and choker".'

The Chairman at the nearby St. George's Hall was Harry Ball,
an ex-Worcester china worker, and the father of Vesta Tilley, who
made her debut on that stage at the age of four in 1868.

Nottingham was rich in music halls. Not far away was 'Mother'
Metheringham's Crown and Cushion 'Free and Easy' music hall,
to which the Queen's jester, W. F. Wallett of Beeston, was a

frequent visitor, often 'obliging' with his Shakespearian quips. Completing the 'Big Three' of Nottingham music halls was Charlie Cox's Talbot Palace, dating from 1876. Charles Coburn began there—at a salary of £3 10s.—and the Palace was the first hall in the Midlands to be lit by electricity, a small gas engine providing the power. The Chairman at this hall was Carl Brennir, who reigned for twenty years. In 1898 the Talbot Palace emerged as the Gaiety Palace, but this did not last long against the powerful Moss' Empire. In 1901 Frank MacNaghten took it over and put in melodrama, but by 1908 it was mostly showing films.

*   *   *   *

The Star Music Hall at Bolton was perhaps the most famous of the old-time 'halls'. Dating from 1832, when a 'singing-room' was established at the Millstones Inn, Deansgate, landlord Tom Sharples moved in 1840 to the Star Inn, in Church Street, and there built on to his hostelry the Star Theatre and Museum. This was always better known as the 'Museum Music Hall' than the Star, and the museum there contained wax figures, stuffed birds and animals, and a historic axe. (According to 'Barton's Historical Gleanings' the Earl of Derby was executed not far from this spot, and this axe was the one preserved in the museum.) The Star Music Hall was burned down in 1852, but the axe was saved from the flames in triumph.

According to a writer in the *Bolton Guardian:*

'The Star Music Hall had a plain stage, and to the left stood the Chairman's box. Mr. Geoghegan, the manager, acted as Chairman, and he had a mallet and called out the names of the performers.

'Performances began at 7.30 each night, and the curtain was wound up by hand. A well-known character named "Museum Jack" lit the lamps and footlights with a taper, and also played the piano. If a "turn" failed to please, Mr. Geoghegan said "You're no good" and ejected the hapless performer.

'There were 2d. and 4d. Checks, or tokens (known as "Wet Money"). These were small coins bearing the inscription of a laurel wreath and a seven point star. The "Mashers" usually had a lemon dash costing 2d. Mr. Geoghegan lived with his wife and seven daughters at the Angel Inn nearby.'

The Star Music Hall was rebuilt after the fire, and re-opened in January, 1855. Later it was known as the Victoria Theatre of Varieties. In the 1870's J. Pittney Weston, who had the Temple Opera House (a converted spinning mill in Dawes Street) was running the Victoria, and many famous 'stars' appeared there. Little Tich and Dan Leno appeared (the latter for 30/- the week) and Tom Hargreaves, who later built the Bolton Empire, was a firm favourite with his song and jest.

In the 1890's the Victoria ceased to function as a music hall, and reverted to licensed premises. Other music halls attached to inns, whose origins were shrouded in obscurity, included Budd's Alhambra at Lincoln (Green Dragon Inn); Bakewell's Empire at Grimsby (Corporation Hotel) and the tiny Royal Standard at Whitehaven.

*　　　*　　　*　　　*

Thomas Youdan, who was responsible for the Surrey Music Hall in Sheffield, was formerly a publican in the city. He came to Sheffield as a labourer from Ireland at the age of 18, saved his wages, and became licensee of one of the many public houses in the populous West Bar area. The Surrey had opened its doors in 1851 as the Casino, and Youdan took it over in 1858 and greatly enlarged it.

It re-opened in 1858 as the Surrey Music Hall, and in its final state was a fine two-tiered building with an imposing tower. The ground floor comprised the music hall, supper room and museum, and above was the ballroom and picture gallery. This place, like the one at Bolton, was completely destroyed by fire, and this occurred on the night of 25th March, 1865. Youdan was reported to be 'completely overwhelmed by the catastrophe'. The fire started in the waxworks, which contained a notable group entitled 'The Judgement of Solomon'.

About the Surrey, the late Alderman Saunders said:

'The Surrey was the best conducted place in the Kingdom. It was a beautiful place and I know of no more handsome hall in the country, except, perhaps Covent Garden.

'There was a splendid ballroom, costly pictures, and a chandelier of great beauty. The museum was unequalled outside London.'

The Surrey had just become a Theatre, only a short time before the fire. The play given on the night of the fire was 'The Streets of London'. The destruction of the Surrey cost Youdan £30,000 but he was undeterred. He immediately negotiated for the Adelphi Circus in Blonk Street, and opened that as the Alexandra Music Hall in October, 1865. The ruins of the old Surrey stood until 1880 when the Union Insurance offices were built on the site.

The Adelphi, which Youdan acquired, dated from 1836 and stood opposite the Cattle Market. When built it had a 42 ft. diameter ring for the equestrian acts and stabling at the rear for 14 horses. The frontage into Blonk Street was most imposing, with handsome Greco-Ionic columns. Youdan enlarged the building and the stage, the old arena being done away with. After the alterations the Alexandra had a stage 40 ft. by 60 ft. and the house held 4,000. It was then renamed the Alexandra Theatre and Opera House.

But in spite of its imposing appearance and name, it was always known as 'Tommy's' (after Youdan). When Youdan died, his manager Walter Brittlebank took it over, and altered it in 1883. About this time there was a stage manager with the curious (real) name of Oliver Cromwell. In 1898 it was modernised and electrified when Wallace Revill took it over. The 'Alex' was Sheffield's 'Home of Pantomime', and most of the operatic productions came there before its demolition in 1914.

There were several well-known halls in the Potteries. In the 'sixties and 'seventies of last century there were 'Free and Easies' at The Old Vine, the Red Lion and The Mitre at Hanley and the Golden Lion at Stoke. In 1868 Rodgers and Warrilow turned an old wooden circus into 'The Peoples' Music Hall' in Glass Street, Hanley.

Perhaps the best-known of all the Potteries halls was the old Gaiety in New Street, Hanley, also known at one time as The Pavilion. Mr. Geoghegan, who came from the old Star at Bolton, was Chairman at this hall for a time. In 1892 the Gaiety became the Empire (with the usual clientele frequenting 'The New Spacious Promenade') but the erection of the Grand Circus by the Elphinstone family (with bookings by Moss Empires) put the proprietors out of business.

*   *   *   *

A famous music hall that sprang from a chapel was the Folly in Manchester, run for a long time by Edward Garcia. The Folly was originally a Methodist New Connexion Chapel and it stood in Peter Street, being erected in 1832. After a Methodist Conference held in Manchester in 1846 it was decided to sell the Peter Street Chapel and concentrate on the new one at Pendleton. This proved a great mistake—hence the name 'Folly'—from which the breakaway New Connexionists never recovered.

In 1897 it was renovated and renamed the Tivoli, under the management of the Lever family. Many famous acts appeared at this little hall, the interior walls of which were covered in mirrors. Thus the 'Pros' could see themselves reflected in all their glory whilst performing, but many artistes found this disconcerting, to all accounts. In 1921 the place was ravaged by fire, after some years in use as a cinema.

Ada Reeve, in her memoirs, recounted:

'In 1936 when I was playing at the Opera House, Manchester, I was passing along Peter Street, and there, displayed on an outer wall, I saw a brass plaque bearing the words: "On this site stood the Folly Theatre of Varieties, where, during the 1880's the following famous artistes appeared . . ." and I found my name among the great ones, which included Pat Feeney, Dan Leno, Marie Loftus, The Great Chirgwin, Charles Godfrey, Lottie Collins, Tom Costello and Marie Lloyd.'

The plaque and building no longer exist for not long after Ada Reeve's visit, the ruins were swept away, and a motor-car showroom erected on the site.

Other early Manchester music halls were the Peoples' Concert Hall in Lower Mosley Street, run by Tom Burton, and opened in 1853. Later it became known as the Casino, and the great Dan Leno made several appearances—clog dancing on a pedestal according to one account. In 1897 the Midland Hotel was built on the site. There was a small theatre incorporated in this hotel, and ten years later Miss Horniman, of the famous tea family, founded the very first 'repertoire' company there, before moving across the way into the empty Gaiety Theatre. On one occasion she was politely asked to leave the lounge of the Midland Hotel, for daring to smoke a Turkish cigarette in public!

Another old Manchester music hall was the Star, at Ancoats, run for a time by Jack Bleakley, later associated with entertainment in Bolton. Then there was the London Music Hall in Bridge Street built in 1862. In 1870 it was rebuilt as the Queens' Theatre, and later controlled by J. Pitt Hardacre. It was closed and sold in 1911.

Another chapel again, which became a 'Theatre Royal', was the old Free Chapel, in High Street, Gateshead. This building dated from 1815, but when the Mission Hall was built, not far away, about 1860, it became the Theatre Royal. It was later run as 'The Royal Theatre of Varieties' and was known by other names, including 'The Queens' '. There was a panic there in 1891, after which it closed for a time. It was rebuilt and re-opened in 1897 as The Queens' Theatre of Varieties. Some years later it went over to films, as the Hippodrome, and ended its career, after a fire, as a Woolworths' store.

But the most famous music hall of all on Tyneside was surely
the old Wheatsheaf in the Cloth Market, Newcastle, a public house
with a built-on 'singing room'. Here, in 1862, George Ridley, a
crippled ex-collier, wrote and sang the immortal 'Blaydon Races'.
The proprietor of the Wheatsheaf at the time was one Balmbra, and
his name is perpetuated in the words of the song:
> 'Aw went to Blaydon Races, 'twas on the ninth of Joon,
> Eighteen hundred and sixty-two, on a summer's afternoon;
> Aw tyuk the 'bus fra' Balmbra's, an' she was heavy laden,
> Away we went alang Collingwood Street—that's on the way
> to Blaydon,' (and so on).

Poor George Ridley died in 1864 at the early age of 30, of
injuries sustained in the pit, but his songs live on. After his accident,
he turned to singing in the public-houses, making his first appearance at the old Grainger Music Hall in 1862. There he sang about
a horse that won the Northumberland Plate that year—'Joey Jones'
—and it was a great success with the 'locals'.

In 1865 the singing-room at the Wheatsheaf was enlarged as the
'Oxford Music Hall' by Messrs. Bagnall and Blakey, who ran it
in conjunction with the Victoria Music Hall, which they established some years later. (The Victoria was probably the old
Grainger under another name.) The late Bransby Williams once
said that he remembered playing at a hall in Grainger Street about
1899 known as 'The Vaudeville', and inferred that this was the
same hall. The Vaudeville was burned down in 1900.

In the 1890's with the rise of the Moss' Empires, the old Oxford
Music Hall at the Wheatsheaf reverted to licensed premises, and
became eventually the billiard room of the Carlton Hotel (as the
Wheatsheaf is now named). In 1937 there was a move afoot to
demolish the premises, but wiser counsels prevailed. In June, 1962
it was used again as 'Balmbra's Music Hall' in connection with the
Centenary celebrations of Blaydon Races.

*   *   *   *

Scotland too, had its share of early music halls, and many
interesting characters and performers were connected with them.

In the 'fifties and 'sixties there were two very well-known 'Penny
Gaffs' in Dundee. The most popular of the two was Fizzy Gow's
house, which was established in the upper floors of a hall in Lindsay
Street. This was known as the Clarence. The rival establishment
was the Seagate, not far away, run by MacKay, later associated
with the Gaiety and the Star in Glasgow.

About 1870 a bright young man named William McFarland took

over a wooden building near the East Station, vacated by Sanger's Circus, and turned that into the Alhambra Music Hall. The place flourished, and five years later McFarland had another Alhambra going, this time in Aberdeen. In 1877 McFarland acquired the Dundee Theatre Royal, and in 1885 built and opened Her Majesty's Theatre to replace it, in the Seagate.

In 1888 McFarland decided to re-open the old Theatre Royal as a music hall, but here his luck failed him. Two days before he was billed to open, the new hall was burned to the ground. McFarland lost a lot of money over this misfortune, and soon afterwards decided to retire, and sold out his interests to Robert Arthur, the noted impresario.

Then, in 1891, the Livermore Brothers brought the music hall back to Dundee when they opened the old Circus in Lochee Road. An old playbill reads:

'The Peoples' Palace, Lochee Road, Dundee, 1891. Proprietors: The Livermore Bros. We are the Pioneers of Refinement!

'The Palace is the only place where you can with safety take your Wives and Families.

'Popular Prices—3d., 6d., 1/- and 2/-.'

In 1893 the Livermore Palace was re-opened on its present site in the Nethergate, and is now known as the Palace Theatre. In 1910, when the Kings' Theatre opened as a variety theatre, with Bransby Williams topping the bill, the Palace went over to films. After a spell of 'talkies' the Palace went back to Variety during the Second World War, the Kings' having become the Gaumont Cinema. Another Dundee music hall, the Gaiety, ran in conjunction with the Greenock Empire and the Star and Tivoli at Glasgow, but in 1911 this also became the Victoria Cinema.

Aberdeen, as previously mentioned, had the Alhambra Music Hall, run by McFarland as far back as 1875. Here, a popular entertainer who later managed the hall, was Harry Clifton who sang 'You never miss the water till the well gangs dry' and also appeared with his wife, May Edwards, a soprano. The Aberdeen Alhambra is still standing, in Market Street, as a carbide factory.

McFarland also had a theatre here called Her Majesty's. When the new His Majesty's was built in 1906, the old one became the Tivoli Music Hall, as it continues today.

Similarly, the Livermore Brothers had a hall here too. In 1892 they bought Cooke's Circus, also known as the Jollity Vaudeville Theatre, and run by 'Baron' Zeigler, and turned this into a Livermore 'Peoples' Palace'. Many famous stars appeared here, including Marie Lloyd, George Lashwood and Little Tich, until the place was destroyed by fire in 1896. Then the new Palace Theatre was built and opened in Bridge Street in 1898; Cyrus Dare, the 'American Entertainer' topping the first bill. Sam Bodie (alias 'Doctor' Walford Bodie) an Aberdonian, made many appearances as did Jack Lorimer, Glasgow born, and father of Max Wall, before it became a cinema. Nowadays the Palace is a ballroom.

*   *   *   *

Edinburgh had several places of amusement in the early days. On the site in Nicolson Street, now occupied by the palatial Empire Theatre, Ducrow's Circus was first pitched in the 1830's. In the 1850's the Amphitheatre was going strong there, and in later years this became the Alhambra Music Hall. Harry West was running it as the Southminster Music Hall when it was destroyed by fire. Then H. E. Moss bought the site and erected the first of the Empires there in 1892. Prior to this, Moss had run the Gaiety Music Hall in Chambers Street since 1875 and acquired an interest in the Waverley Market in 1882.

Other old halls in Edinburgh were the Albert Hall of Varieties, run by MacKay of Glasgow, previously referred to, and the notorious 'Grotto' in Leith Street, run by an ex-medical student at the University named Beaumont, which was soon closed down after complaints to the authorities. There was firstly a wooden circus going strong in Leith, and when this was ravaged by fire, Moss turned an old Presbyterian Chapel into the Gaiety Music Hall. Nearby was a place in opposition to this, called 'The Empire' in Henderson Street. There were other amusements not far away in Portobello.

But Glasgow was really the place for the old-time music hall in Scotland. The residents of the 'St. Mungo' city are really pleasure conscious, now as then, and it is not surprising that there were many places of amusement ready and willing to cater for the Glaswegians' pleasure.

There was the famous Scotia—or the Metropole of later years—which is sadly, now no more. The Scotia opened in 1862 and at that time there was Davy Brown's Philharmonic (or 'Folly') in Dunlop Street; Shearer's Whitebait in St. Enoch's Wynd; Sloan's Oddfellows' in Argyle Street (where James Bayliss was Chairman for a time); 'Free and Easies' called the Jupiter and the Shakespeare in the Saltmarket, and two places run by Willie Campbell (Champion sculler in the West of Scotland)—Levy's at Glasgow Cross and a place in the Trongate, known as 'Campbells'.

The Whitebait was a very curious house—with the performers 'wired in'—so that the audience (usually boisterous) could not jump on the stage and dance with them. At one time the performers at this hall were exclusively female. Mr. Shearer is believed to have been the pioneer of 'Girlie' shows!

Another curious place was the Oxford Cafe Concert Hall, at the top of Hope Street—better known as 'The Garden of Eden'—which was closed down for a time, having acquired a bad reputation. In 1898 Messrs. Gray, Edmiston and Lee turned this into a very respectable music hall, after extensive alterations. It re-opened as the Alexandra Music Hall with T. W. Royal, the Champion clog dancer topping the bill, but this did not last long.

In the 'eighties D. S. MacKay, who came from Dundee, established the Gaiety in Sauchiehall Street and the Star Music Hall in Watson Street, not far from Glasgow Cross. In 1884 there was a frightful panic at the Star, in which fourteen people died. A troupe of foreign acrobats were performing, and one of them is believed to have called out 'Higher, Higher' to a colleague in the pyramid. This was unfortunately misconstrued by the audience as 'Fire' and a mad dash for the exits resulted, with the resulting loss of life. In later years John Wilson opened it (in 1892) as the Peoples' Palace. Later again, it became the Queens' Theatre. James Kirk took over the Gaiety, and then ran it with Moss and Thornton until the new Empire was built in 1897.

The Trongate house, later known as the Britannia, and run firstly by Jack Rossborough and then by Arthur Hubner, was popular with the working-class fraternity. Here Slade Murray ('Far, Far, Away') was a great favourite, and it is believed that George H. Elliott, the Chocolate Coloured Coon (from Rochdale) made his first appearance in Scotland here, completely unknown. The Britannia faded when the 'big guns' of Moss, De Frece and Barrasford opened up in Glasgow during the 1900's and the old house (which bore the inscription A.D. MDCCLVII) ended its days as a place of amusement as the 'Panopticon', run by one Pickard, comprising waxworks, fancy fair and dime museum, etc. It is still standing as a multiple tailoring establishment.

One of the great favourites of the early Glasgow music hall era was a comedian known as W. F. Frame ('The Man U Know'). Frame, who had a poster showing himself grinning through a gilded frame, engaged Harry Lauder as a programme boy, and later gave him his first chance in concert party.

Frame, who had a motto: 'A funny gag, a cheerful shout, is worth more than doctors round about' sang a song called 'It's a

braw, bricht, moonlicht nicht, tonicht, Hooch Aye'. He appeared
for three months at the London Alhambra, where the audience had
difficulty with the language, but he was a great success there and
received many encores. He finished his career as a J.P. for Glasgow.

* * * *

No chapter on the old-time halls would be complete without some
reference to the Chairmen who were such an essential part of that
bygone era.

Of the Metropolitan halls the most notable were 'Baron' Courtney
(with his many rings) at the South London Palace; Sam Sutton at
Deacons; Walter Knowles (an 'Institution') at the Cambridge; Gus
Leach at the Middlesex (of 'Sod's Opera' fame); Frank Estcourt at
the Poplar Queens for Maurice Abrahams; Joe Haynes at the Old
Bedford and John Read at Islington Collins. Harry Cavendish is
said to have officiated at the London Pavilion at one period, while
the redoubtable Rodney Polgraze is connected with several, but
more especially the Star at Bermondsey. Walter Leaver is reputed
to have been the last of these gentlemen of the gavel. He reigned
at the Canning Town Albert until 1906, according to one account.

Turning to the Provincial halls, there was the famed Jack
Geoghegan at the Bolton Star and later the old Gaiety at Hanley;
Sam Sweeney, firstly at the little Argyle at Birkenhead, then the
Effingham at Rotherham and the Varieties in Liverpool, before
finally opening his own 'Empire' in Leicester in 1894.

The immaculate Carl Brennir reigned supreme for upwards of
twenty years at Cox's Talbot Palace in Nottingham; also in Nottingham, Harry Ball (father of Vesta Tilley) wielded the gavel at the
St. Georges' Hall, and Harry Bowser officiated with dignity at
Thornton's Varieties in Leeds at one time. Alfred Roe was monarch
of all he surveyed at the Free Trade in York and at nearby Scarborough a certain Mr. Hardy undertook to see 'that no disorderly
person be allowed to interfere with proceedings' at Reid's Grand
Varieties attached to the old Globe Inn.

Over the border, James Bayliss acted in this capacity at the
Oddfellows' in Glasgow, before founding his own Scotia; Davy
Brown was combined proprietor and Chairman at his Folly, and
Harry Clifton officiated at the Aberdeen Alhambra. Later he was
succeeded by W. J. Ashcroft ('The Solid Man') who later estab-
lished his own Alhambra in Belfast.

Perhaps the most colourful of the old-time Chairmen was Arthur
Orton, the so-called 'Tichborne Claimant', who did several years
in prison for passing himself off as Roger Tichborne, heir to

long-lost estates. In the 1880's Orton went on the halls, reciting his tale of woe, and when folks got tired of him became a Chairman at the old Greyhound in Bradford, which was up a flight of stairs.

The corpulent impostor (he weighed twenty stones) also had a spell at the Crystal Palace in Blackpool before settling down to run a cigar store at Islington, where he was a familiar figure sitting on a chair outside his shop, exchanging pleasantries with performers appearing at the nearby Collins Music Hall on the Green.

Nowadays, in Variety, cabaret or clubland, the function of Chairman is performed by a comperé, should any introduction to the acts be necessary. In television broadcasts from the Leeds City Varieties (in the programme 'The Good Old Days') Leonard Sachs acts and looks the part of the 'Gentleman of the Gavel' in fine style. These popular programmes are ably produced by Barney Colehan, for the BBC.

(Above) The old STAR MUSIC HALL in Bolton, as it appeared over 100 years ago.

(Below) The old SURREY MUSIC HALL in Sheffield after the disastrous fire of 1865.

Plate 1

"LONDON TOWN"
(Right) Finsbury Park
Empire.

(Below) Poplar Queens'.

(Below) Collins Music Hall at
Islington Green.

(Left) The Metropolitan Music
Hall in the Edgware Road.

Plate 2

2

Halls of Fame

RICHARD THORNTON was born at Templeton, South Shields in 1839. When he married Bella Buckham in 1860 he had 4½d. in his pocket (after paying expenses) on which to start married life. When he died, aged 84 in 1922, he was worth £100,000. That is what married life will do for a man—with a wife like Bella Buckham . . .

After some elementary schooling—very elementary—'Dick' as he was always affectionately called, was apprenticed to a joiner. To make more money at the age of 15 he was to be found at weekends fiddling at Marsden Grotto, a well-known beauty spot on the Durham coast, with amusements, run by Mrs. Peter Allen. Dick was no mean exponent of the violin, and he was a familiar figure in the district with his little green bag to hold the pennies, and his violin in its tattered case. At weekends he made sea-trips on the pleasure boats which plied up and down the Tyne, fiddling for coppers.

When he married Bella at St. Mary's, Gateshead, he took another job as violinist at the Theatre Royal, in King Street, South Shields, and gave up the Marsden Grotto pitch. Dick worked in the day-time at a cabinet maker's stores, in Union Alley, at the back of the Theatre Royal. In the 1870's he found himself leading the orchestra at the Theatre Royal, and in 1880, after further 'pushing' by Bella, became 'Mine Host' at a public house in Union Alley, called the Shakespeare Inn.

Dick had seen the 'music-room' at the Locomotive Inn, Mill Dam (in another part of Shields) and indeed had fiddled there himself accompanying the 'turns'. This gave him the idea to establish a music-room at the Shakespeare, which he did, and it was quite successful. In 1884 Mr. Wood, who ran the cabinet maker's stores, told Dick he could have the woodyard cheap if he wanted to expand. Fred Cooke, then manager of the Theatre Royal, when asked for an opinion, did his utmost to discourage Dick from the idea, as he did not want opposition 'in his own back-yard' as it were. Bella, when consulted, had no doubts about the matter at all.

33

B

Mr. Wood was anxious to dispose of his property, there was no
regular music hall in the Shields (apart from Sam Siddal's wooden
Alhambra in Coronation Street) so Dick should go ahead. Dick
went ahead . . .

Mr. Biddick, the architect, was called in to advise on the exten-
sions, and did a great job. Several existing buildings were incorporated in the original 'Thornton's Music Hall' which opened with a
flourish on 2nd November, 1885.

'Thornton's Varieties' was described by the Press as an 'elegant
place of amusement' and it lived up to its title. Mr. Biddick had laid
his plans well. Red plush seemed everywhere. An outstanding
feature was a beautiful cut-glass chandelier which twinkled and
shone in a bewitching manner. There was a sliding roof to ensure
adequate ventilation, and the interior of the hall was beautifully
decorated in a green and gold motif. Capacity was around the
thousand mark, including a spacious gallery for 350 persons.

Performances were once-nightly at 7.45 and the admission prices
were as follows: Pit and Promenade 6d.; Dress Circle 1/- and
Private Boxes 2/- (half-price after 9 o'clock).

Acting manager, under Dick Thornton, was Mr. J. G. Allen, a
member of the Allen family at Marsden Grotto, and a life-long
friend of Dick. Herr Ludwig, late of the Theatre Royal, Manchester,
conducted the orchestra of 'Ten competent musicians—individually
selected'. The scenery was painted and supplied by Mr. Harry
Sharpe.

Hundreds were unable to gain admission on the first night. The
local Press reported: 'Never has such enthusiasm been witnessed
in the Shields . . .' It went on to say that 'thunders of applause
greeted every artiste'. In particular, the antics of the one-legged
'monopedes' Conway and Leyland fairly brought down the house.
Henry Whalling's song 'Mother Dear, the War is Over' was
described as 'the most laughable song ever heard' which was fair
comment indeed. Altogether Thornton's Varieties got away to a
tremendous start.

Later on, when business slacked off a little, Dick engaged the
famous serio Jenny Hill at the (then) fabulous salary of £40 per
week to liven things up a little (which she certainly did). Dick was
fairly aghast when Jenny asked £40 for the week's engagement, but
Jenny was adamant—£40 was her 'very lowest'—and she would
take no reduction! Sportsman Dick paid up and the telegram from
Jenny accepting the booking was proudly displayed in a King Street
shop window for advertisement purposes.

Many 'stars' of the old-time halls made their bow at 'Thornton's' and often the hall was too small to accommodate all who wished to enter that 'Refined place of entertainment'. Therefore, rebuilding was decided upon. The old hall closed down during June, 1898 and in the remaining months of that year a much larger and finer building arose on the same site. By February, 1899 the new 'Empire Palace of Varieties' was ready. The transition from public house singing room to variety palace was complete . . .

The new South Shields Empire opened with a large bill topped by the great Eugene Sandow, with his unique 'Monarch of Muscle' display. Besides his usual and well-known feats of strength, Sandow impressed with a new trick—that of tearing through three packs of playing cards at one time! Also on the bill was a real old-timer in Austin Rudd, the Tyneside comedian and vocalist, who aroused nostalgic memories of the old 'Varieties' with his 'Bobbing up and Down Like This' and other songs he had sung many times at the old hall.

At the opening ceremony Frank Allen, nephew of J. G. Allen, the manager, spoke. (Dick Thornton had 'discovered' Frank Allen working in a small sub-post office in Monkwearmouth, and when he noted Frank's astonishing aptitude for figures, promptly made him Secretary to the Circuit.) Frank Allen said: 'South Shields owes Mr. Thornton a debt of gratitude for his efforts to provide the town with such a fine building' and went on to say that the management of the North Eastern Circuit looked upon the new Empire 'with pardonable pride'. Alderman T. D. Marshall also spoke, and Mr. Thornton suitably responded. The new hall was well and truly launched.

Subsequent bookings proved every bit as popular as the opening bill, and what a stir there was a few weeks later when Diane de Fontenoy appeared with her 'Living Statue' act. The ladies in the Tableaux appeared to be completely nude (or possibly very nearly so), their bodies heavily covered in lacquer! Another 'scoop' by the management was the screening on the Bio-Tableaux (an early form of the cinema) of what must have been one of the very first newsreel films—Scenes from the F.A. Cup Final at Crystal Palace—Derby County v. Sheffield United, in 1899.

The South Shields Empire did very well down the years, and most of the big names in music hall appeared there. However, it suffered with the general decline in live entertainment in the 1930's (against the 'Talkies') and like its neighbour, the Theatre Royal, went over to Pictures eventually. (Dick bought the Royal in 1920 and turned it into a cinema.) He also ran other cinemas at Horden and Jarrow.

About 1900 Thornton relinquished the West Hartlepool Alhambra (never a success). He had erected this place in 1890 but it was too small. A few years later he established an 'Empire Palace' there, on a much larger scale. Still expanding, in 1915 Richard Thornton added the Gateshead Empire to the Circuit. This had b̤en built in 1905 as the King's Theatre. Dick turned it into a music hall.

But Dick Thornton's own favourite 'Hall of Fame' was the Sunderland Empire, which he built in 1907. Whereas the other halls on the 'North East Circuit' had only a weekly visit from Dick (a fine figure of a man, with his stick and red carnation always in his button-hole) the Sunderland Empire was where he spent most of his time. It was a magnificent hall of variety, and the Milburn Bros., who designed it, employed a novel idea with twin-staircases at either side of the stage, where the stage boxes usually are. (The boxes were at the back of the Empire.) The idea was that the twin staircases would facilitate emptying the theatre—to obviate the meeting of the crowd leaving the first house, and the patrons going in for the second. It did not work out too well in practice, but it was repeated at the West Hartlepool Empire and the Liverpool Empire (when rebuilt in 1925), also designed by the Milburn Brothers.

The Sunderland Empire was a huge success. It put the Livermore Brothers out of business at the Palace, on the opposite side of High Street. A curious fact was that the Empire was erected on a site formerly occupied by a Rectory. Famous names that appeared at the Empire during the first year of its life included Harry Lauder, Eugene Stratton, Alec Hurley (the husband of Marie Lloyd), Hetty King, Marie Kendall and George Lashwood.

When the Empire attained its 'majority'—in 1928—unfortunately old Dick Thornton was no longer at the helm (he had been replaced as Managing Director by Col. J. J. Gillespie of Morpeth) but a fine Souvenir Programme was produced that threw interesting light on how the Sunderland Empire came into being.

The Souvenir Programme related:

'Begun under the happiest of auspices, the progress of the Sunderland Empire has exceeded even the most sanguine hopes of its sponsors. The idea of erecting a Theatre on this site originated in the fertile brain of the late "Dick" Thornton— probably the greatest entertainment caterer the North of England has ever produced.

'The foundation stone was laid by Miss Vesta Tilley, now Lady de Frece, on 29th September, 1906, and the building opened on Monday 1st July, 1907. The opening ceremony was of a simple, but nevertheless impressive character. The stage curtain was drawn, disclosing a large assemblage, in the centre of which was Miss Lilian Lea. Among the company were Miss Vesta Tilley, Mr. Richard Thornton, Sir Edward Moss, Mr. Oswald Stoll, Mr. Frank Allen, Mr. W. Milburn, Mr. T. R. Milburn, Mr. J. W. White and Mr. Harry Esden.

'A huge floral horse-shoe emblematic of Good Luck was placed behind. Miss Lea sang 'God Save the King', the orchestra accompanying and the vast assembly joining in. When this was over, the curtain dropped, and was raised again for the first act on the bill, namely 'Astronomy'. Later, when pictures of the stone-laying ceremony by Miss Tilley were reproduced on the Biograph, a huge cheer went up.'

In later years plays and musical productions often ousted music hall from popularity at the Empire, and for a time in the 1930's, films were shown. In 1960 Sunderland Corporation bought the Empire as a Civic Theatre, it having closed down as a Variety theatre (under the aegis of Moss Empires) at Easter, 1959.

*   *   *   *

Perhaps the most famous name of all in Music Hall was the Argyle. Everybody knew about the tiny Argyle Theatre of Varieties in Birkenhead, because in 1930 the owner, Danny Clarke, arranged with the B.B.C. for a weekly broadcast. The very first broadcast of the series, which became a weekly one, was sent out over the old North Regional station on 14th April, 1931.

A tiny place, built on to a public house, it was destroyed by enemy action in 1940. Many famous artistes got their first start at the Argyle, among them George Formby, senior, and George H. Elliott. Gertie Gitana, who hailed from the Potteries, sang there on the stage at the age of ten! It was dear to the heart of every 'Pro' and, through the broadcasts, was known far and wide. People who had never been in a music hall in their lives had heard of the Argyle. It was a place to remember.

Donald Peers, radio's 'Cavalier of Song', who appeared there many times, writes:

'For generations, the Argyle, like so many of its London contemporaries, grew from the "Free and Easy" type of entertainment given in the Argyle public house. It was not too much to say that practically every British vaudeville artiste of note has at one time or another played at Birkenhead.'

The Argyle Theatre of Varieties (to give it its full name) came into being in 1868 when it was built on to the public house of the same name, in Argyle Street, Birkenhead, by proprietor George Arundale. The Argyle opened 21st December, 1868 with a pantomime, and if tradition is to be believed, that pantomime contained the Leno family, with the youthful Dan Patrick doing his stepdance. In January 1869 at the conclusion of the pantomime, which was hardly a success (the profit for the first week came to 11d.!), a Chairman was appointed—none other than Sam Sweeney—later connected with halls in Liverpool, Rotherham and Leicester.

But the Argyle did not survive as an early music hall. In 1876 a dramatic licence was obtained, and Dennis Grannell ran it for some years as the Prince of Wales' Theatre. In 1879 Arundale rebuilt the Rotunda Theatre, in Liverpool's Scotland Road, after a fire, and Grannell and Arundale, in partnership, ran the halls in conjunction with melodramatic fare. The Rotunda, like the Argyle, was built on the site of a 'Free and Easy', and the roof of the new theatre was laid out in curious fashion, like the deck of a ship, apparently as a novelty. Herbert Campbell, the famous Drury Lane comedian of later years, is reputed to have made his first appearance on the boards of the first 'Free and Easy' Rotunda. When the Rotunda re-opened as a Theatre, it began its new career very ambitiously with a season of Carl Rosa Opera.

Grannell's first manager at the Prince of Wales was Philip Clarke, and Grannell married his sister, Alice. Philip Clarke died, leaving a widow and two sons, the eldest being called Dennis ('Danny') after his uncle, Dennis Grannell. In 1889 Danny Clarke became the manager of the theatre, and in 1890 he restored the hall to music hall status, again as The Argyle.

The Argyle Theatre of Varieties was a 'pocket-sized' hall, seating about 800. It was like a shoe-box in appearance inside, with long narrow galleries running down either side, to the stage. There were many pillars in the auditorium, but it had a warm, cosy atmosphere that endeared itself to the heart of every performer. Like the early years, all was not smooth sailing at the Argyle under the new management, one reason being competition arising from Ohmy's Circus, erected in 1888 in Grange Road.

The Circus, erected by King Ohmy, the Flier, and run in conjunction with other halls of a similar nature in Rochdale and elsewhere, was a permanent structure, not a wooden one, and in its original state had a circus arena and stabling for horses at the rear. Later it was reconstructed on orthodox lines as the 'Gaiety'.

There was also the Theatre Royal, lower down Argyle Street, run by Messrs. Stanhope and Vowles, but that building was completely destroyed by fire during June, 1892. The ruins stood for some years.

In 1896, to counter the competition from the Circus, now the Gaiety Music Hall, Danny Clarke tried films to draw in the customers. It was a display of 'Vitagraph Living Pictures' presented by Messrs. Chard and Company of London, and it was claimed that this was the first display of moving pictures outside London. The little Argyle had no electric light in those days, so special cables had to be run along the street to the hall to provide current for the projectors. And so, on a suspended white sheet, the amazed patrons saw (with many a flicker) Persimmon winning the Derby of 1896, card-players in a Paris Cafe, a train entering Calais Station, and other wonders filmed by the Lumiere Brothers in France.

In 1898 the little Argyle really came into its own as a music hall, for in that year William Wallace Kelly (of 'Royal Divorce' fame, and later Alderman W. W. Kelly of Liverpool City Council) converted the Gaiety Music Hall into the Metropole Theatre, and ran it with the very best touring companies and melodrama.

An interesting advertisement for Whitsuntide, 1902 shows that Vesta Victoria was topping the bill at the Argyle, supported by Tom Lloyd, Alice Cooper and an 'All-Star' variety company. Across the water, at the Rotunda, a well-known stock company were giving the Scotland Road patrons a grim lesson in morality with 'The Follies of Youth'.

About this period Danny Clarke at the Argyle gave a chance to several then unknown performers who subsequently became very famous. Among them was Harry Lauder who appeared for £4 a week—singing Irish songs in the first half of the programme and Scottish ones in the second—for good measure! Tom Costello tried out a new song there called 'At Trinity Church I met my Doom' and scored a great success with it. George H. Elliott, the 'Chocolate Coloured Coon' (who hailed from Rochdale) got his first chance there, towards the ladder of fame, and another early 'star' spotted by astute D. J. Clarke was Hetty King, the male impersonator.

Danny Clarke was fond of telling the story of how he 'discovered' the elder George Formby singing in a Manchester 'Free and Easy' called 'The Hen and Chickens', and offered him £2 10s. a week to appear at the Argyle. George jumped at the opportunity. Later, George married a Wigan girl, and one week when he was again appearing at the Argyle as a comedian, the joyful news came through that he had a son and namesake. Danny immediately offered to give the young George an engagement at the Argyle on his 21st birthday! In point of fact young George did keep the 'date' and play the Argyle that week, although it was under the name of George Hoy, as he did not want to trade on his father's good name. Later on, when the old man's name was but a memory, he did adopt it, but by that time he had earned the right to use it.

Mark Sheridan, with his frock-coat and ridiculous bell-bottom trousers, was seen by Clarke in a rival establishment 'across the water'—the tiny Parthenon, run by the Stoll family—and promptly signed him up to play the Argyle. He became a great comedian, with his peculiar old-fashioned style, singing lustily 'I do like to be beside the Sea-side' and a great favourite on the 'halls'. The music hall profession was shocked when he ended his own life so tragically in a Glasgow park in 1917.

After ten years monopoly of music hall entertainment in Birkenhead, the little Argyle once again had to counter a formidable rival, when the New Birkenhead Hippodrome opened in 1908. It was none other than the old Circus-cum-Gaiety-cum-Metropole, resurrected by Walter de Frece! (In 1905 W. W. Kelly had rebuilt the burned-out Theatre Royal and vacated the Metropole Theatre, accordingly.) The Metropole had stood empty for three years until Walter de Frece moved in and revived it again as a music hall.

De Frece altered the old Circus building out of all recognition. The New Birkenhead Hippodrome was described by all as 'a very beautiful music hall'. Walter's wife—Vesta Tilley—topped the bill for the opening week, 7th December, 1908. The 'Hippodrome Pictures' were shown right from the start, and by 1912, when Frank Weston was running the hall, there were more 'pictures' than variety. Not long after this, Clarke bought them out, and turned the Hippodrome over to films exclusively.

In the 1930's when Variety was in the doldrums, due to the 'Talkies' and other attractions, Danny Clarke, always an astute showman, gave the B.B.C. the idea of a broadcast from the Argyle, to stimulate interest in the theatre. The move had the desired effect. The 'Saturday Night at the Argyle' broadcasts were a great hit, and things began to look up. When Danny died, in 1934, his son Tom took over, and maintained the high standards of this long-established family business. He was later joined in management by his brothers Gerard and Herbert.

A black day in British music hall history was 26th September, 1940. On that day Hitler's bombs destroyed the tiny Argyle Theatre at Birkenhead. That much beloved hall was reduced to a heap of rubble. The Argyle public house, which adjoined it, was damaged by blast, and was propped up by wooden stanchions. In spite of it all, a British flag flew proudly over the ruins.

Its old rival, the Circus, alias the Hippodrome, also went under to the bombs (a row of shops now marks the site), while the sister theatre of the Argyle 'across the water'—the Rotunda—was also hit. It had, however, ceased to function as a theatre for some time, having become derelict in the years between the wars, after a long spell of silent films interspersed with variety acts.

Many were the schemes to rebuild the little Argyle and restore the music hall tradition there, but building licences and other frustrating formalities caused constant postponement of these plans. Finally, when the time did come for possible restoration, inflation had raised its ugly head, and put the cost beyond reasonable bounds. In 1960 Tom Clarke received permission to rebuild the Argyle Hotel, and said in a statement issued on behalf of himself and his brothers:

> 'We do not envisage re-opening the Theatre. The Argyle was a family music hall and today there are not enough acts of the type we would want to ensure a weekly variety bill.'

Also, it should be remembered that another formidable rival had arisen to music hall entertainment—Television—and it is doubtful that even if the Argyle had been restored, whether it could have survived.

Perhaps it is fitting that it should remain a gallant and treasured memory . . .

*   *   *   *

When the Argyle was bombed the B.B.C. looked round for another music hall and settled on the Tivoli Theatre, Hull.

Strangely enough, this hall was also run by a Mr. Clarke— Harold Clarke trading as Kingston Varieties—but there does not seem to be any connection between the Clarkes of Hull and the Clarkes of Birkenhead.

Like the Argyle, the Tivoli was a 'pocket-sized' music hall. Actually, it was the stage area of a much larger theatre of yester-year. The main body of the hall of the former Royal Queens' Theatre, an enormous place—said to be the largest place of entertainment in Europe in its day—was condemned as unsafe in 1870. In 1871 the Imperial Hotel was built on the auditorium site, while the stage portion, which was left standing, was adapted as the New Theatre Royal. It had become redundant (the New Theatre Royal) and closed down after the opening of the new Alexandra Theatre in 1902, but in 1912, the Morton family, who owned both halls, adapted it as the Tivoli Music Hall. (George Morton, the founder, died in 1938, aged 100.)

The Tivoli Music Hall opened at Bank Holiday, 1912, with a fine bill including Robb Wilton (then billed as the 'Confidential Comedian', but also completely unknown). Also on the bill was an astonishing contortionist named Yuma, as Mephistopheles (dressed as a Devil in red fleshings) who emerged from a little box amid eerie lighting effects, and threw himself into fearsome postures that frightened people to death. (One young member of that audience had nightmares for weeks after seeing 'Yuma'!)

Hull Tivoli made an ideal hall for intimate broadcasts, and Donald Peers took part in the 1,000th broadcast in the 'Northern Music Hall' series organised by Richard North, from the old North Regional station. Donald tells how this was part of a three-way link-up between the Palace Theatre, Burnley; the Middlesbrough Empire and the Tivoli, Hull. Everyone concerned was on tenter-hooks for fear one of the halls would over-run its allotted time, but everything went off smoothly. Josef Locke, the burly Irish tenor, was on the bill at Burnley, and called out 'Good Luck, Me Bonny Boys!' as a form of greeting.

The Tivoli was badly damaged by incendiaries in 1943, but it was restored in double-quick time, although some of the seating capacity was lost, as the old gallery was not restored, the roof being lowered in the process. The restored Tivoli had now an austere look about it, with its spartan interior, and neon strip lighting round the circle frontage. It lacked the cosy intimate atmosphere of the old Victorian music halls, partly perhaps as it now had a dual-licence, running as a Continental Cinema in the day-time and on Sundays. Also, its future as a place of entertainment was uncertain. In 1951 Mr. Clarke and his co-directors of Kingston Varieties had purchased the bomb-damaged Moss Empire Palace along the Anlaby Road, which had stood empty for ten years, and had spent a lot of money in restoring it. In the early 1950's even, it soon become evident that there was not room for two successful music halls in Hull, even though the Tivoli only seated 825 people. After trying in vain to dispose of the Tivoli as a cinema, the directors of Kingston Varieties closed it down as a music hall in June 1954 and a few months later, after trying to run it as a full-time cinema, it finally closed down for good. (It was demolished in 1959 and Tivoli House—a shop and office block erected on the site.)

*　　　*　　　*　　　*

When the Tivoli closed as a theatre in 1954 the B.B.C. entered into an agreement with Harry Josephs, proprietor of the City

Varieties, Leeds, for the exclusive use of that hall for sound and
television broadcasts. The B.B.C. had in mind the televising of a
series of old-time music hall shows under the heading 'The Good
Old Days'. The City Varieties was a cosy, intimate little hall, just
what the B.B.C. wanted, but it was very shabby. Soon, with the
signing of the agreement with the B.B.C. came a 'face-lift' for the
Varieties, costing many thousands of pounds.

The interior was restored to something approaching its past
glory. There were new curtains, new spotlights, and other fittings,
but the old-time atmosphere was retained. During Television
broadcasts, Edwardian-dressed playgoers (an invited audience) fill
the hall and boxes, while a Chairman's rostrum is erected and the
artistes appear in old-time garb, and the audience join in with the
singing of lusty chorus songs of yester-year. The B.B.C. and Mr.
Josephs spared no pains to reconstruct the glamour of its hey-day.

The Leeds City Varieties is a theatre of mysteries. There are two
ghosts at least. One a woman singer and the other an old-time
pianist. Who they are (or were) seems to be obscure, but watchman
Tommy Atkins has seen them both. Mystery also surrounds a Coat
of Arms over the proscenium arch. No-one seems to know pre-
cisely just how it got there. Legend has it that it was bestowed on
the Varieties by King Edward VII, who was fond of visiting music
halls. He is reputed to have visited the Varieties several times
incognito when on visits to nearby Harewood House as Prince of
Wales. (The attendants will point out the box he is supposed to
have occupied—Box D to the right of the stage.)

Another mystery surrounds the underground passages beneath
the music hall. They are said to extend for miles—one to Kirkstall
Abbey. But there is no mystery about the many autographed
photographs and bills which adorn the circle bar walls. They tell a
story in themselves—the story of the City Varieties.

Here is a bill dated 22nd January, 1886. J. W. Rowley (a Leeds
man) and Marie Loftus topped that one, both of them famous
artistes in their day. Then comes a bill of manager Stansfield's
'Benefit' night in 1878, complete with monologue given by that
famous Yorkshire dialect specialist John Hartley, who founded
'The Clock Almanack'. It is entitled 'Bessie and Dick—or a Visit
to the Varieties'.

The photographs which line the walls of the bar are of great
interest. The young Charlie Chaplin—he played here first with the
'8 Lancashire Lads' in 1897 at the age of eight—and next to him,
black-faced George H. Elliott, the so-called 'Chocolate Coloured
Coon' (he hailed from Rochdale). Then come Nellie Wallace, Will

Hay, and more up to date, Phyllis Dixey, 'The Queen of Strip-Tease'. Below them are signed pictures of Frankie Vaughan and Max Bygraves, both of whom appeared here when totally unknown. Harry Josephs, when proprietor of the 'Verts' (as the Varieties is now nick-named) helped Frankie Vaughan, a Leeds student at the time, to a £150 contract with Bernard Delfont, the impresario.

*   *   *   *

But let us look back to see how it all began. Back to the age of hansom cabs, dram shops, flaring gas jets and feather boas. Not all that hard to imagine when you are in the Varieties . . .

The City Palace of Varieties (to give it its full title—bestowed upon it by Fred Wood in 1905 when he ran it in conjunction with the Queens' Palace of Varieties) has had a full and chequered history. Like so many music halls, the Varieties had its origin in the singing-room of a public house. In this case, it was the White Swan Inn (known locally as 'The Mucky Duck') which was built, or rebuilt in 1799. (Legend says the old coaching inn dated back to 1750, which makes the place over 200 years old), but 1799 seems to have been one certain date. Just when the music-room started is another of this intriguing little hall's mysteries, but it seems feasible that something of the sort existed a long time, perhaps from the very start. What *is* certain, however, is that there has been one since 1857, for in that year Charles Thornton became the licensee. (Just as there are two Clarkes in the history of Northern Music Hall, so are there two Thorntons.)

When Thornton became the licensee of the White Swan Inn during 1857, the Casino was the only music hall of any size in Leeds. The Casino was in King Charles' Croft and next door to it was Billy Thorne's New Theatre, devoted to the legitimate stage. Some time in the 1850's a Mr. Joe Hobson ('Owd Joe') took over the Casino and, in an attempt to make it respectable, swept away the 'wet-money' system, and called the place The Alhambra. Mr. Hobson dearly wanted the Alhambra to become a Theatre, and kept applying for a dramatic licence. In 1864 he was successful, and the Alhambra became 'The Royal Amphitheatre'. This sealed the doom of Billy Thorne's New Theatre, next door, which was bought up by its bigger rival, and after re-building, re-opened at Christmas, 1864, as 'The Princess' Concert Hall'.

The Princess' Concert Hall was very successful, and occasionally, music hall acts took the stage instead of the usual concert singers. One week, early in 1865, Mr. and Mrs. Stephen's Performing Gorillas appeared to good business.

Noting the success of the gorillas, Charlie Thornton decided to enlarge the singing-room at the White Swan Inn, in fact rebuild the place as a music hall. This was done, and the Varieties, in something like the present form, opened its doors at Whitsuntide (7th June, 1865). The first week's attraction appears to have been the Brothers Forrest, singers and entertainers, with a 'Star Company' in support.

In 1865, the Varieties was billed as 'Thornton's New Music Hall and Fashionable Lounge' (patronised by the elite of Leeds), entrance from Briggate. Attached were billiards and supper rooms. The place was noted for its 'attentive waiters' and ladies were admitted free to the music hall, if accompanied by a gentleman.

The year 1868 saw a rival concern of the Varieties removed from the scene—by fire. This was the Prince of Wales' Music and Concert Hall in Kirkgate, not far from the Parish Church. But by 1875 there was other opposition. The Dock Street Music Hall, run by Jack Molyneaux was in full swing: the Rose and Crown hostelry in Briggate had grown a flourishing 'concert room', and by this time Charles Morritt had taken over the Princess' Concert Hall in King Charles' Croft, equipped it with a promenade, museum and picture gallery, and the place was now known as the Princess' Palace Music Hall.

In view of the opposition, Thornton decided to retire from the licensing and music hall trade, and became identified with a shopping arcade in Briggate, which was known as Thornton's Arcade. This contained a novel striking clock, in an alcove above one of the entrances. The figures represented Robin Hood and his Merry Men, and the figures struck the hours. The Varieties was closed and offered for sale by auction, but withdrawn at £10,000 in February, 1876.

It was subsequently bought by Mr. Jack Stansfield, and re-opened as 'Stansfield's Varieties'. A bill, on silk, of 'The first Benefit of Mr. Stansfield' dated 20th September, 1878 now hangs in the circle bar of the theatre. The traditional Chairman seems to have been dispensed with from the re-opening. In the old days of Charlie Thornton, Harry Bowser wielded the gavel for some years.

For the next twenty years, the Varieties had a chequered career. Between 1878 and 1898 the managers and proprietors came and went in quick succession. Mr. Stansfield (who left to try his luck in Halifax) was succeeded by Charles Morritt, who about 1880, ran the Varieties in conjunction with the Princess' Palace.

Apparently this move did not succeed, although alterations and re-building operations were carried out by this enterprising gentleman.

During his regime, a new entrance to the hall from The Headrow
was added, an innovation very much overdue. Mr. Morritt was
followed by Mr. Arthur Greasley, later identified with the
Alhambra Palace, Hull. Then Mr. W. J. Lawrence, the father of
Vesta Victoria, who came from Barrow, tried his luck, but soon
moved to the Old Buck Inn, Briggate, where he became 'Mine
Host' for some years. Early in the 1890's came Mr. Thomas
Dunsford, who was described by all who knew him as 'a perfect
gentleman'. Under his guiding hand, the 'Verts' prospered for a
time, but even he had to give up when the powerful Moss Empires'
Theatre opened in Briggate, during August, 1898.

But it was in 1898 that the Varieties entered into its greatest
days. In November of that year, it was bought at an auction by
publican Fred Wood, who also ran the Scarborough 'Taps' public
house in Bishopgate Street, where the great Dan Leno is said to
have once appeared. With the assistance of Mr. J. C. Whiteman as
booker and manager, the Varieties opened on 1st November, 1898
with a strong bill topped by Alec Hurley, the Coster comedian,
who later married Marie Lloyd. To compete with the mighty Moss
Empires, with their restrictive 'barring clauses' on artistes under
contract to them, Mr. Wood decided to foster unknown talent. And
so there were 'Talent Nights' at the 'Taps', organised by Mr.
Whiteman, and any act showing promise was put on at the
Varieties.

Jack Pleasants, the shy Bradford comedian, and Morny Cash,
'The Lancashire Lad' are reputed to have been discovered here at
the 'Taps'. In addition, Mr. Whiteman signed up a wrestler from
Cornwall, named Jack Carkeek, to give an exhibition of this comparatively unknown 'art' at the Varieties, and found he had started
a wrestling craze which later swept the country in 1904.

Besides unknown talent, many up-and-coming acts, later to
become very famous, made their bow at the Varieties at very small
salaries during Mr. Wood's regime. Three leather-bound ledgers,
recording acts booked and put on at the hall between 1898 and
1904, now in the possession of Mr. Arthur Childs, a retired Leeds
business man, whose grandfather kept the Mitre Inn, provide a
good index to the music hall era of that day.

Bransby Williams and Lily Langtry shared the bill in August,
1898. Bransby got £15 for his week's engagement, but the 'Jersey
Lily'—she was a favourite of King Edward VII—is discreetly
spared monetary mention. George Formby senior only pulled in
30s. about this time, but returned later to 'big money'. Harry
Lauder (later Sir Harry Lauder), the Scots comedian, started at

£6 10s. but soon returned at £22. Really 'Top Money' was paid to Vesta Victoria (£50); Chirgwin, the 'White-Eyed Kaffir' got £75, and Houdini, the escapologist netted a fabulous £150 for a week's engagement. It was now 'Two Houses a Night' at the Varieties, of course, this system being inaugurated in 1902. Mr. Wood was following the successful example of Tom Barrasford, who originated the system locally at the Princess' Palace (now known as the Tivoli) in 1899.

Mr. Whiteman, the manager's comments on the acts appearing about this time at the Varieties make interesting reading. (They were recorded against the fees paid to the various artistes). Charles Coburn (Top of the Bill) was candidly rated 'Not worth the money'. Marie Kendall (at £20) was described as 'extra good', and Rose Daly (£4) 'all right if she would sing clean songs'. Twice Chirgwin failed to appear (comment unprintable); Tom Costello (of 'Trinity Church' fame) was rated 'Good', and Roscoe's Performing Pigs (at £10) warranted 'extra good'.

Mr. Wood later extended his activities to the Queens' Theatre, in the Leeds suburb of Holbeck, when melodrama waned in popularity there, and called that hall 'The Varieties—Queens' Palace' to distinguish it from the 'City Palace'. Morny Cash was a great favourite at the Queens', and the great Dr. Bodie played there also.

Mr. Wood died in 1913, and the Varieties, 'Taps' and Queens' Theatre were sold by auction and passed into other hands. The Queens' Theatre ran a few more years under a new company, with Mr. Charles Bush as manager, until it entered its final phase as a cinema in 1923. The Varieties was purchased by Messrs. Hewitts, the brewers, of Grimsby and Doncaster, and ran in conjunction with their other halls (at those places) until the sad death of their controller, Major Crosby.

Between the wars, the City Varieties was run by several companies, including the White Swan Estates Company, Ltd., who for many years owned most of the adjoining property. In 1941 Mr. Harry Josephs, of the Lewisham Hippodrome, bought the 'Verts' and formed a new company—British Union Varieties—to carry on the great tradition. Under the banner of the Josephs family, the Varieties entered into a new era of prosperity. Famous personalities like John Betjeman paid frequent visits.

Following the Second War, the shows put on have tended to be of the 'Girlie' or 'Strip' type. The titles of some of these are pert, if not actually amusing. For instance, 'Taking Off Tonight' leaves little doubt in the mind of the type of show being put on; 'Fun and Dames' is, however, quite clever. Then we had 'Peek-a-Boo'

several times, starring Phyllis Dixey, the Queen of strip-tease.
Many appearances were made by Miss Dixey, right up to 1957,
when she officially 'retired'.

Whatever we may think of these shows, the Varieties lives on
while other halls have closed down. With all its nostalgia, and no
little help from Television, it has somehow survived to find a
niche in the present-day world of sophisticated show business. It
is, of course, a relic of the past—but an interesting one.

In March, 1960, the 'Bowler and Brolly' men of Whitehall made
sure it will never die. It was then scheduled as a building 'of special
and architectural interest'. This means, in short, that it cannot
be radically altered, pulled down, or turned into a super-market.
It is preserved for posterity.

Now, ten years later, comes a change of policy. Noting the
popularity of the nostalgic 'Olde Tyme Music Hall' type of show,
a resident production entitled 'A Night at the City Varieties' has
succeeded strip-tease. And so, one old Northern Music Hall of the
past era, at least, lives on into the present . . .

                    *   *   *   *

James Bayliss was the man responsible for the erection of the
Scotia Music Hall in Glasgow in 1862, known more latterly as the
Metropole Theatre.

This famous old hall was totally destroyed by fire—on the night
of 28th October, 1961—but the present owner, Mr. Alex Frutin,
purchased the Falcon Theatre at St. Georges' Cross for conversion
into the New Metropole, so that the music hall tradition could be
continued at this new venue. Curiously enough, the New Metropole opened its doors—with the Clark and Murray show 'Scotland
Calling'—to coincide with the Centenary of the old building.

The former Metropole, in Stockwell Street, Glasgow South,
opened as the Scotia Music Hall for the first time on 29th
December, 1862. It was built on to the back of the Scotia public-
house, and, according to one authority, the tradition is really
137 years old, as the 'Free and Easy' singing-room at the Scotia
was first established in the 1830's.

Bayliss, the man responsible for the 1862 development, had
previously been Chairman at the Oddfellows' Music Hall in Argyle
Street, run by Charlie Sloan in the 1850's. Here he had lost an
eye trying to restore order in a fracas, when someone threw a
bottle at him. After this mishap, Bayliss tried his luck as proprietor of two music halls in the Cowcaddens area: firstly at the
old Colosseum, and then at the Magnet (or Milton Rooms) which

stood near the top of Hope Street. It was after the burning down of the Magnet in 1861 that Bayliss moved across the city, purchased the Scotia public-house, and built the new music hall at the rear. One gruesome fact about this, was that the Scotia was built on the site of St. Mary's graveyard, and certain remains had to be removed and re-interred before the foundations could be laid!

At that time there were several 'Free and Easy' places of amusement open in Glasgow, among them the Philharmonic in Dunlop Street; the Shakespeare and the Jupiter, both in the Saltmarket area; the Whitebait in St. Enoch's Wynd, and 'Campbell's' in the Trongate, in addition to those already mentioned.

But under Bayliss, the music hall era proper in Glasgow began to flourish. When he died, in 1870, his widow carried on the tradition for another 20 years, or so. Under the Bayliss' regime there appeared for the first time in the Scottish city such 'stars' of the British music hall as the Great MacDermott; J. W. ('Over') Rowley; Jenny Hill; George Leybourne, and other famous names.

When H. E. Moss (son of James Moss, of the Lorne Music Hall, Greenock) and later of the famous concern, Moss Empires, took over the Scotia music hall in the 'nineties, Tommy Colquhoun, nephew of Mrs. Bayliss, who had been associated with her in the running of the hall, went into partnership with Barney Armstrong and opened two other music halls in Glasgow—the Tivoli at Anderston Cross, and the Palace in Watson Street (formerly the Star and later the Queens'). Bob Singleton, for many years musical director at the Scotia for Mrs. Bayliss, went with them, and was associated in the new ventures. In later years the Tivoli became the New Gaiety Cinema, and the Palace the Queens' Theatre, until it was destroyed by fire.

A great favourite at the Scotia was Vesta Tilley. When she appeared there under the Moss' banner (the proprietors were Messrs. Moss, Thornton and Kirk) in 1895, patrons were so delighted with her performance that they held a collection and presented her with a beautiful floral bouquet at her last appearance there on the Saturday night. Vesta was truly 'Everybody's Favourite'.

When the new Moss' Empire Theatre opened in Sauchiehall Street in 1897, the old Scotia was closed down as a music hall. It was subsequently re-opened at Christmas, 1898 with the pantomime 'Robinson Crusoe' starring Alma Obrey as Principal Boy, and the name changed to the Metropole Theatre, by the new lessees, Messrs. H. H. Morell and Fred Mouillot.

Three years later, Arthur Jefferson (father of the famous film comedian Stan Laurel) took it over, and ran it in conjunction with several theatres, at Motherwell, Blyth, North Shields and other places.

Strong drama was the fare at the Jefferson halls. 'Proof' was one of the first melodramas staged there; then came pieces like 'Maria Marten' and 'The Grip of Iron'. This was known as 'the Burke and Hare' period of melodrama in the theatre. In one of these early masterpieces—'Women and Wine'—the two leading female characters fought each other (after tearing off each other's dresses) in their under-slips—considered very daring indeed at the time. Later there came a more sophisticated type of melodrama, with the emphasis on sex.

Bernard Frutin took over the Metropole Theatre about the time of the First World War, and, upon his death, control passed to his two sons, Hyman and Alex.

The Logan family, whose name will always be associated with the Stockwell Street Metropole Theatre, first appeared there in 1937. Then, 'Pa' Logan and his wife were known as Jack Short and May Dalziel. Jack Short took control of productions in 1943 and in 1947 he founded the famous 'Logan Family', whose shows became an institution at the 'Met.' And so Variety returned to its old home at the Metropole, alias the Scotia, after a lapse of many years.

One reason why the Metropole remained faithful to melodrama so long was that the Palace Music Hall in Stockwell Street (next to the Citizens Theatre, or Royal Princess Theatre as it was then, not to be confused with the People's Palace in Watson Street) had been opened by Rich. Waldron in 1907, and there was hardly room for two music halls in the Gorbals. When the Palace became a 'Talkie' cinema, the Metropole returned to Variety, with conspicuous success.

The New Metropole was built in 1914 as the West End Playhouse, but within six months it had closed its doors as a financial failure. The former Playhouse, which stands at St. George's Cross, in the New City Road area, has a capacity of 1,300. In 1918 Harry Godwin turned it into the Empress Variety Theatre, but after another period of closure, the late George Urie Scott re-opened it in 1933 with Cine-Variety, as the New Empress. In 1956 the New Empress was seriously damaged by fire, but Mr. Scott restored it at a cost of £40,000.

In February, 1960 the building was sold to the Falcon Trust, and re-opened by that body as the Falcon Theatre, as an arts theatre centre. A scheme to re-build the theatre was proposed, at an estimated cost of £250,000, but only £25,000 was raised by a public appeal for funds. It was doomed to close when Mr. Alex. Frutin stepped in and bought it.

And so, Scottish Variety fans, saddened by the loss of their oldest music hall by fire, can rejoice that the old Metropole tradition is being carried on by the same management in a newer building, in another part of the city.

* * * *

If the Argyle was the most famous name in Music Hall, then the Palladium must rank as the equivalent in Variety! It is now known to millions via the famous 'Sunday Night at the London Palladium' on Independent Television, and many notable performers have graced its boards down the years.

It opened on Boxing Day, 1910 with a huge bill of artistes, among them Nellie Wallace, Whit Cunliffe, Ella Shields, Ella Retford and Sir John Martin Harvey in a playlet.

The site of the London Palladium, in Argyll Street near Oxford Circus, was formerly the residence of the Duke of Argyll and Earl of Aberdeen. In 1870 the mansion was pulled down and a building known as the Corinthian Bazaar erected on the site. This in turn was occupied by Hengler's Circus and some reconstruction took place under the supervision of C. J. Phipps, the famous Bath architect, during 1882–4.

F. C. Hengler was a Liverpool circus proprietor, who eventually established circuses in Glasgow, Dublin, Hull and Liverpool apart from the London site. He died in 1887 but his family carried on the circus on the Argyll Street site for some years. In 1895 it was further reconstructed to become the National Skating Palace, with the invention of artificial freezing of water into ice. (The only other 'ice palace' in Europe at this time is believed to have been the Calentarients Rink at Scarborough, in the basement of the old Londesborough Theatre there.)

In 1909 Walter Gibbons acquired the premises on behalf of his company, the London Theatres of Variety ('L.T.V.') and after further reconstruction to the designs of Frank Matcham to the cost of £250,000 the building re-opened as the Palladium. The London Theatres of Variety comprised the Holborn Empire (formerly the Royal, Holborn) and later the Golders Green and Lewisham Hippodromes, in addition to the Oxford and the Tivoli.

Walter Gibbons (later Sir Walter) was a native of Wolverhampton and around the turn of the century was prominent in demonstrating films, known as the 'Gibbons Bio-Tableaux'. He married George Adney Payne's daughter and, with his father-in-law, ran the 'Syndicate Halls'. After Payne's death (by accident) in 1907, Gibbons formed the London Theatres of Variety. In 1914 Walter Gibbons joined the Forces, following the outbreak of the First War, eventually becoming Lt.-Col. Gibbons, K.B.E. and was later knighted.

In 1912, however, the London Palladium had been granted a stage plays licence by the Lord Chamberlain and Charles Gulliver took control, later becoming chief of the L.T.V.

All the big names in Music Hall played at the Palladium under Gulliver, who also gained control of other circuits, including that of De Frece. In the years following the First War the Palladium became a cinema, but reverted back to Variety in September, 1928. This was when Gulliver sold out to the General Theatres Corporation controlled by George Black, son of old George Black of Sunderland. The first star-studded bill under the new order included Gracie Fields, Billy Bennett and Dick Henderson (father of Dickie).

Booking controller at the Palladium in 1928 was a young man destined to play a big part in the fortunes of the building. He was Val Parnell, son of Fred Russell, the old-time ventriloquist, and formerly office boy with Sir Walter de Frece at the Camberwell Empire. Around 1930, when variety theatres were feeling the pinch of the new 'Talkies', Val Parnell persuaded George Black to let him try 'quick-fire' Variety at the Palladium on the American principle. It worked and crowded houses were the rule at the Palladium, in contrast to the rival Alhambra, where Stoll faced an alarming slump.

However, Val Parnell's greatest triumph at the Palladium was his idea for 'The Crazy Gang'. In 1930 he took a trip to Nottingham to see there at the Empire a show called 'Young Bloods' which was a revue put on by Jimmy Nervo, with himself and Teddy Knox as leading comedians. Parnell liked what he saw and persuaded Nervo and Knox to play a week at the Palladium with a 'Crazy Show' routine he had in mind.

However, when it was realised that Nervo and Knox would have to team up with Naughton and Gold, there was trouble because of an old feud between the two teams of comics. Neither would work with the other, but finally Parnell got round them, and the first 'Crazy Week' show was a great success. Nervo and Knox had been a team since 1919 and Naughton and Gold since 1908. Charlie Naughton met Jimmy Gold on a building site at Glasgow and played their first engagement at the old Zoo-Hippodrome in the New City Road, that same year.

Val Parnell's 'Crazy Week' led to a 'Crazy Month' in which Billy Caryll and Hilda Munday (a man and wife team) were brought in, together with 'Monsewer' Eddie Gray, a 'French-talking' juggler with a comedy routine. Then in 1932 Bud Flanagan and Chesney Allen were brought from the Holborn Empire to make up 'The Crazy Gang' which became a British institution for thirty years.

The Crazy Gang reigned at the Victoria Palace for fifteen years solid, being reconstituted in 'Together Again' after the Second War, in 1947, by Jack Hylton. When they finally made their last bow (in May, 1962) they had earned the title of 'Court Jesters' because of their ability to 'warm up' the theatre where the Royal Variety Show was being held—in particular the Palladium their old home —and where most of the Royal Performances were given.

In 1945 George Black died and Val Parnell succeeded him as managing director of Moss Empires and London Palladium. The next year Val Parnell packed his bags for America and the result of that visit turned the Palladium into the World's 'Number One' Variety Theatre.

With the policy of 'Variety is International' he brought over such 'star' names as Danny Kaye, Jack Benny, Frank Sinatra, Bob Hope, Johnny Ray, Ella Fitzgerald, Judy Garland and many, many more. How the crowds rolled in to support this policy, so ably carried on since 1959 by the later 'boss' Leslie MacDonnell.

*　　　*　　　*　　　*

'The Palladium of the North' is how the Gaiety Theatre in Ayr has been described—and for good reason. If you ask the Popplewells (who run this fine Scottish Variety theatre) to name the famous 'stars' who have appeared there, they will smile and remark it is easier to tell you the few that have not!

The Gaiety has been burned down, rebuilt and patronised by royalty, in the 45 years that it has been under the control of the Popplewells, but the family's association with the popular Scottish West coast resort goes back longer than that. In fact to 1913 when Ben Popplewell ('Daddy Ben' to all who knew him) became manager of the Pavilion on the Green for the Council.

But to go right back to the beginning, the Popplewell 'tradition' began in the woollen city of Bradford in the West Riding of Yorkshire, in the 1890's. During those years 'Young Ben' (born in 1870) became fascinated by the 'Saturday Night Concerts' put on by various entrepreneurs at the Bradford Mechanics' Institute.

The son of Alderman John Popplewell, 'Young Ben' was persuaded to enter the family business of Popplewell Brothers, stockbrokers, of Manns Court, Bradford, as junior partner. In 1895 he married Sarah ('Sally') Illingworth, the daughter of another Bradford Alderman. They had four children, but somehow Ben could not give stockbroking his full attention. Those weekly 'Pops' (Popular Concerts) at the Mechanics' drew him like a magnet. In the summer of 1901 he surprised the rather staid members of his family by spending his summer vacation as a member of a pierrot troupe on the sands at Clacton-on-Sea. There as a member of Fred Pullan's 'Yorkshire Pierrots' he strummed away at an old banjo and enjoyed himself immensely.

Fred Pullan, the leader of the pierrot troupe, was a fellow Bradfordian, in fact a member of the family which ran the old wooden 'Pullan's Music Hall' destroyed by a spectacular fire in the 'eighties. Ben and he became great friends and they participated in the running of the concerts at the Mechanics' from time to time.

In 1904 the Bradford Exhibition was held and when it was over one of the temporary buildings about to be scrapped was 'The Concert Hall', an imposing affair with a plaster frontage. Ben Popplewell surprised everybody by purchasing the hall and having it re-erected on land at Frizinghall, near Bradford. His idea was to run the place as an inland concert party pavilion, and so, in partnership with 'The Musical Bentleys', a local man-and-wife team, he opened for the 1905 season with a company known as 'The Dandy Militaires'. Madge Bentley, wife of Walter Bentley, co-partner with Ben, was the soubrette in the company.

'The Dandy Militaires' were a great success at the Frizinghall Pavilion and a youthful and very interested spectator in the early days was J. B. Priestley, who in later years used the concert party idea for the basis of his novel 'The Good Companions'.

After the 1907 season the Bentley's, against the advice of Ben Popplewell, insisted upon moving the Pavilion to a new site. This caused a break-up. Leaving the Bentleys to carry on at Frizinghall, Ben invested money in the Queens' Palace music hall in Shipley, and attempted to give more time to stockbroking.

However, something happened in 1913 to change all that. Curious to know why his shares in the municipally-owned Pavilion Theatre at Ayr were constantly dropping, Ben made a trip to the Scottish resort to find out. The locals called the Pavilion 'The White Elephant on the Green'. It was clear that the Councillors knew nothing about show business and they welcomed his advice. In fact they invited him to stay in Ayr and help them run the Pavilion as manager!

And so in 1913 came the vital decision to finally break with

Bradford and the family stockbroking business. The family moved
lock, stock and barrel to Ayr; the Shipley Queens' Palace being
disposed of as a cinema. Rather curiously, about this same time,
Ben's former partner Walter Bentley entered the cinema business—
at Middlesbrough and Stockton—and did so well he finally had a
suite of offices in the West End.

In 1913 the Popplewell family in Ayr consisted of Ben and
Sally, two sons, Leslie and Eric, and two daughters, Pattie and
Winnie. Came the First War and Leslie, the elder, joined the Royal
Flying Corps, while Eric later joined the Navy. In 1918 the
Coliseum Theatre at Goole came on to the market and Ben, Sally
and the girls decided to return to Yorkshire, to run it. Upon
'Demob.' Leslie and Eric went into the cinema business at Leicester,
where they did everything—from bill-posting to 'turning the handle'.

However, in 1922, Pattie the eldest girl fell ill. The East Yorkshire climate did not agree with her. And so came the decision to
return to Ayr. The Council were glad to see them back. Ben's
first move when taking over the Pavilion again was to put in
Charlie Kemble's 'Entertainers' for the 1923 season. Sadly, in this
year Pattie died, in spite of constant nursing and the best medical
attention.

The year 1925 saw the 23-year-old Gaiety Theatre in Carrick
Street, Ayr, come on to the market, after years of gory melodrama
and spells of 'Pictures and Variety'. Ben decided to buy it and
take his two sons into partnership—and so the great Popplewell
association with the Ayr Gaiety began.

But success did not come all at once. At the end of 1927,
following 18 months' hard work at the Gaiety, the Popplewells
had very little to show for their efforts. Ben then decided that the
time was ripe to employ 'shock tactics'. The Pavilion (leased by
the family from the Council) was converted into a ballroom, to
avoid competition with the new Variety policy at the Gaiety.

A 'Grand Vaudeville Season' was launched at the renovated
Gaiety during the summer of 1928. The biggest names in Variety
at that time were brought to the theatre 'regardless of expense'.
Wee Georgie Wood, Layton and Johnstone, Jose Collins, Will Fyfe
and Harry Lauder followed each other in quick succession. Will
Fyfe, who had played at the Pavilion for the Popplewells as an
'unknown' in 1914 (with his wife Lily Bolton for £8 the pair) came
for a fraction of the fee he could earn in 1928. Likewise, Harry
Lauder (later Sir Harry Lauder) who could command £800 a week
in America at that time, came for a much reduced figure. With the
'Big Name' policy came the big crowds. How the people rolled in

from the outlying districts as motor charabancs were chartered to bring theatre-goers from Maybole, Cumnock and other places. The Ayr Gaiety was successfully launched as a 'Number One' Variety theatre.

In 1929 the 'Grand Vaudeville Season' gave way to 'The Summer Show', and a year later to 'The Gaiety Show'. In 1931 it was named 'The Whirl of Gaiety' and in 1932 the 'Gaiety Whirl' as it is today. So started the tradition which was to make the Popplewells famous.

The first 'Whirl' gave a chance to an unknown comic named Lex McLean. Today he has his own show, which plays to packed houses at the Glasgow Pavilion, in which the Popplewells have acquired an interest. In the 1932 edition appeared Kim Kendall (granddaughter of the famous Marie, who played at the Pavilion in 1917). After the season Kim left Ayr to marry an American millionaire.

Many of those early 'Whirls' were piloted by Dave Willis; then came the late Jack Anthony, Jack Radcliffe, Harry Gordon, Robert Wilson, Jack Milroy and Johnny Beattie. The latter was once very raw material indeed, but has since been billed as 'Scotland's Sophisticated Comedy Star', thanks to 'grooming' by the Popplewells.

Coming more up to date, the Popplewell 'nursery' has produced such talent as Patricia Bredin, Stan Stennett, Margo Henderson, Andy Stewart and Kenneth McKellar. The lovely Moira Anderson, a local girl, also got her first stage 'break' at the Gaiety. Margo Henderson was only fourteen when she was introduced to the Popplewells, but she went on to play the London Palladium in later years.

Royalty has patronised the Gaiety, in the person of the Duke of Kent (husband of the late Princess Marina). The Duke liked the 1942 'Whirl' and said so, but sad to relate, only a few days later he was killed when his war-time aircraft crashed on a Scottish hillside.

In 1955 the Gaiety was badly damaged by fire, but a year later —on 2nd July, 1956—it was re-opened again. Then the Popplewells received a congratulatory telegram from the Queen, of which they are very proud.

Ben Popplewell died in 1950 aged eighty and since that time the theatre has been carried on by his two sons, Leslie and Eric, with sister Winnie co-opted to control the administrative side. Many of the 'Whirls' have been produced by Max and Maisie Norris, who also have Bradford associations.

Although now well into middle life, the Popplewell brothers are still known as 'The Boys'. Eric devises and directs the shows, also travelling extensively in search of new talent, while Leslie assists Winnie and is also responsible for the Pavilion ballroom, where such top class bands as those of Acker Bilk, Kenny Ball, Terry Lightfoot and many others have appeared.

Animal acts are not encouraged at the Gaiety in the light of past experience. Once the stage collapsed under the weight of an elephant; then a chimpanzee ran amok in the auditorium, and in 'Daddy Ben's' time one of Marguerita's 'Forest Bred Lions' remembered his breeding but forgot his manners when he approached the footlights and lifted a leg . . . never have the orchestra beat such a hasty or undignified retreat!

Other incidents since the Popplewell regime began at the Gaiety include the time when the glamorous soprano could not go on because she had mislaid her false teeth; a comedian whose jaw locked in the middle of his act and who had to be rushed to hospital, and the famous lady film star who stopped the orchestra with the words 'I have forgotten my act' and promptly ran off!

The Popplewells are proud of the fact that 'Daddy Ben' was responsible for bringing about one of the most successful partnerships in show business. This was in 1923 when Florrie Forde, rehearsing a new show in Glasgow, telephoned Ben about a partner for Chesney Allen: a man named Stanford having left at short notice. Ben immediately recommended Bud Winthrop, then appearing as a solo comedian at the Kilmarnock Palace. Imagine their surprise when the pair found they had met already—in war-torn France in 1916. Bud changed his name to 'Flanagan' after the theme song sung by Florrie in the show and 'Flanagan and Allen' clicked as a team and never looked back.

Although it is more than fifty years since the Popplewells left Bradford, they still retain an affection for their native city. Occasionally they visit their old haunts, but not as often as they would like—the reason being that they are far too busy running the most successful Variety theatre in Scotland.

3

Stars that made the Halls

WITHOUT A DOUBT, the biggest attraction in the early days of Music Hall was the so-called 'Lion Comique'.

Charles Morton, who has been given the title of 'Father of the Halls', having gained that reputation by 'creating' Music Hall at his Canterbury Arms, in the Westminster Bridge Road, London, around 1850, is credited also with discovering and popularising several 'Lion Comiques'.

'Jolly' John Nash, famous for his laughing songs, was one of the first, but the one whose name stands out is George Leybourne of 'Champagne Charlie' fame. Then there was the Great Mackney, the Great Vance, not forgetting the Great MacDermott (of 'Jingo' fame). Morton was the man responsible for dubbing these men 'Great' when he billed them at his new hall in the West End (The Oxford Music Hall) in the 1860's.

These comiques were known for their songs—especially Vance for his 'Slap Bang!'—which became an early signature tune. The North saw these comiques on tour, of course. There were several lesser known ones, products of the North, such as The Great Mildey and The Great Laroche. J. H. Milburn, an ex-Wearside glass-worker, who made famous 'On the Beach at Brighton', was brother-in-law to Frank Allen, of Moss Empires. Milburn ran a music hall at one period—the wooden Milburn's Varieties which stood on a site later occupied by the Sunderland Avenue Theatre, built in 1882. In later years he managed the Newport Empire for the Moss combine. His son, Hartley Milburn, was a well-known agent.

The comiques were, in fact, comic singers. They all dressed as 'swells' in the very height of fashion, usually swaggering about the stage with a cane, or other foppish appendage. At one time it was considered all the rage to sing patriotic songs. Later on they sang what would nowadays be called *idiotic* songs!

Mackney, perhaps the first of the comiques, graduated from the ranks of the black-faced comedians, and was known for his song 'I wish I were in Dixie', but it was his dramatic recital 'The whole

58

Hog or none' that put a phrase into the English language. He became a farmer after retiring from the halls, and did quite well, which is more than can be said for some of his contemporaries.

The Great MacDermott, famous for his 'We Don't want to Fight, but By Jingo, if we Do . . .' started life as a bricklayer. After a spell at sea he got a job as stage-manager at the old Britannia Theatre, Hoxton, before venturing on the halls as a comic singer. When his fame as a comique dimmed, he ended his career as an agent.

Alfred Glanvill Vance (real name Alfred Peck Stevens) was born in 1840 and in his early days was a dramatic actor in the North. He had experience in stock company at Preston, Manchester and Liverpool, and made his debut as a comic singer at the White Lion (later the Metropolitan Music Hall) in the Edgware Road, about 1864. He then toured with a company of singers, and is known to have appeared at the Leeds City Varieties in the latter part of 1865, the year of its opening in something like its present form. He did Cockney dialect studies, and for a time was known as 'The Chickaleary Cove'. He died of a heart attack on the boards of the old Sun Music Hall, Knightsbridge, at Christmas, 1889.

George Leybourne, the greatest of all the 'Comiques', was born Joe Saunders in Wolverhampton in 1842, and started life as a hammer-man in the local steel rolling mills. After singing in Midlands 'Free and Easies' he made his way to the Metropolis and was discovered by an agent singing in a place called Gilbert's at Whitechapel. After an audition, Old Man Morton put him on at the Canterbury at a salary of £20 (big money then) later raised to £120 per week! He was always immaculately dressed, and commanded big money everywhere he appeared. In the Provinces too, he was a great success. At the old Wear Music Hall, Sunderland, he drove around the town in a carriage and pair (for publicity purposes) and drew £80 a week, which was colossal for a provincial hall. The Wear Music Hall had to stage its performances 'Twice-nightly' in order to accommodate all who wished to see him. His greatest number was always 'Champagne Charlie'. Leybourne perhaps took the words of his drinking songs to heart for he looked upon the wine when it was red, and died (it is said) from the effects of imbibing in 1884 at the early age of 42. His last appearance was on the stage of the Queens' Music Hall, Poplar.

*   *   *   *

The male 'Comiques' had their female counterparts in the so-called Serio-Comediennes, of which there were several who could command big money. The real 'Queen' of them all was the 'Vital Spark' Jenny Hill, who started her career as the hind legs of a pantomime horse, and ended it as a famous Principal Boy.

Much nonsense has been written about Jenny, but it would appear that she was born in 1856, the daughter of a Marylebone 'cabby'. Her first appearance in the Metropolis (as a serio) was at the London Pavilion in the early 1870's when she was put on as a stop-gap turn for the great George Leybourne, who was overrunning his time at another of the 'Syndicate Halls'. Her success surprised Loibl, the manager. She was retained, and her reputation made.

Jenny Hill appeared many times in the North, and was a great favourite at Pullans' Music Hall in Brunswick Place, Bradford. She was always billed as 'The Vital Spark' on account of her abounding energy—a name given her by her agent—Hugh Jay Didcott. She was a small, dynamic little woman, who soon endeared herself to audiences, although sometimes her material was 'questionable'.

A Press report of her visit to Bradford, for the week of 6th October, 1879, makes interesting reading:

> 'Miss Jenny Hill has been delighting capital houses at Pullan's Theatre of Varieties, Bradford, this week. She sings several new songs exceedingly well, and her "patter" is very good. I am pleased to note that she does not indulge so largely in *double entendre*. She is an excellent comedienne and capable of earning a legitimate reputation without descending to vulgarity.
>
> 'The Waite Sisters, the Bros. Poluski, Dick Schofield and others add their quota to the programme, which is a good one.'

One of Jenny's songs, always performed with great success, was 'Masks and Faces', all about a virtuous maiden, and written especially for her by George Lebrunn. She was singing this at the Canterbury Music Hall in London's Westminster Bridge Road on the night a maniac stabbed Letine, a trick-cyclist, at the stage door. Another song success of Jenny's was 'Arry,' written for her by Papa Page, one-time manager of the Brixton Empress.

Later, in 1889, Jenny Hill graduated to the legitimate stage, and appeared at both the Grecian and the Gaiety Theatres in London. In the 1890's her health broke down, and she made a trip to sunny South Africa in an attempt to regain lost vigour, but in vain. She died in England in 1896 at the age of 46.

Jenny, who married at the tender age of 15, left a daughter, professionally known as Peggy Pryde, who also went on the stage and became a Principal Boy. Peggy Pryde made her first stage appearance (as a child, with mother) at the Empire, Hull (when it was known as 'Springthorpe's') in 1877. In later years, Peggy married Maurice de Frece, the agent, and left the Profession.

A great friend of Jenny Hill's was Bessie Bellwood, who sang 'Wot Cheer, Ria', and who had a similar, if noisier, style. She was an ex-rabbit skinner from Bermondsey, and made her debut as a serio-comedienne at Johnny Hart's Temple of Terpsichore (The Star Music Hall) in that borough in 1892. Her real name was Lizzie Mahoney. Although she belonged to a period later than Jenny Hill, she never became as popular in the North of England.

Victoria Monks, another 'serio', who made famous the song 'Won't You Come Home, Bill Bailey?', was on the opening bill at the Lincoln Empire in 1901, when she was very young. When she topped the bill at the Barnsley Alhambra in 1915 the First War was on, and she was then quite famous. She did a lot for the troops, by way of entertainment, in that war, and died while quite young.

Nellie Power, another of the old-time 'serios', had a song called 'The Boy I love is up in the Gallery', made famous years later by the one and only Marie Lloyd. Little is remembered about Nellie Power, who faded quite soon into obscurity, but Marie Lloyd was 'everybody's favourite' in the music hall 'boom' period, which preceded the First War. She was considered by many to be 'The Queen of the Music Halls'.

W. MacQueen Pope, the great theatrical historian, in a tribute, said:

'. . . She was the very essence of music hall, and womanhood . . . She could capture an audience and hold it entranced. She could make it roar with laughter, howl with delight, and bring it very near to tears . . .'

Born in 1870, real name Tilly Wood, Marie Lloyd made her debut, like Bessie Bellwood, at the Star Music Hall, Bermondsey, and got 15/- for her first week's engagement. She was then known as Belle Delamere, but later, with her sisters, became one of the Lloyd Sisters, before branching out on her own.

Marie Lloyd was a forthright, if not definitely vulgar type of comedienne, and was rather pointedly not invited to take part in the first Royal Command Performance in 1912, although at the time she was right at the top of the Variety tree. She married three times, none of them very successfully. One of her husbands was Alec Hurley, the well-known Coster comedian. Marie's last known

appearance in the North was at the Gateshead Empire early in
1922. Not very long after this, she was taken ill whilst appearing
at the Crouch End Hippodrome, and never recovered.

Nellie Wallace was another (perhaps the last) of the so-called
'serio-comediennes'. With her feather boa, sniffle, and suggestive
wink, she topped music hall bills for many years, and more recently,
made a name for herself on sound radio, adapting her style quite
successfully. J. Pitt Hardacre, who ran several theatres in Lancashire, including the old Comedy (or Gaiety) Theatre in Manchester,
is reputed to have 'discovered' her, when he booked her for pantomime. She was on the first bill at the Bradford Alhambra, when
that magnificent white terra-cotta building opened its doors, at
Easter, 1914. Nellie Wallace was born in 1870 and made her very
first stage appearance in Birmingham as a clog dancer in an act
called 'The Three Sisters Wallace' in 1888. She was a very clever
female 'Dame' comedienne in pantomime in later years.

Another popular type of act, presented by the ladies, was that
of 'Male Impersonator'. There were several very famous ones down
the years—Vesta Tilley, Hettie King, and Ella Shields (who made
famous 'Burlington Bertie from Bow') to mention just a few—
and they had many admirers.

Hettie King, who was still making appearances in 1969 well into
her eighties, was born in New Brighton, into a theatrical family. Her
father was a member of a Minstrel troupe and when she was nine
Hettie joined him in an act on the music halls called Will King and
Hettie, in which she did impressions of George Lashwood and
others. While appearing at the Bradford Palace she was seen by
impresario Robert Arthur a few years later and offered £30 a
week to appear as Principal Boy in one of his pantomimes in
Birmingham. However, it is as a male impersonator she is best
remembered—in particular in nautical guise.

Vesta Tilley, the most famous of them all, was born Tilly Ball.
She was the daughter of music hall Chairman Harry Ball, real
name Powles. Vesta, who got her name for being 'the matchless
little Tilly' was always the Darling of the music halls, and was
very well liked and admired. She was one of the 'stars' of the first
Royal Command Performance at the Palace Theatre, London, in
1912, but here a very curious thing happened. Queen Mary, who
accompanied King George V, suddenly indicated 'that the gaze of
the ladies of the Royal Party be directed not at the stage'. It was
not some daring nude, or salacious serio-comedienne that caused
this amazing *contretemps,* but dear little Vesta in trousers! It was
the male attire that perturbed Queen Mary—in her eyes not very

lady-like. Eventually the First War killed such Victorian anach-
ronisms.

Writing about Harry Ball and Vesta Tilley, Emrys Bryson of
Nottingham, says:

'Chairman of the St. George's Hall music hall in Nottingham (where the Co-op. now stands) was Harry Ball. He was
an ex-Worcester china worker, who had designed a tea service
for Queen Victoria. Later he became a comedian, and then
managed the St. Georges' Hall for George Hooper. Ball's
daughter made her debut on that stage in 1868. "Don't be
frightened", coaxed her father, "sing as if you meant it". She
was then four years of age and became Vesta Tilley.

'Billed as "The Pocket Sims Reeves" little Vesta had a way
of making the tears flow from her half-boozed audiences. She
played "Little Willie" in "East Lynne" and entreated a
drunken father to come back to his wife in "Father, Come
Home".

'Under the wing of a neighbour, she used to travel to other
music halls in Derby and Leicester, and later went on tour
with her father in "The Tramp Musicians", sending money
home to Mother in Nottingham.'

The hall in Leicester at which little Vesta appeared, was the
place in the Belgrave Gate, known as 'Paul's' after its proprietor.
Apparently Vesta adopted male attire quite early, for it is known
that when Paul first saw her, he told her to 'Go home and get
dressed'. This place of amusement was noted for its succulent
pork pies in its early days. In later years 'Paul's' became the Tivoli
Palace, until MacNaghten renamed it 'The Pavilion Theatre'.

There were many suitors for the hand of Vesta Tilley when she
grew up, but she settled for the charm of handsome Walter de
·Frece, whom she met while appearing in pantomime in Liverpool in
1889. Her husband later became Sir Walter, and head of that vast
syndicate of music halls known as 'The Variety Theatres Controlling Company', and later again, an M.P. Their marriage was a
very happy one, and the evening of their lives was spent together
at Monte Carlo, where they had a villa.

*   *   *   *

Several Colonials made good on the British Vaudeville stage.
Perhaps the three most famous of them were Billy Williams, Florrie
Forde and Albert Whelan, all now deceased. (Albert Whelan died
while this work was in preparation.)

Billy Williams, known as 'The Man in the Velvet Suit', always appeared in a blue velvet suit, and in the days when he was 'Top of the Bill' drove round the town in which he was appearing in an open carriage, thus attired. This was to draw attention, and so people would say 'There goes Billy Williams—The Man in the Velvet Suit'. In 1902 he topped an early bill at the Tivoli, in South Shields, run by bookmakers Hall and Sweeney. (This hall was not a success, and later became a store.) Billy came from 'Down Under'.

Florrie Forde, also born in Australia, died in this country in 1940 after many years on the music halls. She was in great demand for Principal Boy at one time—she had a buxom figure—and appeared in this role at the York Empire when it opened in January 1902, although in those days it was the Grand Opera House. In this pantomime she wore an enormous hat weighing several pounds in weight, and valued at seven pounds in cash! One of her favourite songs was 'Flanagan' and she sang it in a revue 'Flo and Co.' after the First War. An unknown comedian known as Bud Winthrop joined the show at Glasgow, largely through the recommendation of Ben Popplewell of the Gaiety Theatre, Ayr. Florrie teamed him up with Chesney Allen, and called the pair 'Flanagan and Allen'. They 'clicked' as a team, and never looked back, thanks to Florrie.

Albert Whelan, who hailed from Melbourne, made his debut in London as a scare-crow dancer in revue. He later 'adopted' a tune known as 'The Jolly Brothers' as a kind of signature tune, and used to make his rather leisurely entrance and exit with it, whistling all the while. He was not billed as a dancer—although he did a neat step—but as an immaculately dressed Dandy, with a smart line in patter. There is a story that Sir Oswald Stoll would only allow him eight minutes to do his act at the London Coliseum, which was not enough. Albert got his own back by walking on, to his tuneful whistle, disrobing very deliberately his immaculate white gloves, topper, scarf and overcoat: then (whistling all the while) just as deliberately putting them all on again—time just eight minutes! Sir Oswald was just as amused by this as everybody else 'in the know'.

Ben Leete (professionally known as Harry Rickards) applied lease-lend in reverse. As a music hall performer in Britain in the 'nineties, he went bankrupt. Then he emigrated to Australia and formed a very successful circuit of music halls, eventually paying off all his British debts. As a result he was very well thought of by all ranks of the Profession.

Acrobatic acts have always been popular on the Halls. One of

BRING ON THE DANCING GIRLS!
The Can-Can Girls at Balmbra's Music Hall in Newcastle, 1962.

LA PIA, who appeared in the 1912 Command Performance.

VERONICA, billed as "The World's Champion High-Kicker" in 1933.

Plate 3

THE CAN-CAN!
JANE TERRY
leading the
GAIETY GIRLS
in action at the
famous
LEEDS CITY
VARIETIES.

Photo:
Courtesy of
Michael Josephs.

Plate 4

Photo: Moss Empires

(Above) THE LONDON PALLADIUM. A Royal Event—The Command Performance is the subject of the picture, together with the ornate entrance.

HALLS OF FAME

(Below) THE LEEDS CITY VARIETIES. A Television Event—"The Good Old
Days" being televised from this popular venue in the North by the B.B.C.

Photo: Yorkshire Post

Plate 5

The FOLLY MUSIC HALL, MAN-
CHESTER, as it appeared in the
1890's.

The original GLASGOW METRO-
POLE in Stockwell Street South, before the fire of 1961.

MORE FAMOUS HALLS

The HULL ALHAMBRA as it was
in the Gay Nineties.

The TIVOLI, HULL just before the
closure in 1954.

Plate 6

the very first was Blondin, a real Frenchman, born Emile Gravet, and who was eventually awarded the Legion of Honour. His debut in this country was at the old Crystal Palace in London on 6th June, 1861, and later in that year he did a Provincial tour, appearing at places like Peel Park, Bradford; the Piece Hall Yard, Halifax, as well as at seaside venues like the Raikes Hall Gardens in Blackpool, and the old Summer Gardens at Morecambe. Blondin walked on the high-wire, and had crossed the famous Niagara Falls in America several times.

He was as sure-footed as a mountain goat, but always made some pretence of slipping, to the consternation and horror of the crowd. He complained if the wire was less than 100 ft. from the ground—the nearer to 250 ft. the better—and he wheeled a wheelbarrow across, often with someone in it. Blondin took his small daughter across once, but the authorities later forbade this, so he had to be content with a lion cub. On one occasion at least—at the old Highfield Gardens, near Sheffield—he crossed with the lion cub accompanied by a blaze of fireworks.

In later years Blondin went on the music halls, but often the audience would not believe he was the 'Hero of Niagara'. At the wooden Pullan's Theatre of Varieties, Bradford, in 1879, the management had to announce that '£1,000 will be paid, if not the original and genuine Blondin, etc., etc.' Blondin made a lot of money, but lost it in business speculations. He had to come out of retirement to make further appearances. He walked the wire at Rotherham in 1895 as of old, and again, a year later at a gala in Belfast. Blondin died in 1897 at the age of 73, peacefully in bed at his home (aptly termed 'Niagara Villa') in Ealing. He was a short, stocky figure, with his 30 ft. pole, balanced gracefully on the high-wire. His feats have never since been equalled.

Another curious music hall 'draw' was Arthur Orton, the so-called Tichborne Claimant. Said to be Thomas Castro, a butcher's assistant from Wagga Wagga (New South Wales) masquerading as the long lost Roger Tichborne, heir to wealth and estates, who was lost at sea. In 1866 Orton turned up, and tried to convince everybody he was Roger Tichborne, including relatives of the dead man. There was a court action which began in 1871 and lasted 102 days. The jury finally stopped the case, and the corpulent impostor (he weighed 20 stone) got 14 years for perjury.

When he came out of jail, Orton went on the halls, and in a sonorous voice recited his tale of woe, regarding his alleged wrongful imprisonment. His first appearance was at the Royal Music Hall, Holborn (later the Holborn Empire) where he proved a big

c

attraction. In 1887 he was appearing to fabulous business at Moss'
Gaiety Theatre in Newcastle. Later on, when the novelty had worn
off, he became a music hall 'Chairman' (one hall was the Greyhound Inn Music Hall in Bradford) and later still owned a cigar
store in Islington, not far from the 'Chapel on the Green' (Collins'
Music Hall). He was a familiar figure, before he died at the turn
of the century, sitting on a chair outside his shop, exchanging
pleasantries with the Pro's playing at the famous music hall nearby.

*   *   *   *

There have been many Mesmerists and magicians down the years,
but a famous personality who caused a sensation in Derby in the
early 1900's was Ahrensmayer, an American. He was known as
'The Cowboy Illusionist' and wore a wide-brimmed Stetson hat.
His speciality was hypnotism, when that noble (or possibly ignoble)
art or science was comparatively little known, and truly astonished
the natives by putting a man into a trance by telephone!

Ahrensmayer was engaged at the Derby Palace, and rang from
the manager's office to his 'subject' who was in another part of
Derby, in the presence of medical men as witnesses. Sure enough,
the subject went under the 'fluence'. He was then carried into the
theatre on a stretcher, and on the stage, the hypnotist stuck pins
and needles into him—just to prove that he was insensible to pain.
Surely the subject could have found a less painful way of making
a living?

Another great favourite in Derby was Madame Ella, with her
'Forest Bred Lions'. (Incidentally, most stage lions are invariably
described as 'Forest Bred', no matter how old, tame or toothless,
and Madame Ella's troupe was no exception.) She was a very
daring woman, and her lion act was the big attraction at the
Accrington Hippodrome when that building opened for the first
time in 1903. In Derby she caused a sensation by putting her head
completely in the lion's mouth, and, according to one source, met
her fate by this very trick, which she did once too often it seems
when appearing with a circus on the Continent.

A famous and very graceful act popular on the halls round the
turn of the century was that of Professor Finney and his daughter,
who performed evolutions in the crystal tank, swimming under
water (said to be heated in winter). Later on, high diving was added
to the act, and by this means the worthy Professor came to grief.
He died from injuries thus sustained while appearing with the act
in Grimsby during 1903.

A very peculiar, and somewhat repulsive act was that of Sacco, the fasting man, who went for fifty days (so said the day-bills) without food at Hull in 1897. Admission was 2d. to see this monstrosity, and when poor Sacco was reported to be 'sinking fast' the management felt compelled to raise the price of admission to 6d.! Sacco started his self-imposed torture in the Hippodrome along Porter Street but was later moved to a hall near the Market Place. He lived to fast again . . .

Mr. Graham, the proprietor of the Hull Hippodrome, seemed to have a fancy for the macabre, for in 1911 he was exhibiting articles used by Belle Ellmore, the wife of Dr. Crippen, who, it may be remembered, came to a sticky end. Belle Ellmore was, in fact, a former music hall artiste. She had a loud singing voice, and was ostracised by the 'Profession' for refusing to join the music hall artistes' strike in 1907.

Ventriloquism has always been a feature of music hall programmes, but sometimes it had a varying reception. One of the first, and more successful 'vents' was Lieutenant Cole ('Blow it out, Cole') who appeared on the halls with his nautical dummy about the turn of the century. He was to set a fashion in having a sailor dummy, for he subsequently had many imitators.

A famous 'vent' who followed in his wake, and toured the halls for many years, was Arthur Prince and 'Jim'. Prince's speciality, which never failed to win applause, was to drink a glass of beer while the dummy was talking—a feat never equalled before or since. A new trend in dummies was set by Johnson Clark, with his rustic figure 'Giles'. Johnson Clark played the halls until as recently as 1956. Nor must we forget the 'Grand Old Man' of the V.A.F.—the late Fred Russell—who was father of Val Parnell, of the London Palladium. He was one of the finest of all 'vents' in his day.

Harry Bottles, professionally known as Datas, the Memory Man, was always a big draw. He was a former retort-house man at Anerley Gas Works, and was forced to spend some years in bed in his youth, due to illness. To occupy his time and cultivate a retentive memory, he whiled away his time in bed memorising facts and figures from a large encylopaedia. From this he gleaned innumerable facts about the dates of battles, kings and queens, winning racehorses, shipwrecks, and other things. He was heard by an agent to settle an argument in a London public house, with the result that the agent introduced him to Charles Morton ('The Father of the Halls') who put him on at the Royal Standard, Pimlico (now the Victoria Palace) where he appeared successfully for several weeks.

On tour he appeared at the Bradford Palace and the Huddersfield Hippodrome in 1905. In appearance he looked and acted like a gasworks' labourer. He came on wearing a cloth cap, smoking a 'gasper', and lounging about the stage in anything but an elegant fashion. (It was all part of the act, of course.) Datas surprised everybody by answering, unerringly, the dates of F.A. Cup winners, questions about racehorses, etc., and the people were delighted. He was reported to have sold his head to certain physicians after his death, for £2,000. He outlived the physicians and spent the £2,000!

*   *   *   *

Animal acts seemed to predominate at one period. There were Duncan's Collies; Woodward's Seals, and Lockhart's Elephants. The latter were named Salt, Mustard, Vinegar and Spicy, and their trainer was Captain Joe Taylor. Lockhart's elephants were in great demand during the Variety artistes' strike of 1907, for their trainer said that he had no idea of how they felt in the matter, and that being the case, they went on working. They could not get from hall to hall fast enough.

Captain Woodward, a native of Grimsby, had some very well-trained seals, who did a very good balancing and comedy act. The Captain came from sound Methodist stock, and was a strict teetotaller. It was rare (and still is) to find a performer that does not imbibe.

Another very curious act was that of Consul, the educated ape, who revived theories of the 'Missing Link'. Consul waddled on to the stage of the Wakefield Hippodrome, in September 1909, and twenty medical men with their assistants assembled there to examine the chimp. His manager answered their questions satisfactorily, and Dr. Wade, in charge of the students, put the chimp through various tests. After half an hour, the medical fraternity gravely announced themselves 'satisfied' and retired. The chimp then proceeded to dress, undress, and ride a bicycle round the stage.

At the Southport Pier Pavilion, the Great Consul sat attired in evening dress at a table on the stage, and rang a bell for attention. A waiter then appeared and supplied the chimp with bananas and other delicacies. The poor waiter was kept busy, to the delight of the children present, for Consul appeared to have a voracious appetite. No wonder folks thought there may be something in Darwin's theory!

Musical acts have always 'registered' well, particularly as supporting 'spots' on the bill. There was Kurkamp, the singing conductor, who not only conducted the pit orchestra, but sang as well. His speciality was 'I Wish I were in Dixie' rendered in a rich, full baritone voice.

A different type of musical act was that of Vasco, the Mad Musician, who was billed to play fifty instruments. He had a son called Bert Vasco, who, with one Alexander, did a perch and ladder act, usually on the same bill as his father. Bert Vasco later became a very popular front-of-the-house manager at the old Metropolitan in the Edgware Road. His father, Vasco the musician, came on to the stage at the Burnley Palace in 1908 and played THIRTY instruments (i.e. not fifty) in quick succession, in front of a wonderful back-cloth covered with crotchets. Apparently playing was a thirsty business, for he never stopped drinking from a vessel in the middle of the stage. Vasco was a great success, and took several curtain calls.

*   *   *   *

Magical acts seem to have a perennial appeal and Horace Goldin, who was once a very famous magician indeed, was able to bill himself 'The King's Magician'. This was because in 1902 he had been invited to give a private performance in one of the state rooms at Buckingham Palace, for the entertainment of King Edward VII and his guests.

Goldin, who was assisted by Miss Fransiolini in many of his illusions, caused a sensation with his 'levitation' speciality at the Huddersfield Hippodrome in 1905. Here, Miss Fransiolini was made to rise without apparent agency from a coffin-shaped box on the stage, in full view of the audience. On another occasion, she was seen playing a piano on stage: then Goldin threw a white sheet over her, and when the sheet fell to the ground—assistant and piano had vanished entirely! No wonder Goldin had to take an encore. Goldin, who claimed to have solved the riddle of the Indian Rope Trick, died in 1939—just as he was about to propound a plan to make the British Army invisible in the event of war—which was just too bad as things turned out . . .

Another kind of magician was Harry Houdini, who escaped from handcuffs, bound boxes, etc., in amazing fashion. He was an American—real name Erich Weiss—who read a book on magic by Houdin, the French magician, and decided to emulate him. Houdini's arrival in this country in 1901 was sensational, his debut at the London Alhambra being arranged by Harry Day, then an almost unknown agent. (Later he became Sir Harry Day, a famous Tory politician.) Both Houdini and his agent were of Polish extraction.

The 'sensation' Houdini caused, was to 'slip the Darbies' at Scotland Yard, and to emulate the feat again on the Alhambra stage. It was considered no mean feat to escape from British regulation handcuffs, and Houdini was retained at the theatre a month and was paid £60 a week. Later came a provincial tour, and the astute Fred Wood booked him for the Varieties, Leeds, at £150 a week—very big money indeed for a provincial hall in 1904—but Wood knew what he was doing for Houdini packed the place with his astounding feats. In that same year Houdini escaped from a safe on the stage of the Euston Palace of Varieties—to the astonishment of the safe builders—who declared the feat was impossible. (It was whispered that a confederate slipped him a tiny screw-driver in a hand-shaking episode, and that the master trickster unscrewed the inner part of the lock.) Houdini, who cheated death many times with his sensational feats, died quietly in bed of a ruptured appendix.

In the 1940's and 1950's several of Houdini's tricks, such as escaping from a cabinet, and escaping from a strait-jacket, were emulated by Jimmy Crossini, who claimed to possess several items originally used by Houdini. There was very nearly a tragedy at the Stockport Theatre Royal in 1956. For a publicity stunt Crossini, attired in a strait-jacket was strung up by a rope above the outer verandah of the theatre. The jacket was soaked in petrol, and the stunt was to release himself from the jacket before the flames harmed him. A match was put to the jacket, which flared up, but Crossini had to be cut down screaming, and released badly burned, as the trick went wrong. It was subsequently found that the knots had shrunk in the trappings and could not be undone. Crossini lived to perform again, and not long after this he was in conflict with the management at the West Hartlepool Empire in regard to the billing of a pantomime he was putting on there.

Not so lucky was Lafayette, who died in the fire which destroyed the original Edinburgh Empire in 1911. Lafayette, who became an American, was born Sigmund Neuberger in Munich in 1872. He travelled a large magic and animal show entitled 'The Lion's Bride' on the halls. There were 44 people in the production, apart from two midgets, Lafayette's horse 'Arizona' and his lion 'Prince'. They were supported by an American Jazz Band and Lafayette had with him his dog 'Beauty' which was a gift from his friend Houdini. At Oldham Empire 'The Lion's Bride' went over well, as did Lafayette's own magical act, in which he turned a woman into a bag of dust and then restored her! (Married men in the audience clapped lustily at this.) But at Edinburgh Empire the following week nothing went right. On the Monday 'Beauty' died suddenly, and Lafayette was most upset by the loss of his pet, but that was only the beginning of his troubles.

Lafayette wanted to bury 'Beauty' at Piershill Cemetery but the authorities would not allow this. Then on the Thursday night, 9th May, 1911 Lafayette, holding a flaming torch aloft in the course of the scene with the lion, ignited the drop curtains, which were not fire-proofed as they should have been. The flames spread rapidly and there was a panic. Trombonist Jack Whelan played the National Anthem from his place in the pit to calm the crowd, and Lafayette was seen on the blazing stage appealing for order. For reasons of secrecy, Lafayette kept the door between the auditorium and the stage locked, and this proved his undoing. He was eventually trapped on the stage and burned to death, as did nine members of his company.

There are those who say that Lafayette was seen in the yard outside, and then made his way back with a gun to shoot the lion, but there was some confusion with a drummer named Richards, who 'doubled' for him in some of the illusions. So much so, in fact, that Richards was buried as Lafayette, until a charred body was found on the stage bearing rings which were positively identified as the real Lafayette's. Curiously enough he was buried at Piershill, in a private vault, with the remains of his pet dog 'Beauty'—a strange ending to a strange man. The shock of this great tragedy stunned the music hall world, and it finished Sir Edward Moss, who had banked on the Edinburgh Empire being the venue for the first Royal Command performance, which he had worked so hard to bring about. Sir Edward was never the same again, and died shortly afterwards.

Another illusionist who died on the stage of a music hall was Chung Ling Soo, billed for years as the 'Chinese Magician Extra-Ordinary'. In his repertoire were such astonishing feats as swallowing lighted tapers, producing live fowls out of a boiling cauldron, 'fishing' over the heads of the audience with rod and line (and 'catching' live goldfish) and other wonders. But the trick that brought about Soo's downfall was his famous 'Catching the Bullets' illusion, which went wrong one second house at the Wood Green Empire in 1918, and proved fatal.

In 'Catching the Bullets' Soo stood on the stage holding a plate, while two assistants with rifles fired at his heart from a position in the circle. The trick was for Soo to catch the bullets on the plate, and he had done this for years, to tremendous applause. But on this occasion a war-time audience was horrified to see him stagger and fall, blood pouring from a chest wound. Poor Soo died with

9 MUSIC HALL

a bullet in his left lung, and an inquest was held to discover how it got there. It was revealed that the rifles had false barrels, and the bullets (which were handed round for inspection to each audience) never actually left the rifle. What happened was that by an ingenious arrangement a 'blank' was fired, and the real bullet passed harmlessly into the false barrel. Soo, by sleight of hand, producing bullets on the plate, to give credence to the illusion.

On the fatal night the mechanism failed, and a real bullet was fired, but the whole affair remained something of a mystery. Soo's wife, who assisted in the act, could throw no light on the matter. There was a story of suicide—it was said that Soo had domestic troubles—but a close friend said that shortly before he went on stage that night, Soo was talking enthusiastically about a new illusion he had in mind, and the suicide theory was discounted. 'Accidental Death' was the jury's verdict.

Soo, whose real name was William Ellsworth Robinson, was born at Rishton, near Blackburn in Lancashire, and was the son of a miner. In his youth he studied the manners and customs of Chinamen in Liverpool's Limehouse area before launching himself on the music halls as 'The Chinese Magician Extra-Ordinary'. Probably the nearest he had been to Canton was the Surrey Docks . . .

At one time 'Strong Men' were popular on the hills. There was Eugene Sandow—who tore telephone directories in two—and other prodigious feats of strength. Sandow was popular early in the century and his act was prepared for the 'halls' at Ilkley by Professor Modley (father of Albert Modley the comedian) who had a gymnasium there.

Hackenschmidt was another 'Strong man' who lived to a great age. Described as the 'Russian Lion' he defeated the 'Terrible Turk' in a short, fierce wrestling duel at London's Olympia in 1904. George Hackenschmidt visited Ilkley a few years later and Professor Modley staged an exhibition bout with him at the old Pleasure Grounds in Bridge Lane, before a great crowd.

Samson, whose real name was Alexander Zaas, died while this work was in preparation. He was billed as 'The Russian Cossack' for he was said to have once been in the Imperial Cavalry. Among his feats were such astonishing demonstrations as driving six-inch nails into timber with his bare fists and allowing members of the audience to strike him on the stomach with sledge-hammers!

* * * *

In the old days on the halls, 'Coon singers' were popular for a long time. They had their origin in the Minstrel troupes (all 'black-faced') of which there were several. One of the best-known and popular coon singers was the great Eugene Stratton, born in Buffalo, U.S.A., who came over with the Haverley Minstrels in 1880 and stayed here. He later joined the Moore and Burgess Minstrels, eventually marrying 'Pony' Moore's daughter. He made his debut at the old Royal, Holborn (later the Holborn Empire) in 1892 as a solo act. His famous song 'Lily of Laguna' rocketed him to fame. It was written for him by Southport-born Leslie Stuart, once an organist. Stratton, as a black-faced coon singer, commanded big money on the music hall stage, but he was past his best when he retired from the halls in 1914.

His successor was George H. Elliott, billed as 'The Chocolate Coloured Coon'. George, who hailed from Rochdale, was originally with Harry Reynolds' Minstrels on Rhyl beach in the 'nineties. Then he appeared with troupes at Largs and Prestwick, before he was put on by Moss at the old Scotia Music Hall at Glasgow in 1895. After that he went on the 'halls' as the 'Chocolate Coloured Coon' and was a top-of-the-bill attraction for many years. He made his 'Farewell Tour' of the remaining halls in 1955.

A different type of black-faced entertainer was Chirgwin, billed as 'The White Eyed Kaffir'. Many were the stories of how he got the famous white diamond-shaped patch round his left eye. Some say he got a fly in his eye, and rubbed off the burnt cork in his attempts to remove it, and, when he noted the sensation he made when he went on stage without repairing his make-up, decided to keep the effect. A more likely story is that he had a cast in the other eye, and put the white patch round the good eye to draw the attention.

Chirgwin, who died in 1922, was, in his later years, 'mine host' of a public house in Shepperton. He made his initial debut at the old Swallow Rooms, in London's Piccadilly in 1861 at the age of six. The son of a Cornish boat builder he later formed a double act with another man as 'The Brothers Chirgwin'. In the 1880's he made many appearances in pantomime, notably at the old Britannia Theatre, Hoxton, with lanky Fred Lay as his 'foil'. He also appeared many times during his career in the North of England, but sometimes he got a varied reception. At one well-known hall in the North, the manager used to bluntly say of him: 'Not worth the money', but at other halls he could do no wrong.

Chirgwin always got a good reception at the old Bradford Star (or Palace, as it later became), where he was a striking figure in his black tights, heel-length white coat, and top-hat tilted back. George le Roy, who remembered him well, recalled him playing a peculiar contraption called a 'Bom Bass' at one time. This was a weird affair comprised of bladders and cymbals, which he played with gusto. He talked a lot during the time he was on stage, and interpolated his patter (according to one informant) with gags 'of remarkable daring and potency'. Another beholder suggests they were pitiful stories, and frequently vulgar. He would impersonate a dancer by playing with two clay pipes on a tin tray—a trick used later by Charlie Chaplin with bread rolls in his film 'The Gold Rush'.

Chirgwin, who appeared at the Royal Command Performance in 1912, was famous for his two songs—'My Fiddle and My Sweetheart' and 'The Blind Boy'—and could seldom escape without singing either of them, or frequently, both. He would shout: 'What will it be lads—The Fiddler or The Blind 'Un?' While some audiences received the rendering of these lachrymose ballads with elation (frequently sung in a peculiar shrill falsetto) others were bored to tears. A remarkable instance, which occurred at the Holloway Empire in 1903, was when the pit orchestra struck up Chirgwin's music, eight men with black faces marched solemnly down the gangway to the front singing 'The Blind Boy' loudly. Chirgwin, in the wings, in the act of walking on, walked off again, most upset, and resolutely refused to appear. Charlie Adams, the manager, appealed for order: the eight men left as mysteriously as they had come, the next act was signalled and the show went on . . .

And now the Protean actors . . . Besides Signor Pepi, who later went in for management and controlled a chain of music halls at one time . . . there was dear old Bransby Williams, who passed away while this work was in preparation. Bransby was a great favourite in the North with his character studies. There is a legend that he laid the foundation stone of the Newcastle Empire—the first one—and there were several, but Bransby was no Methuselah, although he lived to a great age.

The truth of the matter is that there were several Newcastle Empires. The first one was built in 1878 out of the old Scotch Arms. It was altered and rebuilt in 1890 and again in 1903. It was at the latter occasion that the disputed incident took place. Early in 1903, when he was 32 years of age, Bransby was appearing at the Olympia Theatre, which was being used by Messrs. Moss and Thornton as 'Empire at Olympia' during the rebuilding of the Newgate Street hall. Richard Thornton, of the famous firm, having actually laid the foundation stone of the new Empire and declared it 'Well and truly laid', was surprised to see Bransby, who was in the crowd nearby, pick up a brick and lay it alongside. But

Dick Thornton, sportsman that he was, seemed amused by the incident, and allowed the brick to remain, saying something to the effect that it augured well for the future of the new Empire. The silver trowel used by Dick Thornton on that occasion is now in the treasured possession of the Reed family of Sunderland.

Dear old Bransby was glad to see the former Newcastle Empire disappear. He always maintained that he was upset by odours arising from the kitchens of the old Scotch Arms, which were directly beneath the stage, and said he did not consider that the scent of frying onions was conducive to the expression of grand emotions.

Bransby had a great affection for the North East, and it was said that his speciality of 'making-up' without actually leaving the stage, for his various parts, was a trick copied from a Protean actor he saw working a hall in Spennymoor in his early days. Actually, one of his first appearances was in Newcastle in 1899, when he is believed to have appeared at the old Vaudeville Theatre there. Bransby recalled playing early in his career at a hall in an arcade at the top of Grainger Street, and inferred it was the Vaudeville, formerly the Victoria. The Vaudeville was burned down in 1900 but later the Newcastle Picture House was built there.

Bransby, whose first appearance on the halls was in 1896 at the old London Music Hall, Shoreditch, was originally a tea-taster, with a firm of Mincing Lane tea merchants. However, the late J. C. Handby, a veteran Bradford journalist, once said to the writer that he distinctly remembered seeing Bransby Williams at the old Tivoli in the Strand in 1893. Bransby did not actually dispute this, but could only recollect playing at smoking concerts, and once at a place near Bow Church called the 'Three Crowns' about 1890. (This would be the place rebuilt as the Eastern Empire by the Marlowe family in 1893, and ten years later turned into the Bow Palace by Frank MacNaghten.)

*   *   *   *

And now the comedians . . . Many famous laughter-makers trod the boards of the music halls, and in a work of this sort it will only be possible to mention but a few of them.

George Robey, who was born in 1869 and in 1919 became a C.B.E. was a well-known figure, with his large eyebrows and swagger cane. His first London appearance was at the old Aquarium in 1891, but J. Pitt Hardacre, who ran the Gaiety and other theatres in the Manchester area, claimed to have put him on at his halls long before that. Robey did a lot of broadcasting.

and became known as 'The Prime Minister of Mirth' in his later days. He was a painter of no mean ability—he used his brushes and canvas between acts in his dressing room—and was hung at the Royal Academy on more than one occasion.

Described as 'The Pure Gold of Music Hall' and 'The Cheekie Chappie' Max Miller became a top comedian between the two wars and at the height of his career earned £1,000 a week at the London Palladium.

Attired in outrageous check plus fours, a kipper tie and a hat set at a jaunty angle, Max could hold an audience in the palm of his hand, not by what he said but the way he said it. He was a master of timing—and also of *double entendre*—which got him into trouble on more than one occasion. Perhaps his great fault—if fault it be—was his tendency to 'ad lib' and say things not in the prepared script and this got him into trouble with the B.B.C. who were particular about those things.

Max Miller was born in 1895 and found he could make audiences laugh whilst serving with the troops in India during the First War. Upon return Ernest Binns, the Northern impresario, gave him a break at the old Lidget Green Pavilion in Bradford in 1921 and a year later at the Shay Gardens in Halifax as a pierrot. Ernest Binns treasured a silver cigarette case given him by Max years later, as a memento of that early booking, for which the comic was paid a modest £5 a week and 'shares'! His greatest song hit was without doubt 'Mary from the Dairy'. Max died suddenly in 1963.

Nowadays discovering new talent on television shows, Canadian-born Hughie Green has been a comedian himself on the music halls and 'knows his business' which is Show Business! He was always popular in the North East and made many appearances when touring with the B.B.C. 'Gang Show' and the 'Discoveries'. Hughie was only sixteen when he first appeared at the Sunderland Empire and at that time he had already had experience as a child actor in films. Another American comedian in Will Mahoney appeared in many revues as well as a Royal Variety Performance at the London Palladium.

A peculiar type of comedian, but a great favourite, was the diminutive Little Tich. He was born Harry Relph in 1868 at Sevenoaks, Kent, and it was a theatre manager who gave him his unusual name. In his early days Harry played a penny whistle in the old Rosherville Gardens, and also for the amusement of queues outside places of entertainment. One night, when he was playing his whistle to a queue outside a Greenwich music hall, the friendly manager roped him in as an 'extra' turn. 'We can't announce you as

"Harry Relph"—that would never do', said the manager. Then, as an afterthought he added: 'I know. We have a very big "Tich" on the bill tonight (20-stone Arthur Orton, the so-called Tichborne Claimant), now we'll have a little one!'

And so Little Tich he became, for the name stuck. He was a great favourite on the halls, although very temperamental, and sensitive about his lack of inches. Little Tich played to fabulous business at the Blackpool Alhambra when Harry Lundy booked him for a week there, early in 1901. He played the 'cello very well, although his fingers were deformed, and he had a rather cute trick of suddenly leaping in the air and standing on the very tips of his very big boots. He had to abandon this in later life, after a bad fall. Little Tich passed away suddenly in 1928.

Another diminutive comedian, but only in stature, was the 'one and only' Dan Leno, who died of insanity in 1904 at the very height of his career. It was thought that the failure of a small circuit of music halls, in which he was a partner, was one reason for his instability.

Dan, born George Galvin in 1860 in a place near St. Pancras' Station, made his very first appearance on any stage at the tender age of four, at the old Cosmotheca Music Hall in the London area. He was carried on to the stage, dressed in a pair of his mother's cast-off tights, to sustain the billing of 'Little George', the Infant Wonder Posturer.

George's father died about this time, but his mother soon re-married. His new father was William Grant, whose stage name was Leno, and the family continued to play the halls as 'The Leno Family'. At the age of eleven, little George became part of the act as 'Dan Patrick Leno—Descriptive and Irish Character Vocalist'. A bill dated 10th May, 1880, for Templeton's Varieties, North Bridge, Halifax, shows 'The Comical Leno's' at the bottom of the bill, with Dan Patrick, the Irish Comic Vocalist, above them.

In that same year (1880) Dan Patrick Leno won a shoulder of mutton in a clog dancing competition at Sherwood's 'Free and Easy' in Wakefield. Clog dancing was all the rage in the North of England at that time, and George (or Dan as he had now become) was very good at this. Joe Hobson, then the proprietor of the Princess' Palace Music Hall in Leeds, promoted a contest to find 'The Champion Clog Dancer of the World'. Actually, this was in fact an astute 'publicity stunt' on the part of wily Joe to bring together at the Princess' Palace, the two acknowledged experts— Tom Ward and Tom Robson.

The prize was a gold and silver belt, suitably inscribed, and valued at £50 which was to be presented to the winner by Joe Hobson. Frank Belton, a comedian on the bill that particular week, persuaded Dan Leno to take part. Dan, to the surprise of all concerned, simply walked away with the competition and, of course, the belt! In fact, 1880 was a lucky year for Dan, for just after the Leeds episode, he married Lydia Reynolds, a ballad vocalist he met in Rochdale.

However, Dan did not hold the Championship Belt for very long, for he was soon challenged by Tom Ward for a return contest. This took place at Ohmy's Circus, in Accrington (where the Hippodrome was later built) and Dan lost.

Soon after this, the belt was stolen, and this led the proprietor of the Peoples' Music Hall in Rock Street, Oldham, to promote another contest, similar to the one held at Leeds. Some of the contests were held in the London Music Hall, Rochdale, for Mr. Jeffereys was proprietor of both halls, but the final was staged at Oldham. The Oldham hall was a wooden place, with a sanded floor, which in later years became an exhibition hall. Dan won back the Belt, or rather a new one, after some terrific contests, and it was suitably inscribed as follows:

'CHAMPIONSHIP BELT WON BY DAN LENO

Champion Clog Dancer of the World

at the

PEOPLES' MUSIC HALL, OLDHAM.

After a Six Nights of Contests

May 14th to 19th, 1883.'

After this, the Leno family settled down for a time in Sheffield, where Leno Senior took over the Tudor Street Circus, erected originally in 1876, and ran clog dancing championships there, with Dan's Prize Belt on full view. No one could touch Dan Leno for clog dancing ability, so the Belt was not likely to be lost again.

Dan's first arrival in London is usually given as 1885, when he appeared for £5 a week at Forester's Music Hall in the Mile End area. Here, he sang 'Going to buy Milk for the Twins' (an Irish ditty) and did his celebrated clog dance. The Cockneys liked his singing, but could make nothing of his clog dancing, as it was new to them.

However, soon after this, he was seen by George Conquest, of the Surrey Theatre, and given his first chance in pantomime there in 1886. At the Surrey Theatre he appeared jointly with his wife for a salary of £20. It was a lucky pantomime for Dan, as the great Augustus Harris saw him, and booked him immediately for panto at Drury Lane the following year. And so success came to Dan Leno, for he subsequently appeared in 15 pantomimes in a row at Drury Lane—a record—and formed a wonderful partnership with Herbert Campbell, with whom he appeared as Dame.

Later he went into partnership with Campbell, and another well-known comedian of the period in Harry Randall, and they erected music halls in Clapham, Croydon and Walham Green. In the early 1890's all went well, but about the turn of the century the big syndicates declared war on them, and the three comedians lost all their money.

Soon after this, in 1901, Dan Leno was commanded by King Edward VII to appear at Sandringham and do his comedy act there. After this, Dan billed himself as 'The King's Jester'. Then, whilst appearing at the London Pavilion, he had a nervous break-down, and never really recovered. The stress caused by the failure of his music halls had affected his reason, and in 1904 he quietly passed away. About the same time, his co-partner Herbert Campbell had a stroke, and he too, died.

Thus ended a famous partnership, both on and off stage. Harry Randall, the other partner, lived until 1932. Never again did Music Hall produce a comedian of the calibre of Dan Leno, whose name became a legend. As a pantomime 'Dame' he has never been equalled, nor hardly likely to be.

4

North Stars and Lesser Lights

MUSICIANS PLAYED a big part in Northern Music Hall. A remarkable case was that of George Burton of Sheffield, who won himself an open scholarship to a London college of music yet never availed himself of it.

George Burton won the scholarship in 1890. When he was 13-years-old he was appearing as solo pianist at the Albert Hall in Sheffield and had won the annual music competition so many times that the promoters barred him from further entry! His first job was in the local steel works, but he soon tired of that and ran away to become pianist to a troupe of nigger minstrels. When they were stranded at Boston, Lincolnshire, without funds, he took charge of them and organised a tour which lasted 22 weeks. After that he was introduced to James Kiddie, a noted Lancashire entrepreneur and pantomime producer. Kiddie was putting on a pantomime in Sheffield and George Burton got the job of writing the musical score. Romance blossomed for George ended up marrying James Kiddie's niece Pollie.

George Burton later ran pierrot troupes up and down the country, but he will always be remembered for his tuneful pantomime songs which put many a performer on the road to success, written under the pen name of Victor Read. He also ran a flourishing variety agency in Fargate, Sheffield, at one period.

Leslie Stuart, who wrote songs for Eugene Stratton, was born in Southport in 1864. His real name was Thomas Augustin Barrett and he was organist and choirmaster at a Lord Street church in his home town at the age of 15. The family then moved to Manchester, and young Barrett was appointed organist at St. John's Cathedral, Oxford Road, a position he held for seven years. In 1888 he arranged sacred and other concerts in the St. James' Hall, which gained some notoriety as 'Barrett's Recitals'. He was the prime mover behind bringing the great Paderewski to Manchester to perform at a concert. As a result, his writing of popular songs for Stratton was done under the pseudonym 'Leslie Stuart' for obvious reasons.

After Eugene Stratton's death, Leslie Stuart lived on as a popular composer of musical comedy melodies. One example was 'Floradora'. Another famous song of his was 'Soldiers of the Queen'. He has been described as the best writer of songs the music hall ever had, although many have tried to claim that distinction. He made his last bow in Variety at the London Palladium in 1928. His song 'Lily of Laguna' (if nothing else) put him among the immortals.

Two of the most famous songs of the First War period were 'Pack up your Troubles in your old Kit-Bag' and 'Tipperary'. Jack Hylton the famous band leader and later impresario had a hand in the latter (together with his father 'Happy Jack Hylton') of which more anon.

'Pack up your Troubles' was written by two pierrots, Felix Powell and his brother George. Felix was pianist in the 'Sundown Pierrots' a troupe appearing at the long vanished wooden Bridge Pavilion at Ilkley, Yorkshire for several seasons before 1914. His brother was vocalist in the troupe which moved to one of the Bradford Pierrot pavilions before circumstances due to the War caused these pavilions to close down. Felix wrote the music and George the words. They were surprised at the success of the song.

But it was really the publishers that 'made' popular songs. Two of the most famous publishers were Lawrence Wright and Bert Feldman.

Lawrence Wright sold songs for a start in Leicester Market in his early days. Many of these he wrote himself, as he considered he could write songs as good as those he was trying to sell. He made money, went to London, and eventually formed the Lawrence Wright Publishing Company. Many of his songs were written under the pen name of 'Horatio Nicholls', perhaps the best known being 'Wyoming' and 'Souvenirs'. Lawrence Wright also gave his attention to Blackpool, where he had a 'song-plugging' establishment, while his summer revue 'On With the Show' occupied the North Pier Pavilion for over 30 seasons.

His chief rival was Bert Feldman, who began in his father's music shop in Whitefriargate, Hull. Armed with his Post Office Savings bank book (containing a modest amount) he made for London and publishing, but had little success until Jack Judge handed him a tattered copy of 'Tipperary'. Then his fortunes took a turn for the better. He had 'song-plugging' establishments in Blackpool like his rival (Bannister's Bazaar, which later became Feldman's Theatre, was his headquarters), but he also prospered in the Isle of Man where the great Florrie Forde was 'Queen' for many years and plugged his songs.

Jack Hylton, the song-writer, bandleader and later great impresario, was born in Bolton, Lancashire, the son of a weaver turned pierrot, in 1892. As a boy Jack joined his father who appeared with Adeler and Sutton's Pierrots at Rhyl and New Brighton. Jack would sweep the stage at Rhyl and help his father dress as 'Happy Jack Hylton—The Diminutive Comedian' for £5 a week and a share of the 'bottle' (collection).

In 1913 Jack left home (his father having taken over the Commercial Hotel in Stalybridge) and is said to have walked to London to get a job as cinema organist at the Stoke Newington Alexandra. (It would perhaps be truer to say that he walked from Old Street tube station.) In 1921, after trying to team up with Tommy Handley in a double act, he formed a dance orchestra and went on to success.

If you look up on the wall of a house on the left hand side of Corporation Street, Stalybridge, you will see a plaque. The plaque reads as follows:

'Remembering with Pride

JACK JUDGE

who in this street and building

was inspired to write and compose

the immortal marching song

'IT'S A LONG WAY TO TIPPERARY'

He was also first to sing it

in public—At the Grand Theatre, opposite

JANUARY 31st, 1912.

The plaque was unveiled in 1953 by impresario Jack Hylton, and the building upon which the plaque is fixed was formerly the Newmarket Inn. Some research was done in 1934 in connection with the making of a film—'Royal Cavalcade'—on the origin of 'Tipperary', and at that time it transpired that Jack Judge had outlined the facts in a letter addressed to a Mr. Whittaker, of that town.

Mr. Whittaker, who was then in business in Stalybridge, exhibited the letter in his shop window. The relevant part of the letter read:

'Dear Mr. Whittaker,

'When I wrote the words and music of "Tipperary" it was

January 31st, 1912, and the place was Stalybridge. The song ·
was actually written in the Newmarket Inn, and I sang it at
the Grand Theatre the same evening. Here is the true
explanation.

'Just after midnight on the 30th (actually the 31st) some
friends and I came out of a club near the theatre, where I had
made a 5/- bet that I would write, compose and sing a new
song on the evening of the 31st. I had not the slightest idea
of my lucky "Tipperary" song until on my way home (to digs
at 20 Portland Place) I overhead one man telling another "It's
a long way to . . ." some place or another about which he was
enquiring the way.

'I was immediately inspired; pounced upon the "long way"
part for the title, added the "Tipperary", did a little thinking
until bed-time, and after a fish breakfast in the morning, I
completed the song in much quicker time than it has taken me
to tell you this story.'

Apparently, during the day of 31st January, Judge hummed the
tune over to Horace Vernon, musical director at the Grand, who
wrote a hasty score to enable it to be played that same evening.
When it was sung, some performing seals on the same bill beat time
to the tune with their flippers. In the film 'Royal Cavalcade' which
had a sequence about this, Jack's youngest brother Ted took his
part, as he strongly resembled Jack as he was at the time the song
was written. Jack Judge was one of a family of nine, and, although
of Irish descent, were all born and brought up in Oldbury, Worcs.

Florrie Forde, the buxom comedienne, gave 'Tipperary' a try-
out in the Isle of Man, during the summer season of 1913, and
Judge plugged it himself on the 'halls' for a couple of years,
together with another number he had thought up ('How are You?')
but without much success. It was on the advice of Bert Maden, an
ex-pierrot, that Judge gave a copy to Bert Feldman, the music
publisher, and history was made. Feldman, who had an unerring
instinct for spotting 'winners' saw its possibilities right away. It
became the immortal marching song of the troops in both wars.

*   *   *   *

One of the greatest names in show business was that of George
Formby—and there were two of them—father and son. Formby
senior was born in 1880 at Ashton-under-Lyne, and at the tender
age of 12 was apprenticed as a blacksmith's striker to a firm of
Manchester ironfounders. The work was far too heavy for his
puny frame, while the sulphur fumes played havoc with his chest.

He was 'very miserable' to all accounts, and only lived for his spare time, when he sang comic ditties and strummed away on an old banjo. Soon he began trying his luck in the 'Free and Easies' in the Manchester area. Then, about 1899, Danny Clarke of the famous Argyle Music Hall, Birkenhead, on a talent-spotting tour, heard him in the 'Hen and Chickens' singing-room, and signed him to appear a week at Birkenhead—salary £2 10s. Danny did not think George's real name of Booth was suitable for the halls, so 'Formby'—a place near Liverpool—was substituted. Not long after this, the great Walford Bodie signed up George to appear with his 'Royal Magnets' company at the old Lyceum Theatre, in Market Street Lane, Blackburn, with a short tour to follow.

About this time, George met and married Eliza Hoy, a Wigan girl, and his luck changed. He made his home with his wife's people in Wigan and got a regular weekly engagement at the old People's Palace in St. Helens, run by a Mr. Tarbuck and Harry Liston, a former comedian. And so, with a regular 30/- a week and his tram fare to Wigan, George Formby started married life. Then, through the kindness of Leoni, the Cat King, George signed up to play the Stoll Tour of nine halls at £8 a week.

But fame really came to old George Formby in 1907 when George Robey signed him for pantomime at Newcastle at £35 a week—real big money in those days. George Formby senior, a figure still well-remembered, with his pallid face, wistful air, enormous boots (bought from the Bros. Egbert for 15s.) and his lugubrious song 'Standing at the Corner of the Street'. Poor old George, always fighting a losing battle with the dreaded pthisis— with his pathetic aside to the orchestra 'Coughing better, tonight?' —had a son of the same name, born 26th May, 1904, the eldest of his many children.

George junior was apprenticed to be a jockey at the age of ten, but increasing weight put paid to that plan. However, during his spell at Ayr stables as a teenager, there came his first meeting with his wife-to-be—Beryl Ingham—then partner in a girl dancing duo 'Beryl and May', at a picnic arranged by the Popplewells on Ayr Green, near their Pavilion Theatre. It was she who persuaded George to launch himself as a solo act upon the halls. This he did, some time later, at the old Earlestown Hippodrome in 1921, under the name of George Hoy (his mother's maiden name). It was not until some time after his father's death that he would allow himself to be billed as 'George Formby'.

Single act George did not cut much ice on the 'Number Two' halls in the North—in fact according to his partner Sam Paul he

got the 'bird' at Blyth when appearing in 'Chip Off the Old Block',
a touring revue—but in 1924 he met up with Beryl Ingham again,
this time at the Castleford Queens'. There George 'popped the
question' and Beryl became his wife and stage partner. Like
Formby senior, his luck changed with marriage and 1924 was an
eventful year. He played the London Alhambra for Sir Oswald
Stoll and there added a catch-phrase to his act which stuck down
the years—'Turned out nice again?'

Then came the famous songs written for him by Gifford and
Cliffe—'Cleaning Windows' and 'Mr. Wu'—followed by Noel Gay's
'Leaning on a Lamp-post' and others by Alf Cotterill of Doncaster. In 1930 he appeared in a film 'Boots, Boots' which cost a
few pounds to make in a converted chapel studio in Manchester.
Then came a series which rocketed him to fame. These included
'Keep Fit', 'Trouble Brewing' and 'Keep Your Seats, Please'. He
made three Royal Command appearances (the last being in 1941)
and had a film contract worth £100,000 in 1938.

But like Formby senior, he fought a long and losing battle
against ill-health. With Young George it was heart disease, and
from 1950 onwards he was under doctor's orders to 'Go Slow'. The
sudden death of Beryl, his constant help-mate (she was more than
just a wife) in 1960 un-nerved him. A few months later, in March
1961, the curtain fell for the last time on one of the most famous
comedians the North has ever produced.

*　　*　　*　　*

There were many well-known Lancashire comedians. One of
these was Morny Cash, who billed himself 'The Lancashire Lad'.
Actually, Morny was 'discovered' in Yorkshire—at one of J. C.
Whiteman's Talent Nights—'Talent at the Taps' ('The Taps' being
the Scarborough Taps public house in Bishopgate Street, Leeds).
This was around the turn of the century, and any budding talent
was put on at the City Varieties, then owned by licensee Fred Wood.
By 1903 Morny Cash was high on the bill at the New Brighton
Palace, and not long after this he 'topped' at the Blackpool Hippo-
drome. Morny, who specialised in old men's parts, sang:

'Hurray, Hurray, I'm going to be married today,

For years I've been upon the shelf,

But now I'm going to slip myself . . .

Hurray, Hurray, I've often heard folks say,

The older the fiddle, the sweeter the tune,

Fancy me—at sixty-three—Having a HONEYMOON!'

Robb Wilton—'The Day War Broke Out . . .'—was another Lancashire comic. Robb, whose real surname was Smith, hailed from Everton, where he was born in 1882. He began his stage career as a comic actor in stock company—in 1899 at the old Theatre Royal in Breck Road, Liverpool (better known as 'Cabbage Hall')—and met his wife, pretty Florence Palmer, in a dramatic season at the New Alexandra Theatre, Hull, in 1903. A few years later he launched out as a solo act in music hall—billed as 'The Confidential Comedian'. He wrote his own scripts, and his wife assisted in the act if need be. One of his first appearances was on the opening bill at the Dewsbury Empire—at Bank Holiday, 1909 —when he shared a line with the Bioscope. A Leeds correspondent says Robb got his first professional 'break' in Leeds in 1911. In that year he was booked to play the City Varieties at a salary of £6 and he had then no other date in his book.

'Fortunately he was seen by Mr. Tom Sherwood, who then controlled the Opera House and Empire Theatres at Wakefield. Mr. Sherwood was able to persuade a syndicate (mainly Harry and Sidney Burns, then operating from Albion Place, Leeds, who had 20 halls in the North East) to put Robb on with star billing . . . The tour began at Stockton, and before it finished Robb was booked to appear in London.'

At this time Robb was specialising in his 'Fireman' sketch— 'Keep the fire going until we get there'—and this stood him in good stead for many years. He was always grateful for Mr. Sherwood's recommendation. In the 1939–45 war Robb Wilton became a National figure with his A.R.P. and other sketches, which were broadcast. He died in his native Liverpool in 1957.

Another National figure in that last war who hailed from Liverpool was Tommy Handley, of 'ITMA' fame. As previously mentioned, Tommy attempted to team up with Jack Hylton in a sketch at the Bedford Palace Music Hall, Camden Town, but it was not a success. Then, while Jack Hylton turned his attention to dance bands, Tommy Handley toured with a sketch entitled 'The Disorderly Room'. This led to a job broadcasting at the old 2LO studios, and from then on, his fame as a broadcasting comedian spread. With 'ITMA' he became a National figure, and with him in that show, was another Merseyside comedian—Fred Yule—an ex-Adeler and Sutton pierrot of years ago.

The name Charlie Olden may mean little or nothing—or even in reverse as Nedlo, the Gypsy Violinist—but think of Ted Ray, and it is one and the same person! Nedlo was 'discovered' by E. C. Jazon, of the agents Jazon and Montgomery, of Lime Street,

Liverpool, and played his first engagement at the Lyric Theatre, Everton Valley in 1927 for £7. He was billed as 'The Gypsy Violinist', and later appeared at the Clubmoor Cinema and the Moss' Olympia, along Boaler Street. At the Lyric, Nedlo shared a dressing-room with Ben Warris, then doing a black-face act. Later, Warris teamed up with his cousin, Jimmy Jewel, and they became a successful comedy pair. Like Tommy Handley, Nedlo (under a new name as Ted Ray) toured the halls and then made a successful career in broadcasting.

'Tubby' Turner, who collapsed and died so tragically on stage at the Halifax Palace in 1952, amid the ruins of his deck-chair absurdity, was another comedian from Lancashire. He turned a breathless stammer into a money-making asset. His catch-phrase 'If it's Ho-kay with you, then It's Ho-kay with Me' was known all over the North.

Born Clarence Turner in 1883 in Preston he worked as a tel- egraphist in the local railway goods yards until he was sixteen. Then, on holiday in Blackpool, he applied for a spur of the moment audition at a show on the South Pier and landed a job as a comedian at £2 10s. a week. In 1906 he married Florence Revill, who became his stage wife in many sketches which he wrote him- self. The climax of his career was when he was invited to play at the London Palladium with the 'Crazy Gang'. Tubby Turner wrote plays between engagements. One of them, 'Summat for Nowt' is nowadays very popular in repertory.

Another popular comedian, who everyone thought was a Lan- castrian, but was actually a Yorkshireman, was the late Dave Morris. Dave, who joked his way through 46 years of ill-health, de- lighted in his deception. He died with one ambition in his life unfulfilled—to appear in a Royal Command Show. It was a bitter pill for Dave to swallow when he found he was rather pointedly not invited to take part in the first Royal Show to be held in the North (at the New Opera House, Blackpool in 1955) in the presence of the Queen and Duke of Edinburgh.

With his straw hat and big cigar, Dave topped Variety bills everywhere, and lived for so long in Blackpool that folk thought he was a native of the place. Adding to the Lancashire 'illusion' was his famous B.B.C. series 'Club Night' in which he made catch- phrases like 'Whacker' and ' 'As 'e bin in?' into household terms. Poor little Dave, who smiled although racked with pain, died in 1960 aged 64. He made his debut on the stage at his native Middles- brough at the age of 11 in 1908, at a talent competition held at the Empire. In those days he was a bare-foot newsboy in the streets.

He was badly gassed while serving with the Green Howards in 1916, and later his eyesight became affected. In his latter years he could not read scripts, even with the aid of his pebble-lensed glasses, which he was never without. His son, Sammy Morris, became a clown in the Blackpool Tower Circus.

Another well-known Lancashire comedian, who passed from the scene some years ago, was Wilkie Bard ('I want to sing in Opera'). Wilkie, who topped bills for many years, and known by his curiously high forehead and spotted eyebrows, was born Willie Smith in Manchester in 1870. He first began singing in 'Free and Easies' in his native city, and in 1893 secured an engagement at Ted Garcia's Grand Circus in Peter Street at £4. But Wilkie Bard really found fame when he landed the part of Idle Jack in panto at Drury Lane in 1908. He never looked back, and was one of those who took part in the very first Royal Command Performance at the Palace Theatre, London in 1912. Wilkie, who made a 'come-back' in the 'Veterans of Variety' show in later years, died peacefully in 1944. His famous tongue-twisting song—'She Sells Sea-Shells on the Sea Shore'—will always live on in the memory.

Remember Whit Cunliffe and Charlie Whittle? Both were popular comedians from Yorkshire in the days before the first World War. Whit Cunliffe was a bit of a dandy. He strutted round the stage in a 'figure-eight' movement with a straw hat jauntily perched upon his head and told us 'I do like to be beside the Seaside'. Perhaps the fact that he had graduated from Adeler and Sutton's Pierrots to the 'halls' had something to do with it, for he always seemed to infuse the bright and breezy atmosphere of the seaside into the stuffy music hall—whatever the weather. On other occasions he asked us 'Who were you with last night?'.

Charlie Whittle was a man of the people. He came from Brad-ford and looked as though he had just dropped his pick some-where and walked on! He had a rough, bluff style which went down very well. He invited us to 'Let's All go down the Strand' and added that if we had a banana as well, everything would be all right. After all, 'We All go the same way Home' or so Charlie kept on telling us.

Another comedian from Bradford was Jack Pleasants, a shy lad, both on and off stage. Jack was 'discovered' in the neighbouring city of Leeds, by the astute J. C. Whiteman. Mr. Whiteman organised 'Talent at the Taps' or in other words Talent Nights in the Scarborough Hotel (or 'Taps') where the great Dan Leno is said once to have appeared. Any artiste showing promise there was given a booking at the City Palace for Fred Wood.

Jack Pleasants did very well at Mr. Wood's halls, and soon got further engagements. His song 'Twenty-One Today' will be sung at every coming-out party for generations to come. Poor Jack died tragically during the run of pantomime in his native city, when appearing there for Francis Laidler. He was playing Idle Jack at the Princes' Theatre in 1923 and suddenly taken ill. He was never of very robust constitution.

Another Northern comedian who died tragically during the run of pantomime was Mark Sheridan, well-known for his absurd get-up of bell-bottom trousers and frock coat.

Mark Sheridan, whose real name was Fred Shaw, and who hailed from Hendon in County Durham (although everyone thought he was a Cockney) strode about the stage, vigorously slapping the back-cloth with his cane. He sang 'Here we are again' amongst other well-tried favourites. Believing he was 'finished' in popularity (quite erroneously) and depressed by events in the Great War, he blew his brains out in a Glasgow park in 1917. He was appearing in pantomime at the Glasgow Coliseum at the time. The Music Hall world was stunned by the tragedy of Mark Sheridan.

Quite a number of successful North Country comedians hailed from Durham. In the old days there was Austin Rudd from Tyne Dock, who made many appearances at Dick Thornton's old Varieties in South Shields. His song and speciality was 'Bobbing Up and Down like This'. From Sunderland came that lanky comic George Doonan who was in 'Casey's Court' and the 'Lancashire Lads' companies with Charlie Chaplin. Of more recent vintage is the rubber-necked Nat Jackley, also from Sunderland.

From Jarrow hails that wonderful little man with the big personality, Wee Georgie Wood, who is still active in the world of Music Hall. Seventy years young he has no thought of retirement, being a columnist in the Profession's own newspaper *The Stage* and very kindly writing the Foreword to this book.

Wee Georgie Wood made his first appearance at the old Jubilee Grounds at Seaham Harbour at the age of five, later joining a pierrot troupe at Barnard Castle, before going on the music halls as a juvenile performer with a Levy and Cardwell company. He made an early solo appearance in Music Hall at the old Empire at Burnley in 1908 at the age of 13, doing impressions of George Lashwood and Vesta Tilley. He was seen by agent George Edelston at Bradford Palace soon afterwards and booked for the Stoll Tour. Around 1917 he formed his 'Black Hand Gang' to play on the music halls; then in 1922 came his long association with Dolly Harmer which lasted until her death in 1956.

Dolly Harmer, who was Georgie Wood's stage 'mother' (in his 'Little Boy' act) was 90 when she died, but did not look a day over 60. It was one of the best kept secrets in show business. In point of fact she was a Principal Boy in 1893 for Walter Reynolds at the Leeds Theatre Royal and other places. About that time she married a scenic artist named Willie Scott, but was soon widowed. Wee Georgie Wood, with whom she was associated for so long, was awarded the O.B.E. in the 1946 Honours List.

Jimmy Clitheroe, Wee Georgie Wood's successor in the 'Little Boy' field, hails from Blackho, near Burnley, Lancashire, and took part in school plays at the local Grammar School. He won a talent competition as a teenager at the Nelson Alhambra and, on the recommendation of an agent, joined a juvenile touring troupe. Following Wee Georgie Wood's 'retirement' from the Variety stage, Jimmy Clitheroe literally stepped into his shoes with his portrayal of 'The Clitheroe Kid' which has been a popular television series. Like Wee Georgie, he has a 'stage mother'. In this case it is actress Mollie Sugden.

Two other boy comedians, who went on to great success, are now that top-class comedy team Morecambe and Wise. Ernie Wiseman made an early appearance as a boy comic in the 'Nignog Revue of 1936' sponsored at the Bradford Alhambra by the local newspaper *Telegraph and Argus*. Shortening his name to Wise, Ernie later teamed up with Eric Bartholomew, who took his stage surname from the popular Lancashire resort. Prior to 1952 they were just another double act in revue, but in that year Richard Stephenson booked them as Robbers in pantomime at the Dewsbury Empire and they never looked back. While other comedians faded with the advent of television, Morecambe and Wise took to the new medium readily and have also made some successful comedy films.

Albert Burdon, whom the great C. B. Cochran 'groomed' for West End musical comedy, was originally a boy comic in South Shields. A competition there won him a six-year contract with Newcastle agent Tom Convery. He made many appearances in touring revue under the Convery banner. Perhaps the most famous of these was 'On the Dole' which began its long run in 1924. C. B. Cochran saw him in this revue, liked him, and offered him better things. Albert Burdon appeared in 'Evergreen' with Jessie Matthews at the Adelphi Theatre, London in 1930 and later was in great demand for pantomime. Nowadays his son, Bryan Burdon, is following father's footsteps in a theatrical career. He appeared as 'Idle Jack' in pantomime at the Leeds Empire just before that hall closed down in 1961.

Leeds has turned out several well-known stage personalities. In the old days there was J. W. Rowley (better known as 'Over' Rowley). This was because he always performed his 'somersault dance' during his act. The audience would call out 'Over, Rowley' and over he would go! Born in 1847 J. W. Rowley was at first apprenticed to a whitesmith. In 1860 he migrated to Huddersfield and soon afterwards began singing at Masonic gatherings, making his first professional appearance at Wakefield in 1870 at Sherwood's 'Free and Easy'.

For some years John Willie Rowley was proprietor of a wooden music hall in Huddersfield, always dubbed 'Rowley's Empire'. In 1892 he booked there for a week 'Charles Chaplin, comic singer' for a modest thirty shillings. Then, the appearance of the father of the world's greatest comedian caused no comment whatsoever! Later on, when the Robinson Brothers took over the Empire, Rowley went back to the 'halls' again, singing with success a ditty called 'Starry Night', which ran:

'Choose a Starry Night for a ramble . . .

Through a shady dell;

A Starry Night for a ramble . . .

A Kiss and Never tell!'

Talbot O'Farrell was a native of the Third Port. He was born Will Parrott and for a time was P. C. Parrott of Hull City Police, but soon got tired of pounding the beat. After this he tried his luck as a pierrot and became known as Jock McIver, the Scottish comedian, with Adeler and Sutton's troupe at New Brighton in 1902. Then a friendly agent recommended he become Irish, and so the music hall stage got Talbot O'Farrell—the Irish comedian and vocalist!

He strode about the stage in a tail suit and a grey topper and did very well for himself. He went to America for some years, but returned—appalled by the high cost of living in the States. In 1949 he came out of retirement to appear in the Don Ross show 'Thanks for the Memory' but died suddenly of a chill in 1952.

Mention of Hull is a reminder that Arthur Lucan died on stage there—on the boards of the Tivoli, 17th May, 1954 to be precise. Arthur Lucan, together with his wife and partner Kitty McShane, were a big 'draw' with their 'Old Mother Riley and her Daughter Kitty' act.

Arthur Lucan married Kitty when she was only fifteen, but their married life was pretty hectic, to all accounts. However, they were great favourites with the children with their 'Old Mother Riley' speciality and made twelve films together, some of which have been screened many times on television. After Arthur Lucan's death, the act was re-formed for a time with Roy Rolland as 'Old Mother Kelly'.

A touching reminder of how much Arthur Lucan meant to the kiddies is the story that his grave, in the East Cemetery at Hull, is invariably covered with flowers. These are put there by children who never knew him, but have seen his many films on television.

A music hall singer who faded out long before his time was Fred Barnes, the son of a Birmingham butcher. He has been described as 'The last of the Lion Comiques'. One of his first appearances was in Leeds where he sang 'Give Me the Moonlight' in 1909. He also danced a little and introduced a song known as 'Mother Kelly's Doorstep' which in later years dear old Randolph Sutton made his very own. Poor Fred Barnes was struck down by misfortune at the very height of his career.

*   *   *   *

What about the feminine element in North Stars? Well, there was the incomparable Gracie Fields, who deserves a chapter to herself, now in happy retirement with her beloved Boris. There was Vesta Victoria ('Daddy wouldn't buy me a Bow Wow') who was the daughter of Joe Lawrence, one-time proprietor of the Barrow Tivoli music hall; Florrie Gallimore, a famous serio-comedienne of the old days, hailed from Sheffield, where she was discovered singing in a weird place called 'Cockaynes'. She made her last appearance on the 'halls' at Huddersfield in 1922.

There was Clarice Mayne, with the blonde hair and gorgeous looks, who was a famous Principal Boy, and who married J. W. Tate, the Manchester song-writer and partner in Wylie-Tate panto-mimes. After Tate's death, Clarice Mayne married Teddy Knox of the famous Crazy Gang comedy team, Nervo and Knox.

Ella Shields, the former male impersonator, who made famous 'Burlington Bertie from Bow' died suddenly while appearing at Middleton Holiday Camp, Morecambe in 1952. She was 73 years of age, and like so many other old-timers, was persuaded to come out of retirement to take part in the Don Ross show 'Thanks for the Memory' which began its first tour in 1949. Ella Retford, who did a similar type of act, and who appeared on the opening bill at the Huddersfield Hippodrome in 1905, was a Wearsider. Her real name was Nellie Flanagan.

Tessie O'Shea, a big comedienne in every way, made a big impact on the music halls in between the wars. She later went on the radio and films with great success. Diane Verne, another big girl, with a similar type of act consisting of cheeky songs to the accompaniment of a banjolele, hailed from Morecambe. She was originally one of the 'Lucky Lancashire Lassies' with Papa Parsons on the beach. Her brother, Charlie Parsons, was a firm favourite with his show at Blackpool.

Gertie Gitana was another 'North Star' and Gitana Street, Hanley, marks her birthplace in the Potteries. She gave us 'Nellie Dean' (which no inebriate ever seems to forget!) and made her first appearance in the Metropolis at the Lyceum when Tom Barrasford was in charge. She was another who took part in the Don Ross 'Thanks for the Memory' revival in 1949.

What about the 'Bottoms and Middles' who made up the music hall bills? Who now remembers Bella and Bijou, that splendid man and wife team from Newcastle—the male partner attired as a flunkey and the woman with her many changes of gowns? They were indeed versatile in every sense of the word.

Then there were the Musical Elliotts—all 'Geordies'—with leader Tommy Varley on concertina and his wife and daughter in the act also.

The Sisters Sprightly hailed from Wigan. First there were two of them—the Long and Short of it—then they were joined by a third girl. They changed their frocks for every number and what smart girls they were, too. The original pair were in great demand for 'Babes in the Wood' in pantomime. (They made their first panto appearance at the Leeds Grand in 1895.) Their father, dapper Jack Lewis, travelled around with them and saw to their every comfort. All the trio had excellent singing voices.

Another three girls—fore-runners of girl acts like the Beverley Sisters of the present day—were the Three Sisters Levey. All were raven-black-haired Jewesses and, if gossip is to be believed, hailed from Lancashire. They all stood six feet tall in their nylons (or lisle, or whatever they wore in those days), but often there were complaints about the material they used. To say the least, it was sometimes cheeky. But they literally 'stopped the show' when they appeared at the Manchester Palace in 1907 and went on to become very successful.

*   *   *   *

And what about the agents that helped to make 'Northern Music Hall'? To mention them all would be impossible, but among the best known were Jazon and Montgomery, of Liverpool; A. G. Hart, of Leeds; J. C. Whiteman of Leeds, and his brother Albert ('Tich')

Whiteman of Castleford. Then there was Harry Selwyn of Harrogate; Bernard Woolley of 'Vaudeville House', Bolton, who booked the Morecambe Winter Gardens for so long; dapper little Percy Hall of Manchester's Oxford Road; and Bert Loman, of Fallowfield, who put many shows on the road.

Another Manchester agent between the wars was the late Jack Taylor, who specialised in 'Long Tours of the Number Two's'. Then there was Jack Gillam, who specialised in pantomimes. Once Jack tried to bring a touch of the West End to grimy Manchester, by opening a night club, but it failed. Later, with more success, there was dapper little Arthur Fox, who began with his 'International Attractions' and finished up by running a lush strip-tease club—'Folies Parisienne'—in a Manchester back street.

No mention of agents would be complete without mentioning Joe Hodgson of Bradford, and his successor, Eric Martin. Mr. Martin, who ran the old Bradford Mechanics' Institute as a music hall between 1940 and 1947 made many 'discoveries'. Perhaps the greatest of his 'finds' was Harry Worth, now a top-line television comedian. Mr. Martin put Harry Worth on at the Mechanics' at a small salary in June 1946. Harry was then a colliery worker at Silkstone Pit, near Barnsley, and did a 'vent' act in his spare time, using two dummies. He was later advised to concentrate on solo comedy, with the eventual result that he became very successful.

During his tenure at the Mechanics' Mr. Martin also gave a chance to a boy comedian from Huddersfield named Roy Castle. Roy was then so young that a special licence had to be applied for before he could appear. A young coloured girl pianist was given a chance after playing at a London party. Her name was Winifred Atwell, and it is said that she got the idea for the vintage piano in the act from playing the ancient instrument at the Bradford Mechanics'!

But the most sensational discovery made by Eric Martin, was the now world-famous hypnotist, Peter Casson. During the 1939–45 war Mr. Martin organised 'Stay at Home' holiday entertainments in Bradford parks, and at one of these, a Bingley youth named Peter Casson was engaged to entertain the children with a little conjuring. He was asked to do a second 'spot' in one programme, and the youthful Mr. Casson said he would oblige with a little HYPNOTISM. Mr. Martin was very sceptical about Peter possessing any hypnotic powers, but let him go ahead, as he considered he had the makings of a good showman. He changed his tune shortly afterwards, when called to the front by an alarmed stage manager, to find the local A.R.P. Chief, a most august personality, who had 'volunteered' as a subject, lying rigid, completely unsupported, by the heels and neck, between two chairs!

No mention of Bradford would be complete without reference to Albert Modley, one of the greatest little comedians the North has produced. Albert, who was once a porter at Forster Square station, in Bradford, used to entertain his colleagues in the porter's room. From this, he got to doing a 'turn' in the pubs to earn a little 'Beer Money'. Ernest Binns, who ran concert parties throughout the North, heard him, liked him, and took him to Morecambe for a season in 1930. Albert never went back to British Railways! He always writes his own material, and never uses a script because he is never quite sure what he is going to say next! Albert's brother, Allen Modley (like Albert a native of Ilkley) also went on the 'halls' for a time. Allen began as a drummer in a cinema orchestra in the silent days. Later he became resident compère for many years at Jack Showers' Stanhope Hotel, Rodley, near Leeds, where many first-class acts were to be seen. Mr. Showers wrote two books about the 'Welcome Inn' (The Stanhope) and its entertainers.

*   *   *   *

Norman Evans was a great comedian 'discovered' by Bradford and Leeds pantomime magnate Francis Laidler. Norman, with his famous 'Over the Garden Wall' scene, made an excellent 'Dame' in pantomime, and appeared in several Royal Command Performances. He was a native of Rochdale and became a travelling salesman. In his spare time he started telling humorous stories at 'smokers' and finally got an engagement at Keighley Hippodrome one week in 1937. Manager Bernard Beard told Francis Laidler that he had never heard such laughter in a Variety theatre, whereupon the great Yorkshire impresario dashed over with a contract. His first pantomime was at the old Princes' in Bristol, bombed out in 1942.

Another well-known Yorkshire comedian is Sandy Powell, who hails from Rotherham. Born in 1900 Sandy was taken by his mother for an audition at the Halifax Palace at an early age. His mother (Lily Le Maine) sat in the back stalls while Sandy did his stuff on-stage. A little deaf, mother would call out 'Speak up, Sandy' whereupon Sandy developed the famous hoarse whisper and would call back 'Can you hear me, Mother?'. This catch-phrase has stuck throughout his career. His first professional appearance (with mother) was at the old Easington Empire in 1912.

More than one North Country comic became a film star. Perhaps the most notable was the late Frank Randle. If he had been born a bit earlier he would have made a fortune in silent films as a

'Keystone Cop' or knockabout comedian. As it was, his rather peculiar and vulgar type of humour was little appreciated outside Lancashire and in the end he formed his own film company in Manchester to make films. With a man called Blakeley many films were made in an old chapel in Dickenson Road on a shoe-string budget. He once tried to put a show on in the West End, but it 'flopped'. However, Gracie Fields once described him as 'the greatest character comedian that ever lived' and that was good recommendation indeed—coming from Gracie.

Born 1902 in Wigan, Frank Randle made his first appearance on the stage at the age of fifteen at the Tower Circus in Blackpool as one of the 'Three Ernestos', knockabout acrobats. His real name was MacEvoy and he adopted the name Randle when he left the trio to become a solo slapstick comedian. Then he teamed up with Gus Aubrey and Ernie Dale to form 'Randle's Scandals'—a road show that ran for years. He was frequently in trouble with the authorities—particularly the Lord Chamberlain—and once there was trouble for burlesquing Handel's 'Messiah' in touring revue. Randle was the uncrowned King of Blackpool, where he lived with his wife Queenie, until he died in hospital in 1957. His 'Baaa . . . I've supped some ale toneeet!' convulsed thousands of Northerners and will live on in the memory of Northern Music Hall.

Another comedian who made good in films was Stanley Jefferson, born in Ulverston, and the son of Arthur Jefferson who ran the Theatre Royal at North Shields, the old Scotia in Glasgow (as the Metropole), and other halls. As a youth Stanley Jefferson toured with Will Murray's 'Casey's Court' and Fred Karno's 'Mumming Birds' companies, together with Charlie Chaplin. In 1910 he sailed to America with the Karno company at the same time as the great Charlie. While Chaplin was taken under the wing of Mack Sennett, the latter's rival Hal Roach annexed Stanley Jefferson and turned him into the slimmer half of the film comedy team Laurel and Hardy. Like his partner, Oliver Hardy, Stan Laurel died of a stroke in Hollywood some years ago.

Another comedian from the North East, who made good on television, after many years on the music halls, was Jimmy James. Born in Stockton-on-Tees, he was the son of Will Netta who ran pierrots at Belle Vue Gardens in Manchester. With a cigarette rolling about his mouth, and 'assistance' from two particularly dense 'stooges' in Bretton Woods and Hutton Conyers (both named after unusual places) he appeared in touring revue for many years. He was originally a Thomas Convery 'discovery' and made his first appearance in Newcastle.

THE FABULOUS POPPLEWELLS

Above: "The Dandy Militaires" in the Frizinghall Pavilion at Bradford, 1905. Ben Popplewell ("Daddy Pop") is at the back (left) in boater. His associate Walter Bentley is at the back in trilby.

Below: The famous Gaiety Theatre, Ayr restored after a fire in 1955.

Below: "The Boys" today. Leslie on the left, with Eric Popplewell.

Plate 7

LADIES AND GENTLEMEN!

(Above) The Lucky Little Lancashire Lassies at Happy Mount, Morecambe in 1925.

(Below) Fred Pullan's all-male "Yorkshire Pierrots" at Clacton, 1901.

Plate 8

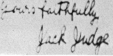

(Top left) JACK JUDGE.
(Top right)
TALBOT O'FARRELL
outside a Blackpool song
plugging establishment.

(Above)
Two Blackpool rivals—
Bert Feldman and
Lawrence Wright,
also known as
Horatio Nicholls.

(Right) Original
manuscript of Jack
Judge's song
"Tipperary".

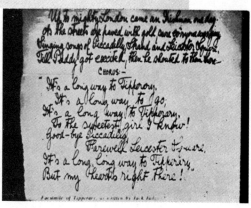

Plate 9

George Burton and his "BOHEMIANS" Concert Party at South Shields in 1909.

DOWN MEMORY LANE

COSY CORNER: The Marquee on the Sea Front at South Shields in 1909 used by "BURTON'S BOHEMIANS".

Plate 10

(Above) FREDDIE FRINTON is the first man on the left of this picture taken at Cleethorpes in 1935. This was when he was a member of Jimmy Slater's "Super Follies".

FROM THE FOLLIES TO FAME

(Below) No prizes for guessing who the zany guy is at the back of this picture! Yes, it's the unknown KEN DODD when a member of the Fairfield Concert Party run by Don Ellis (next to Doddy's tuba) at Liverpool in 1952.

Plate 11

WYLIE-TATE PIERROTS at the Central Pier, Blackpool in 1924. The Company includes Jimmy Pullen, surrounded by "We Three" (Dorothy and Susie Belmore and Vera Vere).

BESIDE THE SEASIDE

THE PICCADILLY REVELS—A notable Scarborough Company of 1933 at the Floral Hall. Included are The Western Brothers (Kenneth and George); Webster Booth, Vi Stevens and Edgar Sawyer. Can you spot them?

Plate 12

Also from Stockton-on-Tees came Will Hay—who made his first stage appearance with a Fred Karno show in Manchester during 1908—who went on to make many films in the role of a comic schoolmaster. His daughter, Gladys Hay, became well-known as a comedienne. Other names in the comedy business hailing from the North East include Frank E. Franks and Bobby Thompson.

A character comedian from Redcar, who formed a concert party for the beach there in 1947, is Alan Gale who now runs 'Old Tyme Music Hall' shows at several South Coast resorts. His study of a Chelsea Pensioner is in a class apart. Also adept at comedy characterisation (and bearing a remarkable resemblance to the late Carl Brisson) is Ken Palmer, who adds lightning sketches for good measure.

The late Freddy Frinton, so popular at the London Palladium, was born in Grimsby and appeared on the sands at nearby Clee-thorpes with Jimmy Slater's 'Super Follies' in 1935. After years on the music halls he teamed up with Thora Hird (who hails from Morecambe) in 1960 and became very well-known as a comedian on television in the 'Meet the Wife' series.

Ken Dodd is another who began with concert party. A member of Don Ellis's Fairfield Concert Party of 1952 in Liverpool, he graduated to the boards of the music halls some two years later, when he topped the bill at the Hull Palace as 'The North's New Star Comedian'. His first real break came in pantomime at Brad-ford in 1959 at the Alhambra for Gwladys Stanley Laidler. Then, success came rapidly, for with his 'Diddy People' and famous 'Tickling Stick' he brought a new style of humour to Variety and television.

Agent Bill Watts summed up the Knotty Ash comic's success very well when he said: 'He is a funny man who brings all the red-plush, smoke-laden atmosphere of the British Music Hall back to us with all its warmth, its tears, its humanity . . .'

*   *   *   *

There were quite a number of music hall personalities from 'over the Border' that made the grade in Music Hall. Remember Harry Tate, with his walrus moustache and comedy sketches, such as 'Motoring'? He was a Scot, born Ronnie Hutchinson, but took his stage name from his first employers—Messrs. Tate and Lyle—the sugar refiners. He made his first appearance as a mimic at the Oxford in the West End in 1895. Later Wal Pink, the famous script writer, wrote his 'Fishing' and then 'Motoring', together with other successes.

Sandy MacNab was another Scottish comedian. He toured with an Egyptian mummy scena, and was a particular favourite in Doncaster, where he appeared several times at the Palace. It is said that he purchased 39 Hilldrop Crescent at Finsbury Park, the former home of Dr. Crippen, for the sum of £100, opening it as a museum for relics of the notorious murderer. When the novelty of this faded, he let the place off as digs for Pro's appearing at the nearby Finsbury Park Empire!

A Scottish comedian who became a Knight of the Music Halls (in 1919) was Harry Lauder. Born in 1870 in Portobello, Harry Lauder worked in the Lanarkshire pits as a youth, then for some years joined a touring concert party. Then in 1899 Dennis Clarke of the Argyle in Birkenhead gave him his first real 'break' on the boards as a solo turn. He did two 'spots' in the programme—singing Irish songs in the first half and Scottish ones in the second—just for good measure!

His first London appearance was at Gatti's-in-the-Road in 1900 when manager Tom Tinsley put him on as a deputy and Lauder never looked back. At Christmas of the years 1900 to 1903 he was booked to appear in pantomime at Newcastle, and wrote a new song for each of the shows. First came 'Roamin' in the Gloamin' '; followed by 'Just a Wee Doch and Doris' and 'I love a Lassie'. All were 'hits' and outstanding ones, too, as was 'It's Nice to get up in the Morning', which came later. He had a son killed in the first World War, and felt this loss very keenly. It is said that he wrote 'Keep Right on to the End of the Road' in memory of his son. Sir Harry Lauder was 'careful' with his money, and died a comparatively rich man in 1950.

Will Fyfe was more a character actor than a Scots singer or comedian. His studies were really lifelike, particularly those of a Railway Guard, a Poacher and a Gamekeeper. He was born in Dundee in 1887 and in his youth, like Sir Harry Lauder, gained his experience with 'Fit-Up' touring companies in the Highlands. Just before the First War he scored heavily at the Glasgow Pavilion with a song entitled 'Glasgow belongs to Me'. That song, which passed into Scottish history, was given birth by an incident Fyfe witnessed at Glasgow Central Station, in which a tipsy Scot gave Fyfe his 'cue for song'. Lots of Will Fyfe's material was written for him by Neil Kenyon, and he made many appearances in pantomime. He was awarded the C.B.E. for his work for E.N.S.A. in World War II. Will Fyfe passed away in 1947.

But the Scot who made the most money out of Music Hall down the years was the great Walford Bodie, miracle worker and hypnotist. Born Sam Bodie in 1871 he was apprenticed to the National Telephone Company in Aberdeen, which accounted for his familiarity with electrical apparatus. At one time there was talk of him joining the Presbyterian ministry, and then training for surgery, but actually he did neither, as he was averse to discipline. He became interested in 'Saturday Evening Entertainments' in his native Aberdeen, and took part in several shows. But his interest in show business was well and truly stimulated when his sister married H. Werner Walford, proprietor of the Connaught Varieties music hall, in Norwich.

That was in 1897, and Bodie assisted his brother-in-law in the running of the hall, and did an act himself—conjuring and a little ventriloquism. In 1898 Bodie tried his luck as a theatre proprietor —in Macclesfield—but the venture failed. He then went on the halls with his 'Royal Magnets' company, which consisted of himself doing conjuring and ventriloquism (in his vent. act Bodie used ten dummies, dressed as nigger minstrels, with himself as interlocutor); his wife, Princess Rubie, doing a second-sight act and singing for good measure; his sister, Mystic Marie, playing the piano and assisting in the mystery, and a galvanic young lady known as 'La Belle Electra' who took part in all kinds of weird electrical experiments. Soon Bodie changed his name to 'Dr.' Walford Bodie, having adopted his sister's married name, and obtained an American degree in Materia Medica. An early report of one of these appearances, at the Circus of Varieties in Rochdale, 14th January, 1901, reads as follows:

'Dr. Walford Bodie and his talented company are packing the Circus of Varieties in Rochdale, this week. Dr. Bodie, who has appeared here before, gives a remarkable demonstration of ventriloquism and hypnotism.

'His electrical experiments were of a most remarkable character, but Mesmerism is now the principal feature of his entertainment. Under this influence a man became convinced that he was General Buller, and spoke well of the South African campaign. (Boer War.)

'Miss Marie Walford assisted at the piano and Mr. J. Izatt conducted the Circus orchestra in his usual smart fashion.'

But Bodie's great success came a few years later, when he appeared at the old Britannia Theatre, Hoxton, under Tom Barrasford's control, in 1903. His act was now billed as 'Electric Wizardry' and cripples and other deformed persons were brought to him in the hope of a cure. The late George le Roy told the writer that he recalled the front of the Britannia Theatre festooned with sticks and crutches people had thrown away after receiving the 'Doctor's' treatment.

By 1906 Bodie was earning £400 a week on the halls—on a par with Paderewski—and had formed a limited company to manufacture 'Electric Liniment' for general sale to the public. A report in the Variety Theatre Annual for 1906 makes interesting reading:

'The gentleman of the pen found the Doctor in his dressing-room at the Surrey Theatre, and after waiting until the healer had dismissed a number of patients and other consultants, was accorded the interview he craved. He elicited the fact that his victim was originally intended for the Church, but kicked over the ecclesiastical traces. Then he embraced the study of medicine, the desire to alleviate the sufferings of others by the introduction of new and little-known methods, and the annihilation of old-fashioned theories and grand-motherly nostrums, being his incentive.

'Dr. Bodie's first London appearance was at the Britannia in 1903, and caused such a furore that he played three engagements there within six months. Since then he has been booked and re-booked everywhere, also with the Stoll, Payne, and other combinations. This in itself is not an un-mixed blessing, as he has lately received an offer from America at a salary of £300 a week, with the option of his services being retained for an extended period at £400 a week, which he has accepted. Little wonder that he is in such demand, as his name on any bill spells record business.

'His cures of paralysis by means of massage, electricity and hypnotic suggestions have been the wonder of the world, and he has been patronised by clergy, medical men, and the elite of society in every part of the Kingdom. Moreover, he has been the means of drawing to our music halls a class of people who have never before entered their portals, and who, in all probability, would never have done so had it not been for the fame of his miracles—beg pardon—the Doctor emphatically rejects the idea of anything miraculous. Everything he does, he claims, can be explained by natural scientific means.'

In 1907, whilst appearing at the Doncaster Grand Theatre, Dr. Bodie was accused of 'barbarity' by the local Press. Apparently he had on one occasion upon the stage a small boy with a stiff leg, who had been turned out as incurable by Doncaster Royal Infirmary. The worthy Doctor appeared to lose patience with the lad and to all appearances smashed the little boy's stiff leg against his own in a determined attempt to make it move. Considerable animosity was aroused in Doncaster towards Bodie by this apparent lapse, as the small boy was well-known.

In later years came frequent 'brushes' with the medical profession. For example in 1912 Glasgow University medical students wrecked the electrical apparatus when the Bodie Show was playing at the Coliseum. 'Doctor' Bodie—who always said that the letters 'M.D.' after his name stood for 'Merry Devil'—carried on with his 'Electric Wizardry' for many years, having many replacements of his young ladies in the process. His first wife having died, Bodie then married Florrie Robertshaw, a 22-year-old chorus girl in his show, at the age of sixty. He then bought a house-boat on the River Thames and gained a reputation for throwing extravagant parties there. The boat was aptly named 'La Belle Electra' and a fine sight it looked when lit up at night.

Bodie made (and spent) vast sums of money during his lifetime, but there was some doubt about his final financial state when he died in 1939 at the age of 68 after appearing for the season at the Blackpool Olympia. He was said to have invested large sums of money in a London night club venture which did not succeed. Be that as it may, he was the most colourful charlatan ever to grace the boards of the country's music halls.

And with those words we must leave this brief review of those 'North Stars and Lesser Lights' who made up the hey-day of Music Hall . . .

5

Gracie and Charlie

TWO OF the most famous names in show business—Gracie Fields and Charlie Chaplin—both sprang from roots deep in Music Hall.

Gracie was born in Rochdale and Charlie without doubt a Cockney. He was, however, discovered by a Wigan man—J. W. Jackson—who taught him the fundamental tricks of the trade with his troupe as a youngster in the 'Number Two' music halls which abounded in the early years of the century.

The principle 'Ladies First' had better apply; so let us first take a look at the origin and the rise to fame of the North's very own 'Queen of Song'.

*   *   *   *

Grace Stansfield was born in a little room over a fried fish and chip shop in Tweedale Street, Rochdale, Lancashire on 8th January, 1898. Her mother Jenny, who was only 19 when Grace was born, used to scrub the stage at the old Circus of Varieties in Newgate, and also take in 'Pro's washing'. In those days the old Circus was run by Messrs. Smith, Lee and Hargreaves (Smith being the real name of Ohmy the Flier) and the curious wooden building had done duty since 1882.

Gracie had two sisters, Betty and Edie, and later there was brother Tommy. But it was Gracie, the eldest, that had the voice, and mother was determined that the stage should be her career. When mother went to collect the washing from Mr. Grindrod, the commissionaire and doorman at the theatre, Gracie went with her. Often they were allowed to go backstage when the show was on, and from that vantage point watch the performers.

Gracie, on instructions from mother, used to sing loudly outside the 'Pro's digs' nearby, in the hope that one of them would hear and notice her. One day mother's tenacity was rewarded. Lily Turner, a music hall singer from the Midlands, and professionally known as 'Rose Bush', heard her. Lily was what is known as 'resting' at the digs, and she suggested that young Grace should go in for a singing competition being held that week at the Circus.

Although only seven, Jenny dressed her daughter up to look at least twelve, and with singing lessons from Lily (who taught her to sing 'What makes me love you as I do') young Grace entered the singing competition organised by Mr. Pringle, the manager, and won it. The prize was 10s. 6d. and everyone was impressed by this accomplishment. It made Mrs. Stansfield more determined than ever that the stage should become Gracie's career.

Lily Turner, the singer, who was 'resting' indefinitely in the digs at Rochdale in the hope of eventually marrying a rich local stock-broker, was a frequent visitor to the Stansfield's kitchen. Mrs. Stansfield was anxious to obtain all the information she could about the stage. Over cups of tea Jenny and the singer talked about life on the halls, and then came the day when Lily, as Rose Bush, got an engagement to play at Burnley, 18 miles distant.

It was decided that Gracie should join the act with her, and this meant playing truant from school. One of Lily's old stage dresses was cut down for her, and a few ribbons added. And so the young schoolgirl Grace Stansfield fulfilled her first professional engage-ment at W. C. Horner's old Empire Music Hall, in Cow Lane, Burnley.

Gracie did not actually appear on the stage, to all accounts, but sang the second chorus back to Lily from a seat in the gallery. It was a start, and soon after this she literally 'sang for her supper' at smoking concerts in her native Rochdale. The reward was often a few pork pies which were taken home and eaten.

After some experience with a juvenile troupe—and a spell in a convalescent home as a result—Gracie went back to school for a year. Then at the age of twelve, came her big chance. A neighbour called at the Stansfield home to say that singer Jessie Merrylees, billed to appear at the Rochdale New Hippodrome, had been suddenly taken ill and could not appear. The manager wanted to know if Gracie would deputise? Would she! She was down at the New Hippodrome in an instant and the deal was fixed.

And so Miss Gracie Fields was billed to appear for the rest of the week at a salary of 35s. She was so good that she was retained for a second week. It was on the advice of a friendly printer that her surname was shortened to Fields, and sound advice it turned out to be. The New Hippodrome was a brick-built music hall built on the same site as the old Circus of Varieties, in Newgate. It was erected and opened in 1908 and run by the Jackson family, who had formerly toured the halls with a musical act.

After the Rochdale Hippodrome engagement came a spell with Haley's Juveniles, a song and dance team, and one of the halls visited on this tour was the Hull Hippodrome in Porter Street. Then came nearly two years in Blackpool with a troupe called 'Charburn's Young Stars' followed by a spell at home.

At Christmas, 1914, Mr. Ernest Dotteridge, manager of the Oldham Palace gave her a small singing part in the pantomime he was producing there. Mr. Dotteridge was impressed, and recommended her to Freddy Carlton (better known as 'Cousin Freddy') who ran a concert party troupe at Cosy Corner, St. Annes-on-Sea. And so she spent a happy summer season with the Pierrots at a salary of £3 per week and 'Benefits'. The principal comedian with the troupe at this time was Fred Hutchins.

But bigger things were in store for Gracie Fields. After the summer season was over, mother took Gracie to see Percy Hall, a well-known Manchester agent. Mr. Hall, a dapper little man, who also ran a hat and bonnet shop in the Oldham Road in addition to his agency, had the reputation of being a shrewd judge of talent. He offered Gracie six weeks engagements at local halls at a salary of £5 per week. Gracie was IN.

After this, came a meeting in Mr. Hall's office in the Oxford Road, with the cast of a new touring revue entitled 'Yes, I Think So'. The principal comedian was a pale-faced young man named Archie Pitt. Archie had been on the halls for years, and had risen from the working men's clubs in the North. He was destined to be Gracie's first husband.

The time was 1915 and 'Yes, I Think So' went on the road for 18 months, under the banner of Percy Hall. The first circuit the show was booked to play was the Broadhead Tour, which then comprised a dozen or so halls in workaday Lancashire towns. (The Broadhead Tour was known among the Pro's as 'The Bread and Butter Tour'.) 'Yes, I Think So' opened at the Hulme Hippodrome, followed by the Preston Kings' Palace and other Broadhead halls. It was fairly successful.

Then, in 1916, Archie Pitt branched out with his own revue, 'It's a Bargain' which he had written himself. The leading lady was Mona Frewer, and in it, apart from Gracie, were Archie's three brothers, Edgar, Pat and Bert, who did a comedy act together as the Aza Brothers. Bert very soon dropped out of the act and became manager for the show. He proved himself to be very capable and shrewd, and in later years found fame for himself as an agent. (It was upon his advice that a scrap-metal dealer named Jimmy Brennan took over the old Tivoli Theatre in Barrow which was going for a song, and from that small beginning became a successful theatre and cinema proprietor.)

The Pitt revue 'It's a Bargain' ran for over two years, not without some difficulty, and played most of the 'Number Two' dates in the North. It was at the Selby Hippodrome very soon after its opening in 1916 in the short period before it went over to films. (The Hippodrome was built by the Tuck family, who had the tiny Globe cinema in Gowthorpe.)

The hour of Destiny for the little touring revue came in 1917 when the 'It's a Bargain' company was stranded without funds after a particularly bad week at the old Victoria Theatre in West Stanley, Co. Durham. They had no money to get across country to play their next 'date' in Liverpool. However, kind-hearted Arthur Williams, managing director of the Garston Empire loaned Bert Aza enough money to pay the company's fares. From then on, 'It's a Bargain' never looked back, and went on to play bigger and better theatrical 'dates'.

Then, in 1918, Archie wrote another revue to keep the company together. It was entitled 'Mr. Tower of London' and was destined to run for seven years, and to boost Gracie Fields, from an obscure comedienne in touring revue to a big West End 'star'. In it, Gracie took the part of Sally Perkins, and she was joined by her sisters Edie and Betty, and then by brother Tommy, who sold programmes for a time, until a part was found in the cast for him. In 1922, after four years of touring, Gracie married Archie Pitt. She was 25 and he 43.

But, apart from marriage, the greatest thing that happened to Gracie during the tour of 'Mr. Tower of London' was when Sir Oswald Stoll booked it for one week at his Alhambra Theatre in London's Leicester Square. A letter of encouragement from Miss Evelyn Laye to Gracie on her first night was a nice gesture on the part of Britain's most famous musical comedy star.

The Press verdict on Gracie Fields the next day was 'Brilliant', and so, at the age of 27, the girl from 'Chip Sarah's' in Tweedale Street, Rochdale, had really made the grade, and became a West End star.

Sir Oswald Stoll kept her on at the Alhambra, paying her £100 a week, in 1925. Then came engagements at the Coliseum, and at the Cafe Royal. Sir Gerald du Maurier was taken by her style, and engaged her for the part of Lady Weir in his production of 'S.O.S.' at the St. James' Theatre. In addition to all this, Gracie was in demand for making gramophone records. She made such favourites as 'Walter' and 'The Biggest Aspidistra in the World' all about this time.

King George V saw Gracie's performance in 'S.O.S.' from the

Royal Box at the St. James' Theatre, and not long after that came
the invitation to appear in the Variety Artistes' Royal Command
Performance, the first of several such appearances Gracie subsequently made. The girl from Rochdale had come a long way.

But in 1932 came even more fame—with a screen contract. In
that year she made 'Sally in our Alley' with its haunting song,
'Sally', her first 'Talkie' film. This initial success was followed by
more films—'Looking on the Bright Side', 'One Week of Grace' and
many others. Fame had really caught up with Gracie Fields, for
she is reputed to have made £400,000 in seven years.

Sisters Betty and Edie both married and raised families. Betty
married artist Roy Parry, and Edie, Duggie Wakefield, the long-
toothed comedian.

Soon Gracie's marriage to Archie Pitt broke down. They were
not really compatible, quite apart from the difference in ages. Then
came the Divorce courts and subsequent re-marriage to Monty
Banks, the film actor and producer. She was happy with Monty
Banks, but he died tragically in her arms aboard the Orient Express
after less than ten years of marriage. After two years of widow-
hood—in luxury—she met and married Boris Alberovitch in Capri,
when she was over 50 years of age.

There will always be controversy connected with Gracie Fields,
'The Queen of Song' and without doubt, the North's greatest
comedienne. Theatre critic R. B. Marriott summed it up very well
when he said this in tribute:

'There are those among us who deeply regret that the vast
sums of money she earned from her films took her away from
Variety, and that Capri virtually took her away from the
Theatre altogether.

'After the early revues she never again appeared in a production in London or the Provinces, although until a few years
ago (this written in 1960) she made fairly regular appearances
in Variety.'

And so we leave this resumé of the career of Gracie Fields, the
North's very own Queen of Comedy, who became a legend in her
own lifetime.

Today she still lives peacefully with husband Boris on the very
lovely Italian island of Capri, a rich woman in her seventies. Rochdale to Capri is a big stride, but she made it by her own talent, plus
the determination of her mother Jenny, and of course, her first
husband, Archie Pitt. ·

King George VI made her a C.B.E. and a Member of the Order
of St. John of Jerusalem. She is a Freeman of her own home town

of Rochdale, and she has had a ship named after her. But to all
Northerners, she is still 'Our Gracie'.

* * * *

Charlie Chaplin first saw the light of day in a little back room
of the 'Pro's digs' at 287 Kennington Road, London, on the 16th
of April, 1889.

Another notable event occurred in that year in another part of
the world. It was the patenting of the first movie camera in
America by Thomas Alva Edison. A strange coincidence perhaps,
as one made a fortune out of the other.

Although Charlie Chaplin found fame with his Little Tramp
character in America, through the medium of the silver screen, the
basis of his success in comedy films was laid here in this country.
It was learned the hard way—on the boards of the music halls.

One of his first appearances on the stage was in Leeds, at the
City Varieties. This was during the week of 15th March, 1897,
when the eight-year-old Charlie was the youngest member of the
Eight Lancashire Lads, clog dancing and doing the 'Cake Walk'.
The Lads were then on tour, but they were back in Leeds again
at Christmas, supporting Miss Edith St. Clair, Principal Boy in
Walter Reynolds' comedy pantomime at the Theatre Royal, 'Babes
in the Wood'.

How Charlie came to join the Lads at that tender age is a
poignant yet fascinating story.

Both Charlie's parents were theatricals. His father, Charles
Chaplin, a comic singer, was an habitual drunkard. He died of a
disease brought on by excessive drinking at the age of 30 in
St. Thomas' Hospital, London, leaving his wife to support two
young children—Charlie, and his half-brother Sidney, the child of
his mother's former marriage to a bookmaker named Hawkes.

Mrs. Chaplin (Hannah), whose stage name was Lily Harley, was
a rather temperamental singer and dancer of Spanish-Irish descent,
who became mentally deranged by the loss of her second husband.
The result was that Charlie and Sidney were sent by the authorities
to the Old Cuckoo Schools, Hanwell, then a poor boys' institution.
That was early in 1895 and his teacher at Hanwell was said to have
been a Mrs. Rogers.

In a Sunday newspaper during January 1951 an interesting letter
appeared from a Mrs. E. Turner-Dauncey, written from an address
in Southend-on-Sea. It read:

'I taught Charlie Chaplin at the Victory Place Board School,
Walworth, when he was between four and five.

'I well remember his large eyes, his mass of dark, curly hair, and his beautiful hands. He was very sweet and so shy.

'He copied his famous walk from an old man who gave oatmeal and water to horses in cabs and carts outside the Elephant and Castle.'

The Chaplin brothers are reported to have spent a most unhappy period at the Hanwell Institution. Sidney, the elder by four years, was released first. The entry reads:

'Sidney Chaplin handed back to mother, 10th March, 1896.'

Sidney went to sea as a naval cadet and made good. Charlie, who was released later, returned to the care of his mother, who had now taken a room at 3 Pownall Terrace, Kennington.

Mrs. Chaplin was able to subsist by doing sewing, and Charlie helped out by selling papers at Ludgate Circus, and fetching free pea soup from the old Church in the Waterloo Road.

Charlie was fond of dancing in the street to the tune of the barrel organs, and it was while dancing in this manner that he was spotted by J. W. Jackson, who ran the Eight Lancashire Lads troupe on the music halls.

* * * *

The story of Jackson's Eight Lancashire Lads is equally fascinating, and it is true to say that had there been no Lancashire Lads, there may well have been no Charlie Chaplin of film fame.

John Willie Jackson was a white lead worker at Golborne, Newton-le-Willows, near Manchester, who in 1895 taught clog dancing to youths in the village, assisted by his school-teacher wife. In the summer of 1896 the Jacksons, with their five children were on holiday in Blackpool. A talent competition was being held on the Central Pier, organised by Robert Bickerstaffe, the manager. The Jackson children were persuaded to enter, and won easily with their clog dancing speciality.

The result was that Mr. Bickerstaffe offered them a 12-week engagement at the Central Pier. As Mr. Jackson's health was being affected by the lead process work, it was decided to accept, and that Mr. Jackson would remain in Blackpool to look after the children and act as manager. Three other children, sons of a widow with 13, were brought from Golborne, to bring the troupe up to eight. The Jackson children were four boys and their sister Rosie, who had her hair cut short, to make a fine 'boy'.

The original 'Eight Lancashire Lads' were:

John Willie Jackson, junior; Herbert; Alfred; Stephen and sister Rosie; George Cawley and Jim and Billy Cawley (twins).

After their successful season at the Central Pier, Charlie Morritt, then manager at the Blackpool Empire in Church Street, booked them for a week, and succeeded in getting them a further week's booking at the Circus of Varieties, in Rochdale.

This led to a 'trial matinee' at Gatti's-in-the-Road, London, followed by a short tour of London's 'Syndicate Halls'. Late in 1896 came a booking at the Canterbury, in the Westminster Bridge Road, and it was then that Charlie joined the Lads.

One of the twins fell sick, and Mr. Holden, the manager at the Canterbury, who had booked Chaplin senior many times at his hall as a comic singer, remembered young Charlie and his dancing prowess, and recommended him to Mr. Jackson.

'J.W.' was delighted with him, and upon his assurance that Charlie would be well looked after, together with his own children in the troupe, Mrs. Chaplin let Charlie go. The Lads got £1 each per week and their keep. And so it came about that Charlie appeared in Leeds in March 1897 as the youngest member of the troupe.

Although the work was hard and the travelling arduous, Charlie enjoyed his spell with the Lads, with whom he made several tours. He liked to do a 'Dude' speciality where his flair for mimicry could be given full rein. Following the Leeds Theatre Royal engagement, which made them famous, the 'Lads' were booked solid until 1900, about which time Charlie left them.

Before we leave them it is of interest to state that many famous personalities were connected with the Lads, down the years, with their constantly changing personnel. There was Arthur Millis, who later became a member of an outstanding American comedy team —Handers and Millis. Then Jack Edge, who rose to be a famous comedian in this country, not forgetting Tommy Handley, of later years.

But it was in Paris that J. W. Jackson and his troupe found real fame. That was in 1909 when the Jaxon troupe were presented at the Folies Bergere. So successful were they, that the following year Mr. Jackson was requested to supply a girl troupe, and so the 24 English Dancers were formed.

Then came the Eight Grecian Maids who were a great hit in the comic opera produced by the great Max Reinhardt at the Munich Theatre of the Arts. At one time Jackson had troupes working at the London Hippodrome, the London Alhambra, the Folies Bergere, Paris, as well as the touring Lancashire Lads and the Jaxon troupe. In 1925 one of his troupes was honoured to appear in the Royal Variety Performance of that year, before H.M. King George V and Queen Mary.

The 'J. W. Jackson' of recent years, was, of course, the son. This 'J.W.' passed away in 1952 and since then the Jackson Girl troupes (the Lads having been disbanded with the 'Talkies') were carried on for a time by his widow and her son John. In 1934 the 'Bluebell Girls' were formed, to become very famous.

A most interesting letter was received from Tommy Graham, one of the Lads of 1906. He writes:

'The troupe I joined in 1906 had very few of the original lads in it. Most of them were on the Continent in a unit formed and taken there by J. W. Jackson, junior. Even at that time they had toured Germany and Scandinavia, and I believe, Poland and Russia.

'The dress of the Lads I joined in 1906 was "Country smocks and hats for a vocal number; then into short velvet pants, with shirts and bows, for the clog dancing speciality". It was the custom, by the way, of all "Clog Dancers" of those days to do their solos on a slate or marble slab, whether they were professional or amateur.'

*   *   *   *

After one of his tours with 'The Lads' Charlie went the rounds of the London agents' offices, and succeeded in getting a small part in a pantomime ('Puss in Boots') at a London theatre. In this he played the part of a dog, and had the management of that particular theatre in a frenzy when he suddenly included some impromptu realistic 'doggy' business, involving a prop tree, to the great delight of the audience!

From clog dancing to drama was the next step, and at the age of 14 he landed a part in the touring production of 'Sherlock Holmes, or the Strange Case of Miss Faulkner'. This had been put on by Charles Frohman, the American impresario at the Duke of York's Theatre, London, and was an adaptation for the stage by William Gillette of a play by Arthur Conan Doyle.

The tour opened at the Shakespeare Theatre, Liverpool, at Easter, 1903, with Charlie's half-brother Sidney in the part of Count von Stahlberg, and H. A. Saintsbury, well-known on Mersey-side as a stock company actor, as the famous detective. It was Charlie's job to provide a little comedy relief in the last act as Billy the Page. His wage was now £2 10s.

The Yorke family of Blackburn distinctly remember the play being there during 1903, with the Chaplins in the cast, and by

Christmas of that year the touring play reached Dewsbury. At the apartment house where Charlie and his brother stayed, he wrote in the visitors' book:

'We have been exceedingly comfortable and spent a very happy Christmas.'

Charlie was not always so fortunate in his choice of 'Pro's digs' for he subsequently acquired a mongrel bitch on this tour, which in turn gave birth to five pups, and he insisted in travelling these around with him, to the consternation of landladies!

A curious incident occurred years later in Dewsbury, which seems to suggest an affinity between the great comedian and that town. In 1942 a framed photograph of Charlie—in the popular guise of the Little Tramp with baggy pants of film fame— disappeared from its place in the foyer of the Tudor Cinema. The manager—with a touch of Chaplinesque humour—put up a notice which read as follows:

'If the person who stole this photograph will call at the office he will be supplied with a photograph of Mrs. Chaplin to make a pair.'

Monday, 1st February, 1904, saw the play reach York, where it was put on at the Theatre Royal, but it cannot have been very successful there, for after only three days it was taken off and transferred to the Grand Opera House at Harrogate.

The bills read:

'Mr. Charles Frohman presents William Gillette's famous play in four acts "Sherlock Holmes—or the Strange Case of Miss Faulkner".

'The cast included H. A. Saintsbury as Sherlock Holmes, Charles Mussett as Dr. Watson, Robert Forsyth as Professor Moriarty, Sidney Chaplin as Count von Stahlberg and his brother Charles as Billy the Page.'

For the week of 16th May, 1904, the play was at the Bradford Theatre Royal, which is also a cinema nowadays. The Bradford Exhibition has just opened a few weeks previously in Lister Park, and the city was thronged with visitors. To all accounts the play had a much better reception than at York or Harrogate.

That week Saintsbury was making his 500th appearance in the name part, and Fred Inwood had replaced Charles Mussett in the part of Dr. Watson. A report of the play reveals that Saintsbury 'made the part of Holmes live' and that other parts were played by Miss Theodore Dicke as 'the repulsive Madge Larabee' and Ernest Ruston did well as James Larabee. As the gentle Miss

Faulkner, Miss Lucille Milner played the role with 'sympathy and understanding'.

The play was still running in September 1905, for in that month it visited the Huddersfield Theatre Royal, with the two Chaplins still in the cast. By that time, however, H. Lawrence Leyton had taken over from Saintsbury the role of the great detective.

There was another tour a few years later, when there was an attempt at revival, following a London run. In the second tour H. Hamilton Stewart played the great detective's part and Cedric Walters was in Charlie's old part of Billy the Page.

In October 1905, another version opened at the Duke of York's Theatre in St. Martins' Lane, entitled 'The Painful Predicament of Sherlock Holmes' in which Charlie again played Billy the Page. At Christmas there was a version of Barrie's 'Peter Pan' at the theatre and Charlie appeared as one of the wolves.

Then came a lean spell for a time, enlightened by an episode in which the frantic manager of an East End hall—believed to be the old Cambridge in the Mile End Road—called on him to deputise when his leading comedian fell ill. Thus Charlie made his appearance in the East End as 'Sam Cohen, the Jewish Comedian'. In this role he wore the original comic's baggy pants (a forecast of things to come?) and fell into a tub of water on stage, to great merriment.

In May 1906, Sidney Chaplin, four years older, and acting as his guardian, signed a contract on Charlie's behalf for him to appear in a show called 'Casey's Court' being run on the halls by Will Murray. This was a representation of Cockney children playing in a slum alley (a fore-runner of the 'Dead End Kids') with Will Murray in the part of Mrs. Casey. Ernest Cadle ran the show.

'Casey's Court' opened with Charlie in the cast, at the Bradford Empire during the week of 14th May, 1906 where it was described as 'funny and quaint'. It was at the Halifax Palace a few weeks later, but this time it was being billed as 'Casey's Court Circus'. A little later again it was under the heading of 'Casey's Court Nibbs'. In this show Charlie did an impersonation of the great 'Doctor' Walford Bodie, who was at that time causing a great sensation on the music halls with his Mesmerism and weird electrical experiments.

A critic who saw the show at the Burnley Empire said some of the characters were hideously deformed and inferred that the whole show was in very poor taste. However, Mrs. Casey's 'second sight' act always went down well causing roars of laughter everywhere the show played.

There were 30 or so youths at one time in 'Casey's Court' and it proved a great training ground down the years for budding comedians. Among those who later became famous can be named George Doonan, Stan Laurel, Tom Gamble, Jerry Verno, Tommy Trinder, Jack Edge, Jack Mayo, Dave Morris and Robbie Vincent ('Enoch').

For a time Bob King took over the part of Mrs. Casey, but after the First War Will Murray resumed and toured the show off and on until 1934 and then again for a few years prior to 1952. In 1934 Will Murray and his son Roy Leo (who took part of 'The New Warder') acquired the Grand Theatre at Blackburn and re-opened it as a music hall. They also established an agency in Jubilee Street, next door to the theatre, and ran this until 1956.

Charlie remained with the company for some time, appearing with them at the Folies Bergere in Paris, where he revived his 'doggy business' with success.

During 1908 brother Sidney was playing a part in Wal Pink's comedy sketch 'Repairs' and Charlie joined the company. They were seen by Fred Karno, who was literally 'King' of the comedy sketch business on the music halls at that time. Karno, real name Fred Westcott, was an ex-acrobat, and actually had a 'fun factory' in Camberwell, and was running what amounted to a repertory company of comedians who played in his sketches on the various music halls. Among such masterpieces were titles like 'Jail Birds', 'Early Birds', 'Saturday to Monday' and 'The New Woman's Club'.

Karno liked Sidney, but was not impressed with Charlie. Sidney was given the part of the Drunken Dude in a piece called 'Mumming Birds', but Charlie got only a small part in 'The G.P.O.' in which he played opposite the great comedian Fred Kitchen.

In point of fact, Charlie learned a lot from Fred Kitchen, who was Karno's leading comedian. Kitchen had joined Karno's 'speechless comedians' in 1897 and was a master of mime. He wore big boots—which no doubt Charlie noticed—and was famous for his catchphrase 'Meredith, We're in' which was the last line of a previous Karno sketch called 'Moses and Son' (or 'The Bailiffs').

Karno was surprised by Charlie's progress with Kitchen, and promoted him to a better part in a sketch called 'The Football Match'. In this, Charlie played the part of a dastardly villain in slouch hot and voluminous cape who attempted to persuade Stiffy the Goalkeeper (played by Harry Weldon) to sell the game. In this scene many famous ex-footballers took part, usually players with local interest wherever the show was playing. This sketch was later re-titled 'The Cup Final' and as such was at the Bradford Empire during February 1909, with Charlie in the cast. Across the road Wee Georgie Wood was making an early appearance in music hall at the Bradford Palace the same week.

In April 1909, Karno put a new production on the road, entitled 'Jimmy the Fearless' which opened at the Willesden Hippodrome. Karno offered Charlie the name part but at the crucial time Charlie lost his voice—probably due to nervousness—and the part was given to Stanley Jefferson, son of a North Shields theatre proprietor. What to do with the voiceless Charlie was something of a problem, but Karno solved it by giving him Sidney's old part, as the Drunken Dude in 'Mumming Birds', which was played entirely to mime.

'Mumming Birds' was the most famous of all the Karno sketches, and in its time it made a lot of money for its originator. It was first put on in 1904 at the old Star Music Hall, Bermondsey, as a substitute item under the title 'Twice Nightly'. It was written at a few hours' notice by Charles Baldwin, who sold the rights to Karno for £5. The first 'Dude' was Billy Reeves, the baggage man, the only person available at the time.

'Mumming Birds' consisted of a stage within a stage, and was actually a skit on the 'mashers' at the old London Alhambra. In this sketch, the 'Dude'—a red-nosed inebriated patron occupying a box—nearly falls out of the box trying to get a worm's eye view of the dancing girls. The Dude also interferes with actors on the stage by throwing things at them and poking fun; finally tangling with a wrestler known as 'The Terrible Turk', usually played by Jimmy Aubrey.

It did not catch on at first, under its original title of 'Twice Nightly', principally because many music halls at that time were only once-nightly: then someone suggested an ornothological touch. Karno had 'Jail Birds' and 'Early Birds'—why not 'Mumming Birds' for the mime show? So 'Mumming Birds' it became and an instant success. Soon afterwards, Frank Allen, a most astute booker, paid a large sum to obtain the contract rights for 'Mumming Birds' to play the Moss Tour, then the largest and most powerful syndicate of music halls in the country. (Once at the Boscombe Hippodrome the inner stage collapsed, fortunately without serious result to cast or audience.)

Chaplin was in his element in the Dude part, as he had done something of the sort with 'Casey's Court' and also as a member of the Lancashire Lads. At which music halls Charlie played the Drunken Dude part has always been a topic for argument; the fact being that several comedians played the part down the years ('Mumming Birds' was going strong as late as 1922). The first was

Billy Reeves in the original offering 'Twice Nightly'; then the
Chaplin brothers, Sidney and Charlie, followed by Billie Ritchie
and others. Charlie certainly played the part at the Dewsbury
Empire, shortly after its opening at Bank Holiday, 1909, and later
at the Keighley Hippodrome for Francis Laidler.

But Charlie's greatest triumph on the British music hall stage
was his star part in 'Jimmy the Fearless'. Karno offered him the
part again, and this time, Chaplin, now in good voice, jumped at
the opportunity.

His first appearance in the role was again in Bradford, this time
at the Empire, during the week of 29th August, 1910. On the same
week's bill at the Empire was the great Eugene Stratton, the coon
singer, who was then reported to be 'past his best' (he retired in
1914). Charlie is said to have played a trick on a local chemist
that week, so delighted was he at getting the part.

'Jimmy the Fearless' was about a youth who carried out all sorts
of feats of daring, only to wake up from a dream at the end. Years
later Danny Kaye exploited the same idea as 'Walter Mitty'. Truly,
there is nothing new under the sun . . .

Charlie was in his element as Jimmy, and he was still playing the
part when a few weeks later the Karno touring company got its
sailing orders for America. His last appearance on the British
music hall stage as a comedian was at the Oldham Empire in
September, 1910: then he set sail to find fame and fortune.

It was while playing the part of the Drunken Dude in a refined
version of 'Mumming Birds' (re-titled for American consumption
'Saturday Night at the English Music Hall') that he was spotted
by the great Mack Sennett at the Morris Theater, New York.

Actually, Charlie made his American debut in the Karno show
'The Wow Wows' at the Colonial Theater, New York, in the week
of 3rd October, 1910. Two weeks later he was in Brooklyn. The
Karno company returned to England in the summer of 1912 for
Charlie saw the Carnival of Flowers in Jersey during August, and
later played in Paris at the Folies Bergere.

Early in 1913 the company returned to America, and the famous
telegram sent by Kessel and Bauman (on Sennett's instructions)
was dated 12th May, 1913 and addressed to Alf. Reeves, manager
of the Karno show, at the Nixon Theater, P.A. It referred to a
comedian called 'Chapman' who played the Drunk, which was, of
course, Charlie. In due course, Charlie Chaplin signed a film contract with Sennett's Keystone Company, at a salary of £25 a week.
His last appearance in Vaudeville was at the Empress, Kansas City,
on the 28th November, 1913. In December 1913 he reported to

Sennett at Keystone as a film comedian. A rival concern (Hal Roach Comedy Pictures) signed up Stanley Jefferson, also of the Karno Company, and turned him into Stan Laurel, the slimmer half of the film comedy team of Laurel and Hardy.

Charlie's first film, 'Making a Living', was released in February 1914, and in it he appeared in his Dude outfit from Vaudeville, but it was not a success. It was not until he adopted the guise of the Little Tramp that he found fame in pictures. Some say that Charlie had done something of the sort in a Karno absurdity called 'London Suburbia' but the popular American version is that one day in the dressing room, which he shared with the Keystone Cops, Charlie tried on Charlie Avery's tiny coat, Fatty Arbuckle's enormous trousers and Ford Sterling's giant cop boots. Then he added for effect a prop bowler, a small moustache and cane, and strutted around.

The effect was electric. Charlie had found a new personality. His room-mates roared with laughter. Sennett came in to see what all the noise was about and could hardly get the Little Fellow on celluloid quick enough.

The rest of the story is well-known. Success, fame and fortune.

The antics of the great little comedian brought joy to millions of people the world over, through the medium of the silver screen.

Interval . . .
Accolade . . . By Royal Command . . .

IN 1912 MUSIC HALL reached its zenith. Then the highest honour possible was bestowed upon the Profession. King George V commanded that his subjects, the performers of Variety, should appear before him and his Queen (Queen Mary) at the Palace Theatre, London, on 1st July, 1912.

Sir Edward Moss had worked hard for this to be brought about. He always wanted his beloved Empire Theatre in Edinburgh to be the venue, but that was no longer possible. The Edinburgh Empire was destroyed by fire in May 1911 when The Great Lafayette and several members of his Company 'The Lion's Bride' perished in the flames which engulfed the stage part of the building. And so it came about that the Palace Theatre, London (formerly the Royal English Opera House) was chosen to hold the great event, which resulted in a knighthood for its controller—Alfred Butt.

This, the Royal Command Performance of 1912, was perhaps the only *real* Royal Command Performance in the full sense of the term. True, there have been many Command Performances since, but they have been more in the style of Royal Performances at which a representative of the Monarchy has been present.

In the early part of 1912, when the news leaked out, the Music Hall fraternity was in a ferment of excitement. Who would be 'in' and who would be left 'out'? The Music Hall Profession was a very over-crowded one, and a dozen Command Performances would not accommodate all the 'stars' who could appear. And so, a Committee was set up, representing the various branches of the Profession, to decide on what form the Royal Show should take.

On the Committee were such figures as Sir Edward Moss, Walter de Frece, Frank Allen, J. Laurie Graydon, Walter Gibbons, Oswald Stoll and others, and, of course, Alfred Butt of the Palace Theatre.

No matter how much the Committee pondered and deliberated, many artistes would be disappointed. What was wanted was a bill

117

representative of the Music Hall as a whole. There would have to be acrobats, dancers, ventriloquists and others in addition to the top comedians and singers of both sexes. Then someone had a brainwave. Why not make the last 'turn' a vast gathering of artistes on stage? It would be 'Variety's Garden Party' and there would be 150 of them in it. In this way, many artistes who, in the normal way, would not get a chance to perform, would still be able to say that they had 'appeared before their Majesties'. It was a superb 'face-saver'.

But even so, one very great artiste was omitted. It was Marie Lloyd—a comedienne at the very top of the tree—but very unpredictable, and known for her incursions into occasional vulgarity. There seems no reason why she should not have appeared in that vast gathering at the end, but the strict conventions of the period should be borne in mind. Before the First World War things were very circumspect, but how little did those at the time know that two years later Europe would be plunged into a war from which very little of the security and decorum of the early years of the century would emerge.

Of course, Marie Lloyd was hurt by this snub, and many of her brother and sister artistes felt strongly also, but she got some consolation by billing herself 'The Queen of Comediennes' from then on. The same week as the Royal Performance she was appearing at the London Pavilion, not far from the Palace!

But what of the Royal Command Performance itself? On the night of the great occasion the vast Palace Theatre was packed with everybody who was anybody in the Music Hall world. The Royal Box was beautifully decorated with what appeared to be a solid mass of national flowers. The audience were eager and expectant, but at the same time very much on their best behaviour. This 'starchy' atmosphere has been evident at most of the Royal Command Performances, but never more so than at this one—the very first.

The King, to indicate this was an informal affair, wore evening dress, with a flower in his button-hole. Queen Mary wore a dress of pale lavender. The Royal Party included Princess Victoria, Princess Christian of Schleswig-Holstein, the Grand Duchess of Russia, Princess Victoria of Schleswig-Holstein, Prince Arthur of Connaught, The Duke and Duchess of Teck, together with Prince Alexander and the Princess Henry of Battenburg. A Royal Party indeed. A tremendous ovation greeted their Majesties as they took their places in the Royal Box.

The performance was a very long one and lasted several hours.

There was a tense atmosphere for most of the time, and many of the artistes were nervous and far from at their best. Poor old Chirgwin came on and fairly gibbered at that august assembly. Then a galleryite came to his aid—shouting a word of encouragement from the 'gods'—and he was at his ease, and usual self. Harry Tate, with his 'Motoring' absurdity, caused roars of laughter, and it was obvious that King George V was highly amused by the antics of the car that did not go, in spite of many 'Goodbyees' from the passengers. George Robey and Alfred Lester were others that 'scored heavily' in the theatrical jargon.

But just before the interval there occurred that amazing *contretemps* in which the Queen intimated that 'The gaze of the Ladies of the Royal Party be not directed at the stage'. What was it that offended the gaze of the Royal Ladies? Not some daring nude, or suggestive serio-comedienne, but the sight of dear little Vesta Tilley wearing trousers! (Vesta, of course, was a male impersonator and wore male attire for her impression of 'Algy, the Piccadilly Johnny'.) This was a totally unexpected development, quite unbargained for by that very careful selection committee. Apart from this, and the fact that one comedian over-ran his time, were the only untoward incidents on that gala night.

But the real great success of the first Royal Command Performance was that vast gathering at the end, entitled 'Variety's Garden Party' in which 150 artistes took part. How that vast assembly sang 'The King' led by Harry Claff ('The White Knight') in his shining white armour. It was a night to remember.

That first Royal Show raised over £2,700 for charity, but the King made it known that at subsequent Performances less should be spent on decorations, floral and otherwise, so that more money would be made available for charity. Nowadays the sum raised is far in excess of that first night's figure.

*   *   *   *

Subsequent Royal Variety Performances have been held at the Alhambra (now no more); the Hippodrome (now the 'Talk of the Town' night-club); the Coliseum; the Victoria Palace and the Palladium. The Palladium holds the record for no less than twenty Royal Variety Performances have been held there. These Royal Shows were suspended during both wars.

Many artistes have appeared at the Royal Shows. Gracie Fields holds the personal record, having appeared in five, the last time being at the Palladium in 1950. Nowadays the Show is not only representative of Variety (that form of entertainment being but a shadow of the great days of 1912) but 'stars' of radio, television, cabaret and screen take part, as well as American and Continental artistes.

It was as though that first Royal Show of 1912 caught Music Hall at its peak, for soon afterwards it began to decline in popularity. The Great War came, and with it Rag-time, revue and the big-scale musicals. Then came the improved 'pictures' moving from the old flea palaces and fairground Bioscopes into improved 'Picture Houses' and, finally with sound, into the super-cinemas. Then came radio, dog racing and finally television as competitors.

The North had to wait until 1955 until it got a Royal Variety Performance. On that occasion it was held at the superb New Opera House in Blackpool, one of the finest theatre buildings in the country, erected in 1939.

Two other Royal Shows have been held in the North. In 1957 H.M. Queen Elizabeth and H.R.H. the Duke of Edinburgh saw a Royal Variety Show at the Glasgow Alhambra, where (as might be expected) Scottish talent predominated the bill. In 1959 H.M. the Queen Mother graced the Manchester Palace Theatre with her presence. On this occasion a special Royal Box was built into the auditorium.

And so, with the Royal seal of approval, Music Hall can truly be said to have emerged from the public house singing rooms to the all-so-very-respectable Palaces of Variety . . .

6

The Moss Empires

HORACE EDWARD MOSS, later Sir Edward Moss, founded the largest and most successful chain of variety theatres in the world—Moss' Empires—controlling at its peak thirty-three music halls. Like other great concerns, it had a small beginning: in this case a tiny place called the Gaiety in Chambers Street, Edinburgh.

Sir Edward, who was 60 when he died in 1912, was a J.P. and a Deputy Lieutenant. In his later years he lived at Middleton Hall, Gorebridge, Midlothian, the former home of Lord Rosebery of Dalmeny. He was the eldest son of James Moss, diorama proprietor, of Ashton-under-Lyne, Lancashire, and married twice. His first wife was Ellen Bramwell of Guernsey, who died in 1893, and his second Florrie Craig, of Peterborough, whom he met and married in 1902.

Knighted in 1906, Sir Edward was to be denied his greatest wish—that his beloved Empire Theatre in Edinburgh should be the venue when Music Hall gained its Accolade—on the occasion of the first Royal Command Variety Performance—which took place in 1912, in the presence of Their Majesties King George V and Queen Mary, and other distinguished Royal personalities. Instead the Edinburgh Empire was burned to the ground in that great catastrophe involving the loss of life of Lafayette, the illusionist, and several members of his company, in 1911. Consequently, the Palace Theatre, London, was chosen for the Command Performance, resulting in a Knighthood for its controller, Alfred Butt.

*   *   *   *

Educated in Manchester and Glasgow, while still in his 'teens Horace Edward Moss travelled with his father's diorama show, playing the piano to accompany the Franco-German War scenes which were unfurled on the moving canvas rolls. In the 1870's Moss the elder became proprietor of the Lorne Music Hall, Greenock, Scotland, and here Horace Edward gained some experience in management.

121

In 1877, at the age of 25, Moss broke away from his father to acquire a music hall of his own. This was the tiny Operetta House in Chambers Street, Edinburgh, opened in 1875 by impresario Carl Bernard, but later run by George Grant as the Gaiety Music Hall. Success was hard to come by in those days, but Moss kept up the Variety tradition at the Gaiety and in 1880 he managed to accquire another hall—a wooden place at Leith—where the turns 'doubled'. He also staged seasonal shows in the Edinburgh Waverley Market.

In 1883 Moss crossed the border into England, intent on trying his luck in the North East. His first acquisition was the Sunderland Theatre Royal, where he took over the lease from Alfred Davis, another well-known theatrical manager, and turned that illustrious theatre into the Royal Music Hall.

The reason for the astonishing decline in the fortunes of the Sunderland Theatre Royal was that the new Avenue Theatre had opened in 1882 and had captured all the business. Davis had run both the Theatre Royal and the Lyceum (the hall where Sir Henry Irving made his very first professional appearance) but fire had destroyed the old Lyceum in 1880. Alfred Davis left Sunderland in 1883 to try his luck in Bradford, at the Princes' Theatre there.

But it was in 1884 that Moss's really successful music hall venture took place, and the scene was Newcastle. The hall concerned was the New Tyne Concert Hall in Nelson Street, a curious place, up a flight of stairs. It was the former Lecture Room of the Musick Hall (in the classic sense) built originally as a place of culture for Novocastrians by Robert Grainger in 1838. In 1861 Dickens had given a reading there and other famous notabilities had appeared.

The *Newcastle Journal* of 17th November, 1884, commented:

'Mr. H. E. Moss, of the Gaiety Theatre, Edinburgh, and the Theatre Royal, Sunderland, has acquired the building in Nelson Street known as the Tyne Concert Hall. This hall has now been entirely reconstructed as the Gaiety Variety Theatre. An attractive act-drop has been provided by Herr Sveder, while Messrs. Dobie and Sons, of Edinburgh, have been responsible for the decorations.'

The Bohee Brothers, of Haverley Minstrels fame, topped the bill at the opening of the Gaiety Varieties, Newcastle, and on the same bill was Bonnie Kate Harvey, a great favourite of the period. Jack Pellow was manager for Mr. Moss, and Tommy Henderson wielded the orchestral baton.

The Gaiety was a success from the start. One report described it as 'The Eldorado of the North' and said that Moss was making money 'hand over fist'. On opening night there was standing room only as 'applause shook the building'. It was soon obvious that the tiny Gaiety was far too small to accommodate all who wished to attend. The Tichborne Claimant (Arthur Orton, the corpulent impostor) caused a sensation when he appeared in 1889, reciting his usual tale of woe, and packed houses greeted the top-line artists booked by the astute Moss for this popular little music hall.

About this time, Moss sold his interest in the Sunderland Theatre Royal to Richard Thornton, the South Shields showman. Thornton had made money at his 'Varieties' in Union Alley, South Shields, and was anxious to expand. A friendship struck up between the pair, and as both wanted to open a new music hall in Newcastle, a joint venture seemed the ideal solution, as neither wanted competition from the other.

Both Moss and Thornton had had their eyes on the Royal Scotch Arms, an old posting house, in Newgate Street. This had a singing-room which was very popular, and the site seemed ideal for a new music hall venture. Very soon an arrangement was entered into with Mr. Farquhar M. Lang, the proprietor, to build there the first of the Moss-Thornton 'Empires'. But Mr. Lang imposed a condition that the public house should stay in existence and be incorporated in any rebuilding. (The Royal Scotch Arms was an old coaching inn dating from the 1850's to which a new frontage had been added in 1878.) In consequence, architects Oliver and Leeson were called in to prepare plans for the new Empire Music Hall to be built on top of the Royal Scotch Arms, the 1878 frontage to remain.

The first Newcastle Empire, built above the inn was, according to a contemporary description, 'a large, square and lofty building, with its circle built in the style of the Leeds Grand Theatre'. The upholstery was described as 'sumptious'. Mr. William Glover painted the new scenery, while Mr. John G. Allen was brought from South Shields to manage the property for Messrs. Moss and Thornton. One feature, apparently not taken into account by the architects, was that the stage of the music hall was right above the inn's kitchens, and often succulent smells would invade the auditorium, but this was only found out by subsequent experience.

After the Mayor and Sheriff of Newcastle had inspected the premises and expressed themselves 'satisfied with the arrangements' the Empire Music Hall opened on 1st December, 1890 with a big bill headed by Don Juan A'Caicedo, from the Folies Bergere, Paris. Among the supporting acts was Peggy Pryde, the daughter of Jenny Hill, the famous serio-comedienne.

The old Gaiety closed down at the same time the new Empire opened, and several of the acts were transferred to the new hall. Moss and Thornton appeared on the stage of the Empire together, at the opening ceremony, and solemnly declared that they would cater with pleasure for Newcastle audiences . . . 'With first-class matter, free from any objectionable features'.

*   *   *   *

Returning to the Scottish scene, the position in 1888 was that the little Gaiety in Chambers Street was still going strong; there were seasonal activities still at the Waverley Market, but in that year the old wooden circus in Leith which served as a music hall was burnt to the ground.

Moss, who had built up a good connection with his Variety shows in Leith, did not want to lose his patrons' goodwill, so he acquired an old Presbyterian Chapel in Kirkgate and, after reconstruction, opened it as the Princess' Theatre at Christmas, 1889. However, in the meantime, a rival manager, taking advantage of the situation, opened an Empire Music Hall in Henderson Street, so Moss had to open the Princess Theatre as a drama house—it opened with the play 'False Lights'—but in later years, when its namesake in Edinburgh had closed, the Princess' Theatre became the Gaiety Music Hall.

Turning his attention to Glasgow, Moss, in colloboration with Dick Thornton and James Kirk, acquired an interest in the Scotia and Gaiety Music Halls in that city. The Scotia, in the Gorbals area, was one of the oldest halls in Scotland, dating back as it did to 1862 when it was built on to the back of a public house (although there was an old singing-room on the site long before that); while the Gaiety in Sauchiehall Street had been erected by one Mackay, who ran it in conjunction with the Star Music Hall in Watson Street, and the Albert Hall of Varieties in Edinburgh. Both halls did well, and soon the bills put on by 'Messrs. Moss, Thornton and Kirk' began to make a big impression on the people of the St. Mungo city.

Equally successful was the original Gaiety in Edinburgh, in fact, so much so that expansion become a necessity. As it was not possible to enlarge on the site of the original hall, Moss looked round for another one. A site in Nicolson Street appeared to present possibilities, for it was firmly rooted in entertainment history. In 1820 Ducrow's Circus had tented there, followed by Newsome's Circus; then a wooden Alhambra had occupied the site, and finally the Southminster Music Hall, which had been destroyed by fire.

Moss acquired the site towards the end of 1891 and following the demolition of the ruins, work on the erection of a new hall began immediately.

The new house, which was to be called the Empire, was designed by Frank Matcham, who subsequently designed most of the Moss' Empire theatres. The first Edinburgh Empire was a very beautiful building, and a contemporary description of the hall reveals the following:

'On 7th November, 1892, the Empire Palace Theatre, Edinburgh, was opened to the public. Nicolson Street was thronged with sightseers gaping at the brilliantly illuminated entrance and dome . . . gazing with envious eyes at the mortals who had gained admission.

'To a packed auditorium when all the electric lights were put full on, just before the performance, the effect was magical. The Theatre, with its stately proportions and beautiful decorations, stood revealed in all its grandeur, and the audience, charmed with the brilliant spectacle, broke out into a loud and hearty cheer.'

That enthusiastic audience saw a first-class bill on that auspicious occasion. Giving the proceedings a good send off were the massed bands of the Argyll and Sutherland Highlanders, with the Carabineers; then came Evans and Luxmore in their speciality 'Musical Madness'; Professor Maud's Canine Wonders charmed everyone with their astonishing sagacity, and Miss Cora Stuart and her Company appeared in a series of entertaining sketches, and there were other fine acts, all adding to the enjoyment of a memorable evening. A very young assistant stage manager at the opening of the Edinburgh Empire was Mr. A. S. Cruikshank, in later years to become managing director of Howard and Wyndham Theatres, Ltd.

With the opening of the new Empire, the tiny Gaiety in Chambers Street was closed down, Marie Loftus topping the last bill. After being closed for some time, the Gaiety was revived for a few years as the Operetta House, until it was sold as a warehouse. (It was finally demolished in 1952 when Knox House, an adjunct of the University, was built there.)

Now, at the beginning of 1893, with several Scottish ventures established and well under way, it was time for the invasion of England by the all-conquering Moss Empires' combine . . .

*   *   *   *

The first 'conquest' in England was in the Midlands—the old Crystal Palace in Birmingham—which fell without much resistance being offered. The Crystal Palace, which stood in Hurst Street, had opened its doors in September, 1862 as Day's Concert Hall, but it closed down at Bank Holiday, 1893 upon being sold to Horace Edward Moss and Richard Thornton. However, it was decided to stage a benefit performance for Harry Day, son of James Day, the original proprietor, so the old hall was re-opened for one night to allow this to take place. A sizeable sum was raised at this performance. Then, the demolition contractors moved in, to clear the site for the erection of another ornate 'Empire Palace' designed by Frank Matcham, on the lines of the one erected in Edinburgh the previous year.

The Birmingham Empire which arose on this site was a large, ornate building, accommodating 2,000 persons. The stage, very well equipped, was 56-ft. wide and 34-ft. deep, with a 30-ft. proscenium opening. Opening with a flourish at Whit, 1894 the Empire offered its new patrons a big bill topped by Chirgwin, the White-Eyed Kaffir, then at the peak of his career. In support were Wal Pink and Company in a comedy sketch entitled 'The Parrot'; Gus Elen, the Coster comedian, the Two Macks, knockabout acrobats, and many other fine acts. The Empire got away to a good start and the music hall tradition on the Hurst Street site was being maintained with first-class fare.

No sooner had the Birmingham venture been successfully launched, than Messrs. Moss, Thornton and Co. turned their attention to Sheffield. Here work began on the erection of an Empire upon land opposite to where Walter Cooper's Alhambra music hall had once stood, in Charles Street. It was to be a bigger house than that of Birmingham, for the new Sheffield Empire was to hold 3,000 persons and would be built at a cost of £65,000—a very big sum indeed in those days.

A Prospectus issued in 1895 described the new building as 'The finest in the Country, with all the Latest Improvements: Sliding roof, electric light, Fire-proof Curtain, etc., etc.' and patrons were promised a programme 'replete with all that is Excellent, Refined and Entertaining, always Guaranteed . . .'

The Sheffield Empire Palace, which had a most imposing frontage into Charles Street bearing the words 'Music and Art', was carried out in the Moorish style then so popular, and opened for 'High Class Music and Varieties' on 4th November, 1895 with a big once-nightly bill, topped by Cora Stuart and her Company (who had appeared on the opening bill at Edinburgh) in a sketch entitled 'The Fair Equestrienne'. Supporting acts included Will Evans, the 'Musical Grotesque'; Lettie Lynne, descriptive vocalist;

Nellie Christie, the 'Dandy-Coloured Coon' (from the original Christy Minstrels), and others. The Grand Orchestra of 20 musicians was conducted by Mr. Ralph Booth and the opening was a huge success.

As a result of the opening of the Moss' Empire Palace, several small music halls in the West Bar district went out of business, among their number the Grand Theatre, run by the Welding Brothers, from Aberdeen. The Grand was not out of action long, for it was taken over the following year by an energetic music hall proprietor from Northampton in Frank MacNaghten, who lost no time in re-opening the Grand on the then virtually unknown 'Two Houses a Night' system, as a counter-attraction to the expensive bills staged at the Moss house.

*   *   *   *

Merseyside was the next part of the country to receive attention, and in January 1896, Messrs. Moss and Thornton at an auction bought the 30-year-old Royal Alexandra Theatre and Opera House in Lime Street, which had been closed for some time, for £30,000.

Erected in 1866 as the Prince of Wales' Theatre, on the site formerly occupied by Charles Garner's Livery Stables, the building had closed down after barely a year's existence. It had been subsequently re-opened as the Royal Alexandra Theatre and leased for the next 20 years by Edward Saker, only to close suddenly again in 1888. Some time later John Hollingshead, of the Gaiety Theatre, London, tried his luck, with disastrous results, one story being that in the end the bailiffs tried to enter the building for purposes of distraint and were kept at bay by the staff with hose-pipes, until the water supply was cut off!

Now, following the auction, it was in the hands of Moss and Thornton, who immediately began converting the hall into yet another 'Empire Palace'. After complete internal re-construction, including the installation of the new electric light, the 'Empire Theatre of Varieties' opened on the 19th December, 1896 with Mr. Oscar Barrett's 'Fairy Pantomime—Complete with Harlequinade—Cinderella'. The large cast included Florrie Harman as Cinderella, Marie Campbell as Dandini, Reuben Inch as the Clown, and Fred Emney (Snr.) and Victor Stevens as the two Ugly Sisters.

The new Liverpool Empire was a conspicuous success, and drew crowds from a very wide area to see the magnificent pantomime, which ran until February 1897, when Variety took over. A very prosperous house, that old Liverpool Empire functioned until 1923, when it was closed and demolished. Then a completely new Empire was built on the site, opening in 1926.

The Scottish scene was changing also with the advent of 1897. In Glasgow, where the Scotia and the Gaiety were considered small and outdated, it was decided to demolish the Gaiety, which occupied the best position (in Sauchiehall Street) and build there a huge Empire, on the lines of those erected in England. Accordingly, this was done, and the Glasgow Empire, a large music hall holding 2,000 opened at Easter, 1897 with a big bill, topped by Glasgow's own girl from Stockwell, Marie Loftus. When this occurred, the old Scotia in the Gorbals was closed down, but it reopened again shortly as a home for melodrama, known as the Metropole Theatre, by the well-known touring managers, Morell and Mouillot. (Just to further complicate matters, a small music hall at Anderston Cross, hitherto known as the 'Argyle Street Varieties', became the New Gaiety Music Hall, and then the Tivoli, but its final state was the Gaiety Cinema!)

In 1897 work was also going ahead with the erection of another large music hall in England—this time in Kingston-upon-Hull. This was sited along the Anlaby Road in Hull, but the new building could not be called the 'Empire' owing the existence of Messrs. Bosco and Downs' Empire Music Hall (the old Mechanics' Institute in Grimston Street) once known as 'Springthorpe's'.

It was decided to call the new building in Hull 'The Palace Theatre of Varieties' and it would be designed by Frank Matcham in the usual Moorish style of decoration, and embody the now essential sliding roof, electric light, etc.

According to a contemporary description the Hull Palace Theatre was '. . . an elevation of classic design, with an entrance divided by stone columns and pilasters. It embodies a glass-roofed conservatory, crush-room and entrance of Indian design complete with palms and ferns, etc. There are tip-up plush seats in most parts, and arrangements have been made with the Railway Company to run a late train to Bridlington after the performance.'

Performances were once-nightly at 7 o'clock and prices were from 4d. to 2/6d. The theatre held 2,000 persons and the stage dimensions were 55-ft. across, by 35-ft. deep; proscenium opening 30-ft. across.

The Palace Theatre of Varieties, Hull, opened on 6th December, 1897 with a very distinguished audience. According to a newspaper report 'The best families of Hull and district were represented in the boxes' and Mr. Frank Allen, associate of Messrs. Moss and Thornton, spoke on behalf of the directors of the 'Liverpool, Leeds

LAUGHTER MAKERS

TWO FAMOUS FORMBY'S
Left: Young George and (right)
George (Senr.).

TWO FAMOUS STARS
Below: Albert Whelan and (right)
George Robey (offstage).

Plate 13

**SOME FAMOUS LADIES
OF THE HALLS**
Above: Daisy Dormer and (right)
Gertie Gitana.

Below: Mona Vivian and (left) Nellie
Wallace.

Plate 14

Photo: D. Worrall

(Above) The big fire that destroyed the Rochdale Royal in 1954 (Gracie cried when she saw this picture).

GRACIE FIELDS—The North's Greatest Comedienne

(Below, left) Gracie as she appeared in "Mr. Tower of London" and (right) In her dressing room at Bradford in 1956 on her Farewell Tour she inspects an old bill unearthed by Mr. F. D. Taylor, at nearby Keighley. This shows "Pit 4½d" and makes Gracie laugh.

Photo:
Courtesy of Lou Warwick

Gracie in 1921.

Photo: Bradford Pictorial

Plate 15

(Above) As a member of the EIGHT LANCASHIRE LADS in 1898 (Charlie is the "Dude" out in front).

THE GREAT CHARLIE CHAPLIN as a youngster

(Below) The teenage Charlie as one of the members of CASEY'S COURT in 1906. (Stan Laurel is the second from the left in the middle row).

Plate 16

(Top left) SIR EDWARD MOSS—founder of the famous Moss Empires.

(Top right) NEWCASTLE EMPIRE. The first of the Moss - Thornton Empires in England.

(Below left) The SUNDERLAND EMPIRE as it was at the time of the Farewell Visit of G. H. ELLIOTT.

(Below right) RICHARD THORN-TON—An early partner in the Moss Empires.

Plate 17

(Above) ALBERT MODLEY, who appeared in 15 pantomimes for Francis Laidler, and GWLADYS STANLEY, who became Mrs. Laidler.

PANTOMIME FAVOURITES

(Below) The "King of Pantomime" with his "SUNBEAMS" of 1938, and his favourite Bradford Alhambra.

Photo: Courtesy of Rowland Hill

Photo: B. Middleton

Plate 18

CHARLIE WHITTLE "The Day we Christened the Baby".

JACK PLEASANTS—the Bradford-born comedian who made famous the song "I'm Twenty-One Today!"

FAMOUS MUSIC HALL FIGURES
(Left) George H. Elliott, the "Chocolate Coloured Coon". (Right) "Doctor" Walford Bodie, Hypnotist and Miracle Worker.

DR. WALFORD BODIE, THE FAMOUS SHOWMAN

Plate 19

ALAN GALE — A Yorkshire-born Talent spotter who now runs "Old Time Music Hall" shows in the South of England.

STAR MAKERS

ERIC MARTIN—The West Riding agent who "discovered" such personalities as Harry Worth, Roy Castle and many more.

KEN PALMER

KEN PALMER—A favourite Northern compere, cartoonist and entertainments manager of wide experience.

ERNEST BINNS who ran Concert Parties throughout the North and gave a start to many later famous performers.

Plate 20

and Hull Empire Palaces, Ltd.' which was the new holding company. Miss Lilian Lea, the ballad soprano, sang the National Anthem and the show was on.

The 'Best families in Hull and District' saw a big bill topped by Gus Elen, the Coster comedian; Captain Slingsby, ventriloquist; Nellie Christie, 'The Original Susie-Tusie'; The Glen-Roy Dancers, and others. Bob Singleton conducted the pit orchestra and Alfred Graham was the house manager.

It was a notable opening bill in many ways, for Captain Slingsby later joined Moss Empires as an adviser, after managing the Hull Tivoli for Messrs. Mortons. Bob Singleton, the musical director, came from the old Gaiety at Glasgow, while Alfred Graham, who came from a 'legitimate' theatre at Sheffield, stayed in Hull and joined the 'opposition' by becoming manager for Tom Barrasford at the Hull Alhambra. (When that old hall was reconstructed as the Hippodrome, Graham ran it himself for a time, in conjunction with the old Oxford Palace at Middlesbrough, but the ending was sad—both halls closed down suddenly when it was announced that Mr. Graham's affairs 'were in Chancery'.)

The Hull Palace was a great success, and outlived several of its rivals as a music hall. It was a very draughty building, and there were many who said that Matcham should pay more attention to such fundamental matters and less to non-essentials such as conservatories, ferneries, etc. The fate of the Hull Palace in later years was that it had to be closed because of air raid damage in 1940, only to re-open ten years later under new management entirely, later still to be converted into a 'Continental' type music hall. Manager here for a long time, during the Moss Empires' reign, was that doyen of managers, Jesse Challons, in later years so ably connected with the Sunderland Empire.

* * * *

In February, 1898 came the opening of the Nottingham Empire Palace—which brought Oswald Stoll into the picture. Both Moss and Stoll had designs on Nottingham, and rather than enter into competition with each other, decided to amalgamate. The Empire in that city was jointly controlled, and the first of the Moss Empires to be run on the new 'Two Houses a Night' system. Oswald Stoll was made managing director of the 'Nottingham Empire Palace Co. Ltd.' and this was to lead, in time, to the unification of all the Moss Empires.

Next hall to open in the ever-growing Moss Tour was the Leeds Empire Palace. This hall was situated in Briggate, Leeds, and like so many of the theatres, was designed by Frank Matcham. It was due to open on Monday, 29th August, 1898 but the contractors cut things rather fine. A big crowd gathered in Briggate outside on opening night, but could not be admitted until the plasterers—working feverishly in the auditorium—had finished their job. The Leeds Empire was hardly as large as many of the other halls in the circuit, for it seated only 1,750 but there were three tiers and the height gave an illusion of spaciousness. Stage dimensions were 66-ft. wide by 38-ft. deep, and the usual Moorish style of decoration was very much in evidence.

There were fifteen 'turns' on the opening bill and the first programme bore the words 'Elegance, Safety, Comfort and Respectability'. Among the acts taking part was that of Harry Tate, then at the beginning of his career. In later years he recalled the instance quite vividly, saying that he *cycled* from Manchester to Leeds that weekend! In those days Harry Tate was described as a mimic, but at the height of his career took part in several famous sketches, such as 'Fishing' and 'Motoring'. The latter was especially popular. for the car never made any progress whatever, in spite of many 'Good-Bye-Ees' from the occupants.

Also on the early bill at Leeds were the Onda Brothers, one of whom some years later ran several places of amusement in Preston. Arthur Grimmett, the musical director, had already run two theatres in Halifax—the old Gaiety at North Bridge, and the Grand Theatre—which was built on the same site. The Northern Theatres Co. bought the Grand Theatre in 1897 and Grimmett then joined Moss Empires as a musical adviser.

The opening of the Leeds Empire had a disastrous effect upon the existing music halls in the city—the Varieties and the Tivoli—both of which closed down for a time. Both revived in sensational fashion, however, the Varieties becoming the now famous City Varieties under the able guidance of publican Fred Wood (with assistance from booker J. C. Whiteman); while the Tivoli rose again as the Hippodrome due to the efforts of an energetic Tom Barrasford from Jarrow.

After many years as a music hall the Leeds Empire went over to 'Talkies' in 1931 when Charlie Chaplin's first sound film 'City Lights' was shown there. But Variety soon returned—for the rival Hippodrome closed down in 1933—and the Empire went on to do very good business in the music hall 'boom' following the Second War.

*　　*　　*　　*

In the nearby city of Bradford another Moss Empire was in the course of being erected in 1898. This was not ready for opening by Christmas, as had been the intention, but was opened on the 30th January, 1899.

Unlike the other Moss halls, the Bradford Empire was not designed by Matcham, and it was unusual in so much that it was built on the back of licensed premises, rather in the fashion of the old-time singing rooms, but in this case it was the rather superior Alexandra Hotel in Great Horton Road.

According to a contemporary description:

'The Bradford Empire is a palatial and sumptuous hall of variety. The figured-style vestibule pierces the entrance to the Alexandra Hotel and the body of the hall is constructed on the cantilever system—that is to say without supporting pillars— and embodies two tiers, being carried out in an Arabesque style of decoration.'

The architect responsible for this departure from the usual style was Walter Sprague, who had at that time been responsible for the design of several London Theatres, including the Aldwych, the Strand and the New Theatre. The Bradford Empire had an Oriental look about it, but it was not so ornate as those planned by Matcham. There was no upper circle, just dress circle and gallery, with seven large boxes at either side of the stage. Instead of a sliding roof, the large domed centre ceiling was capable of elevation for purposes of ventilation. Six amber muranese lamps hung from the ceiling (instead of the usual shower electroliers) and the hall had a cosy look about it, the colours being red, cream and gold, with gold-bas relief. A completely new feature, the first installation in any theatre or music hall, was the employment of electric battens.

Sandor's Stage Circus was the opening attraction at the Bradford Empire, where Philip A. Lennon was brought from Leeds to manage the property. In support was a large variety bill, including Addie Conyers (serio-comedienne); Herr Gross and his Educated Baboons; the Two Finneys (in the Crystal Tank); The Eight English Roses (dancers, together with the sensational American dancer 'La Sylph'); Rumbo Austin and his 'Nippers', the Sisters Johngmanns, and others. Performances were once nightly at 7.30 p.m.

At the opening ceremony Frank Allen, on behalf of Moss Empires, spoke to a packed house. He said:

'The Bradford Empire will warrant the support of all classes of society. Nothing will be seen or heard here that will raise a blush or put modesty to shame. Bring your wives and daughters . . .'

And so the Bradford Empire was launched with music hall. While business was good it could have been better, and after a few months it was decided to follow the example of Frank McNaghten who controlled the nearby Palace, and go over to 'Twice Nightly' programmes. The Palace had a hard time when the Empire first opened, but later on there was good natured rivalry.

However, a situation arose in 1913 which spelled 'Finis' to the Bradford Empire as a music hall. Francis Laidler, who owned the Princes' Theatre and other halls, decided to erect a magnificent new Alhambra Theatre of Varieties on some spare ground only a few yards from the Empire. This would be run in conjunction with the Variety Theatres Controlling Company, directed by Walter de Frece, which was by this time in direct opposition to the Moss Empires' combine.

The new Bradford Alhambra was built, and opened on the 23rd March, 1914 with the Wylie-Tate production 'A Year in an Hour', together with supporting acts, including Nellie Wallace, the well-known comedienne. The Alhambra was designed by Messrs. Chadwick and Watson, the Leeds architects, and was carried out in the English Renaissance style, with a most pleasing white terra-cotta exterior. It was a medium sized house, accommodating 1,800 but with an exceptionally wide stage and proscenium opening, capable of taking the largest touring productions.

The effect of the Alhambra upon the Empire was pretty much the same as the effect the Empire had had on the Palace in 1899. A solution had to be sought, as it was perfectly obvious that there was not room for three music halls in Bradford, and all within a few yards of one another. A meeting was held, at the instigation of Moss Empires, the outcome of which was that from 1916 the Empire would be leased to Mr. Laidler as a 'Number One Touring Company Theatre' and Moss' Empires would assume booking control for the new Alhambra, upon expiry of the present arrangement with the Controlling Company.

At August Bank Holiday, 1916 the Bradford Empire re-opened as a playhouse; Voilet Fairbrother appearing in 'Romance'. This was followed by other good touring productions, and such famous personalities at Matheson Lang, Weedon Grossmith and Jack Buchanan appeared, but after only 15 months this brilliant season of plays was brought to an end by a disastrous fire, in which the stage end of the theatre was completely destroyed.

After reconstruction, the Bradford Empire opened in 1918 as a cinema, and for a number of years it was leased to and run by several controllers. In 1952 there was another serious fire, after which the Empire closed down for good as a place of entertainment, since being used exclusively for storage purposes. In passing, it is of interest to note that in 1946 Mr. Harry Buxton, of the Buxton Cinema Circuit, Burnley and Manchester, made application for permission to convert the Empire back again to a music hall. This raised very strong objections indeed from both Mr. Laidler and Moss Empires, and the scheme was abandoned.

*   *   *   *

Another hall which was booked 'in conjunction with Moss Empires' for a long time was the Grand Theatre and Circus, at Hanley, Staffs., owned by the well-known Elphinstone family. This was the first hall in the country convertible either for a circus or music hall, and gave Edward Moss the idea for the London Hippodrome.

Designed by Frank Matcham, the Hanley Grand Circus was carried out in Renaissance style, with busts of Shakespeare and Goethe, and there were notable paintings by Signor Buccini. Seating 2,594 persons, the Grand had a stage 63-ft. long by 40-ft. wide, with a 32-ft. proscenium expanding to form a 40-ft. circus ring. (In strict point of fact, Matcham had designed one other circus before this—the Grand Cirque at Bolton—erected in 1894 by the Newsome family, afterwards converted to the Grand Theatre by structural alterations.)

The Hanley Grand Circus and Music Hall, with bookings by Moss Empires, was opened on 22nd August, 1898 with a typical circus bill, including The Valdares, cyclists; the Two Franks, on the horizontal bars; John Higgins, the 'Human Kangaroo', and other acts. Signor Bianchi, who conducted the Grand Orchestra, was related to the Bianchi who once ran the old Waxworks in Liverpool, taken over by the Stoll family.

The Hanley Grand did big business, and the Elphinstone's were able to buy out the 'opposition' (The Leeds and Hanley Theatre Co.) at the Empire, or former Gaiety, music hall. In 1901 the Elphinstone management reopened this house as the Kings' Theatre, with dramatic fare, but in later years it was to become a cinema.

In later years the Hanley Grand forsook circus fare, and became an orthodox music hall, where all the 'big names' in music hall appeared, but in 1932 came the decision to convert it into a cinema. No sooner had the Grand gone over to 'Talkies' than it was completely gutted in a disastrous fire, said to be a 'Judgment' by many Potteries folk, who did not want to see Variety banished from the district where Gertie Gitana had such close associations. (The final outcome was that the Odeon cinema was built on the Grand Theatre site, while Moss Empires acquired an interest in the Theatre Royal, Hanley.)

*   *   *   *

The year 1899 was a big year in the history of the Moss Empires, for it saw the tentacles of the combine reach London, with the formation of the London District Empire Palaces Co., and it also saw the unification of the various companies under one head.

The London District Empire Palaces Co. embraced three suburban halls in the Metropolis, the first of which, the Holloway Empire, was opened on 4th December, 1899 and the others, the Empires at Stratford and New Cross, quickly followed. However, the Holloway Empire had a very short life, of just over a decade, when it was closed and sold as a cinema, the reason being that the much larger Finsbury Park Empire was opened in 1910 as a replacement. The Stratford and New Cross Empires were to continue until about the time of the Second War, the former being damaged by bombs and not rebuilt, and the latter leased to other controllers.

December 1899 also saw the unification of the ten existing companies under the one heading of 'Moss' Empires, Ltd.' with share capital in the region of £1 million. Oswald Stoll became managing director of the new group of companies, a position he held until 1910. One of the ten companies in the merger related to the new London Hippodrome, a building designed by Matcham convertible either as a circus or music hall, and this opened on 15th January, 1900 with a combined water, variety and circus spectacle, entitled 'Giddy Ostend'. This was the first Moss Empires' hall in London's West End.

One result of the incorporation of the various Empires' companies was that Dick Thornton 'opted out' of the main circuit with the entry of Stoll, stating that he preferred to keep the new South Shields Empire under his own control. As a result Thornton subsequently built up a 'North East Circuit' of halls, allied to, but not part of the main circuit of Moss Empires. In the administration of the North East Circuit, Dick Thornton was ably assisted by the Gillespie family of Morpeth.

Apart from the South Shields Empire, which was opened on 13th February, 1899 Dick Thornton had the old Olympia in Northum-

berland Road, Newcastle, which he acquired in the same year
from Linden Travers, and retained his directorship of the Newcastle Empire. When the Newcastle Empire was demolished and
completely rebuilt in 1903 the Olympia was used as 'a temporary
Moss Empire' and the bookings transferred there. Upon the opening of the later Newcastle Empire—with the ill-fated Chung Ling
Soo topping the bill on 14th December, 1903—the Olympia Theatre
was leased to Ralph Pringle and the North American Animated
Picture Co., to become Newcastle's first regular cinema.

Three other 'Empires' were added to the North East Circuit by
Richard Thornton down the years. They were the Sunderland
Empire, opened by Vesta Tilley in 1907; the West Hartlepool
Empire, added in 1909, and the Gateshead Empire, adapted from
the former Kings' Theatre in 1915. In addition Thornton ran
several cinemas, including the former Theatre Royal in South
Shields, before he died in 1922.

* * * *

Reverting to 1900, a time when many music hall circuits had
scarcely begun, the Moss Empires combine was almost complete.
Certainly it was flourishing.

The success of the London Hippodrome as a home for circus and
water spectacles was undisputed. The building held 1,340 patrons
comfortably and represented a long-cherished ambition of Sir
Edward to give Londoners an opportunity to view first-class fare
at moderate prices. The Hippodrome cost £250,000 to erect and
was built to plans prepared by Frank Matcham, embodying the
latest methods and experience gained at the Grand Circus at
Hanley.

In fact the success of the London Hippodrome, and the opening
of a similar building in Manchester by Stoll, led Moss to believe
that a circus on these lines would be an investment in Liverpool.
The result was the Liverpool Olympia, opened in 1905, on a site
not far away from where Hengler's old circus had stood. The building opened with 'Tally Ho!' a hunting extravaganza, direct from
the London Hippodrome.

Another enormous house on these lines was the Glasgow Coliseum, erected in 1906, but, like the Liverpool Olympia, this hall
soon outlived its usefulness, being one of the first buildings
acquired by the Scottish Cinema and Variety Company, later
merged with the mighty A.B.C. combine.

In 1907 the Birmingham Grand Theatre, then run by J. W.
Turner as a home of opera, was added to the circuit, and opened

in December of that year, as a music hall. In 1909 the old Grand
Theatre in Cowcaddens, Glasgow was added, but this house did not
remain in the combine for long, as it was damaged by fire and its
subsequent resurrection was as a cinema. Another Glasgow house
controlled for a short period was the Hippodrome, the hall adjoining Bostock's Zoo in the New City Road, but this was relinquished
to become 'Joy-Town' and then an exhibition hall.

Oswald Stoll left the combine in 1910, to concentrate upon building up a Tour of his own. In the next few years he erected Empires
or Hippodromes in Wood Green, Chatham, Chiswick and the
Bristol area. He left behind in the Moss Empire concern his original
Empires at Cardiff, Newport and Swansea, all of which had been
rebuilt since their original inception.

In 1911 the disastrous fire which destroyed the first Edinburgh
Empire took place, and the shock of this put Sir Edward (he had
been knighted in 1905) on his death-bed. He had been in failing
health for some time, not improved by the resignation of Stoll.

The death of Sir Edward Moss in November 1912, brought to a
close a notable chapter in the history of British Music Hall, which
lost one of its greatest figures, while the North lost one of its
greatest sons. Sir Edward was succeeded by Frank Allen, former
associate of Dick Thornton, as managing director, a position he
held until 1919 when he retired.

Before his death Sir Edward had noted the changing tenor of
events in the entertainment world. An up-and-coming young man
named Albert de Courville had been co-opted to the booking side,
and was responsible for bringing over to England the American
Ragtime Octette in 1912. With the subsequent production of such
shows as 'Hullo! Ragtime' the American influence was beginning
to be felt in British entertainment. The old circus and water
spectacle shows it seemed had had their day.

At the time of Sir Edward's death, the Moss Empires' Tour was
at its height. Some 30 properties were owned by the combined companies, and several others were booked or run in conjunction.

A Moss Empires' letter-heading *circa* 1912 gives the following
information:

> (*Properties Owned*). The Empire Palaces at Birmingham,
> Bradford, Cardiff, Edinburgh, Glasgow, Hull, Leeds, Liver-
> pool, Newcastle, Newport, Nottingham, Sheffield and Swansea.
> (*Also Owned*). Metropole Theatre (Glasgow); The Andrews'
> Hall, and Philharmonic Hall (Cardiff); the Grand Theatre
> (Glasgow); the Grand Theatre (Birmingham); the Bordesley

Palace (Birmingham); the Coliseum (Glasgow) and the Broadway Theatre (New Cross).

(*North Eastern Circuit*). The Empire Palaces at Gateshead, South Shields, Sunderland and West Hartlepool.

(*London District Empires*). The Empire Palaces at Finsbury Park, New Cross, and Stratford, together with the London Hippodrome.

(*Booked in Conjunction*). The Grand, Imperial and Her Majesty's Theatres at Walsall; Dublin Empire; Belfast Empire; Grand Theatre, Nottingham, and Stoke Newington Alexandra Theatre.

In 1913 the Moss Empires' Circuit was supplemented by the addition of two Cine-Variety Theatres, in the Summerhill Palace (Birmingham), and the New Empire Cinema (Newcastle). Later the Andrews' Hall at Cardiff became known as the Olympia Cinema and control passed to the A.B.C. Cinema Circuit, as was the case with the Glasgow Coliseum. About this same time, the Bordesley Palace, a Birmingham suburban house, built in 1904 and subsequently acquired by Moss Empires', was leased to impresario T. Morton Powell, and later to Messrs. Kimberley, for the purpose of running stock company and melodrama.

During the First War, Stoll's old Philharmonic Hall in Cardiff was closed and sold; the Grand Theatre, Glasgow, damaged by fire, was disposed of as a cinema, and control of the Metropole Theatre, Glasgow also passed out of control of the circuit. The Stoke Newington Alexandra Theatre, which became a cinema in 1913, had a notable organist in Jack Hylton, the noted impresario of later years.

*   *   *   *

In the 1920's many changes took place. In 1928 the General Theatres Corporation was formed, with George Black (son of the George Black who ran the waxworks and Monkwearmouth Picture Hall in Sunderland) as general manager. This Corporation was subsequently merged with Moss Empires' and this merger brought in such famous music halls as the London Palladium, the Victoria Palace, and the Holborn Empire.

In 1933 the Variety Theatres Controlling Co., the mighty syndicate originally formed by the merger of the Barrasford, De Frece, and other circuits in 1911, was taken over. Charles Gulliver, manager director of the Controlling Company, joined the directorate of Moss Empires, as did George Black, of the General Theatres Corporation.

The dissolution of the Controlling Company meant that such halls as Barrasford's old Hippodrome in Birmingham, the Leeds Hippodrome, and Sheffield Hippodrome, were no longer in deadly opposition to the Moss combine.

Several of the merged halls were sold as cinemas, including the Hippodromes at Sheffield and Liverpool, while others, including the large Hippodromes at Leeds and Newcastle, were sold for purposes other than entertainment. On the other hand, halls of the calibre of the Glasgow Alhambra, the Edinburgh Theatre Royal, Brighton Hippodrome and the Portsmouth Hippodrome became valuable links in the 'chain' of Moss Empires' ever-growing strength.

The year 1933 saw the winding up of the affairs of the North Eastern Circuit. The Empire Palaces at South Shields, Gateshead and West Hartlepool were all sold as cinemas, while the Sunderland Empire Palace became a separate holding company running in conjunction with Moss Empires. For some years, following 1933, the Sunderland Empire pursued a 'Pictures and Variety' policy, but the Second War and the period following brought about a 'boom' in Variety, and the film part of the programme was soon discontinued. The Avenue and Theatre Royal buildings in Sunderland, formerly the properties of Richard Thornton, were closed down. The former was taken over by a brewery, and the latter, after alterations, was re-opened as a Black's Cinema.

The Second War came, and brought about a revival of interest in the music halls, but it also brought about the destruction of several halls. The Stratford and Holborn Empires in London were destroyed, as was the Portsmouth Hippodrome. The Hull Palace was damaged, and subsequently sold, while a fire (not ascribed to enemy action) finished the Newport Empire.

In 1945 Val Parnell, son of the famous old ventriloquist Fred Russell, became managing director of Moss Empires. Two years later Prince Littler became Chairman of the company. Prince Littler is also Chairman and managing director of the Stoll Theatres Corporation, having succeeded to that position upon the death of Sir Oswald Stoll in 1942.

Under the control of these two energetic personalities complete reorganisation of the Moss Empires' circuit has taken place. While several new properties have been acquired—notably the Winter Gardens, Morecambe and the Palace Theatre in Manchester—other halls have been closed and sold.

In 1959 Leslie MacDonnell succeeded Val Parnell and further changes and closures have taken place. However, with the famous

London Palladium in the ranks, the Moss Empires' syndicate still rates as the premier music hall syndicate in the world.

Now Leslie A. MacDonnell, O.B.E. (described as 'The Friend of the Stars') has retired, and his place at the helm of Moss' Empires has been taken by Louis Benjamin, formerly managing director of Pye Records.

7

The Stoll Tour

IF THERE was one music hall magnate who looked the part less than any other, it was Sir Oswald Stoll.

Stoll, who joined the select brotherhood of Knights of the Music Hall in company with such distinguished brethren as Sir Walter de Frece, Sir Alfred Butt and Sir Walter Gibbons in 1919, was an exceptional man in many ways. For example, in 1904 he was responsible for the publication of a book entitled 'The Grand Survival: A Theory of Immortality by Natural Law', which proved him to be something of a philosopher.

In appearance, with his gold pince-nez, he looked more like a Sunday School superintendent, and he often acted like one. Not for him the free and easy Bohemianism of the music halls. He was a stickler for respectability, and seemed obsessed by the idea that the music hall should be raised to the level of drawing-room entertainment. His staff had orders to report anyone using any expletive beyond a mild 'Damn' and woe betide anyone who did. All material used in the acts was subject to rigorous censorship, and performers like Arthur Roberts who slipped in an occasional naughty word had to be on their guard. They never 'ad libbed' on the Stoll Tour!

Quiet, studious and shy, Stoll was a perfectionist, and a hard man to work for. He could never bear to be told that he was wrong, even when the error was a glaring one. There is a well-known story about one of his managers who once pointed out a mistake, to which Stoll replied: 'Do not ever tell me that I am wrong. If it occurs again, you will be dismissed.'

Some time later, the unfortunate man had reason to point out another discrepancy. Stoll breathed hard and said: 'Mr. Manager. I told you once before never to dispute my orders. Kindly now go and draw three months' salary from the cashier in lieu of notice.' A hard man, and difficult to please.

On another occasion there occurred a remarkable incident, which, if nothing else, proved him to be a man of few words. (Several performers claim to have been the recipient of what came to be known as 'The Famous Telegram' but usually this distinction, such as it is, is credited to Espinosa, the well-known dancer.)

In the 1900's Espinosa, who had not been in this country long, was living outside London, and was booked to appear for a week at the Shepherds Bush Empire, an outlying London hall. Stoll, who on Monday evenings was generally to be found in this, his favourite music hall in the Metropolis (and 'try-out' hall) insisted that Espinosa and his Dancers occupy the last position on the bill. This incident upset Espinosa, as he was living some miles outside London and, with the second house ending late, found difficulty in getting transport home after the show.

Espinosa complained to Sam Gethin, the manager, but the latter inferred that it would be as much as his job was worth to change the timing of the show. Gethin suggested a wire to Stoll in Cardiff on the matter.

The wire was duly dispatched, and ran:

'Oswald Stoll, Empire Theatre, Cardiff.

'Will you kindly alter my time. I am last act on and live eighteen miles from Theatre. How can I do it?'
—Espinosa. Shepherds Bush Empire.

Back came the famous reply:

'Move.'—Stoll.

Sir Oswald, who died at his Putney home in 1942 at the age of 75, was born in Melbourne, Australia in 1867. His mother, Mrs. Adelaide Gray, was later widowed, and returned to England to her native Liverpool, together with Oswald and another younger brother Roderick.

In Liverpool she met and married John G. Stoll, a Danish wax-work show proprietor, in 1875, whereupon the names of the boys were changed to Stoll. The waxworks and music hall run by J. G. Stoll was in the Parthenon Assembly Rooms, Great Charlotte Street, 'six doors from Ranelagh Street' (according to the bill matter).

The Parthenon Rooms had been erected in 1845 and for a time were occupied by Bianchi's Waxworks. Then Mr. Stoll had taken over and supplemented the waxworks show with live performers to stimulate business. An old bill dated 1850 shows 'Models of Art. The Tableaux Vivants and the Poses Plastique' as an attraction there.

In 1880 John G. Stoll died suddenly, and 14-year-old Oswald had to leave school to assist his mother, Mrs. Adelaide Stoll, run the Parthenon Music Hall. In his own words of later years 'She

knew very little about the business, but I know even less'. He
recounted how he found his youth a handicap, and how, to impress
visitors and agents, '. . . he ran back and forth between his mother
and a fictitious manager with instructions'.

Hannen Swaffer, the writer, in a tribute to Oswald Stoll, wrote:

'Oswald Stoll started his training as a music hall manager
early. When only fourteen he left school to help his mother
run the Parthenon, a 'beer and sawdust hall" in Liverpool,
with prices so cheap that the most expensive ones were the box
seats at a shilling. These box seats were actually right on the
stage, and people were locked in to prevent boisterous spirits
getting on to the stage, to tickle the dancers' legs.'

Stoll acted as his own agent, booking acts with only his late
stepfather's books to guide him. His younger brother Roderick
assisted with 'front of the house' management. Many times Oswald
offended artistes by offering them salaries ridiculously small, but,
more often than not, if the performers had no other date in their
books, the bluff came off, and they were glad to accept.

A popular favourite at the Parthenon was a young male impersonator in Vesta Tilley, in fact Vesta was 'everybody's favourite'.
It was no secret that Oswald Stoll was 'sweet' on Vesta and he had
high hopes of winning her. But there were many suitors for the
hand of the attractive Vesta, and she fell for the charms of a handsome young Jew from the Roscoe Arcade in Liverpool—Walter
de Frece. The de Freces were Stoll's rivals in Liverpool; apart
from the agency in the Roscoe Arcade, they ran the Gaiety Theatre
in Camden Street, and the Theatre Royal in Clayton Square. It was
while appearing in the annual pantomime at the Gaiety that Vesta
Tilley met Walter de Frece, in 1889.

It is perhaps true to say that had there been no Vesta Tilley,
there might have been no 'Stoll Tour'. Oswald, who had written
several songs for Vesta, was literally heartbroken when he heard
of her engagement to his rival, and his reaction was to put as much
distance between himself and Liverpool as he could.

And so it came about that in 1890, at the age of 23, Oswald,
together with his mother and brother, moved lock, stock and barrel
to Cardiff, to try their luck at what had been Levino's Music Hall,
opened in 1887, but now closed. (The Parthenon was carried on for
a time by a Captain Slater. Then it became the Theatre Moderne,
with melodrama, but in 1907 it was closed and sold as a warehouse.)

The first thing Stoll did upon arrival in Cardiff was to change
the name of Levino's Hall of Varieties in Queen Street into the
'Cardiff Empire'. On the first Saturday night only 25/- was taken

at the box office—where Mrs. Adelaide Stoll held sway, as in Liverpool—and drastic action was necessary. The first move was to
bring the name of the 'Empire' to the minds of the public. Stoll
did this in no uncertain fashion by painting huge posters with the
words 'Support the EMPIRE' in large letters, above his bill matter,
and sticking these up all over Cardiff. (There was trouble about
this, but all came right in the end.)

Another move was to change the Empire over to the 'Two Houses
Nightly' system, and Vesta Tilley, hearing about the plight of the
Stolls, agreed to appear for a week's booking at the Empire for a
very small salary. Oswald Stoll never forgot Vesta's kindness, and
reciprocated by writing more songs for her, which she sang with
great success. (Among them were 'Bachelors' and 'Oh, You
Girls!'),

In regard to the 'Two Houses Nightly' system, there has been
much controversy in music hall circles as to where this originated.
Several entrepreneurs claimed this distinction for themselves.
including George Belmont (also known as 'Barnums Beauty') who
introduced it at the Sebright's Hall, Hackney, in 1885; Oswald
Stoll (Cardiff Empire, 1890); Frank MacNaghten (Sheffield Grand,
1896) and Tom Barrasford (Leeds Tivoli, 1899). But in addition to
these, there was the Wear Music Hall in Sunderland, where
proprietor and ex-scene painter S. H. Bell had put on 'Two Houses
a Night' to try and accommodate all the patrons who wished to see
the Great George Leybourne, the 'Lion Comique', when he played
a week's engagement there in 1875. Another early contender for the
title was Barnard's Music Hall in Chatham, also going in the 1870's.
This hall catered for the Navy, and here there were often two
'houses', one for the Officers and another for 'Jack Tar and
Company'.

Although it is generally accepted that Henry de Frece (father of
Jack and Walter) claimed to have originated the idea at the old
wooden Alhambra in Manchester Street, Liverpool (erected in
1866), there was no definite date when the system began.

However, this same controvery arose when Barrasford died in
1910 (he claimed to have made the system practical—which he
certainly did) and an interview conducted between a theatrical
journalist and George Leglere, the old-time pantomimist at that
time, appears to set the matter at rest for good and all:

'The "Two Houses Nightly" system originated at a place
called Rigden's Alhambra in Sandgate during 1860. My father,
Louis Leglere, was booked there and told me this.

'Not long after this there were two houses each night at the

Victory Theatre in Aldershot, to cater for the troops, and also at Browning's Theatre in Dover in respect of the Navy.

'When I was very young I recall appearing with my father at a place called "Harwood's" in the Pitfield Street area of Hoxton. This would be in the 1870's and here there was two houses each week night and FOUR on Saturdays, including the matinee, of course.

'We were a double act then and the agent that booked us was called Maynard, I believe.'

Be that as it may, 'Two Houses a Night' saved the tiny Empire at Cardiff and very soon the place was firmly established. Oswald Stoll opened an agency for the booking of artistes, which was quite successful, and in 1892 at the age of 25, his broken heart apparently mended, met and married a young Welsh girl in Harriet Lewis. The Stolls made their new home in the fashionable Newport Road area of Cardiff where their little daughter was born. By 1895 music halls had been added in Swansea and Newport. Prosperity and happiness had been found by the Stoll family in South Wales. They had worked hard and deserved their success.

In 1896 Stoll turned his attention to the Midlands. The Theatre Royal in Nottingham, built 1865, was up for auction, and Stoll bought it with the idea of turning it into a music hall. But the local citizens were horrified at Stoll's intention and there were cries of 'Sacrilege'. Wiser counsels prevailed, and Stoll decided to erect a new music hall on an adjacent site. The Theatre Royal was then leased to Robert Arthur, the West End impresario, who undertook to continue dramatic fare.

Stoll called in Frank Matcham, the eminent architect, for advice upon the erection of the proposed Nottingham Empire. The site in mind was at the side of the Theatre Royal, consisting of some unsightly wooden shops, which had been purchased for purposes of demolition.

Matcham disclosed that agents for Edward Moss were looking for a suitable site to erect an 'Empire Palace' in Nottingham, and that he had been approached for advice from that source also. This led to a conference between Moss and Stoll, the outcome of which was the famous 'working agreement' between the two, to avoid a clash of interests. It was decided that a new 'Empire Palace' should be erected in Nottingham, booked in conjunction with the Moss Empires, but that Stoll's site in Sherwood Street should be used, and that Stoll should be managing director of the 'Nottingham Empire Palace Co. Ltd.'.

The Empire Palace was duly erected and opened on the 28th

February, 1898. The design of the new hall was Matcham at his ornate best. It was described as '. . . a hall to vie with the home of an Eastern Potentate . . .' At either side of the stage were boxes surmounted by 'pagoda-like domes, with grinning idols representing the Indian God Kriska'. At each corner of the vast auditorium 'Four elephant heads in gilt stare out at all and sundry'. There was a sliding roof on the lines of those in operation at the Canterbury Music Hall and the London Pavilion, and there were six boxes either side of the stage, at circle level. The lighting arrangements were particularly pleasing, for no less than 40 'shower' electroliers lit the auditorium, while the colour motif was blue, cream and old gold. Capacity was almost 3,000 and the stage dimensions were 60-ft. wide by 35-ft. deep, with a 29-ft. proscenium opening.

Lydia Yeamans, the noted ballad vocalist ('the Original Sally in our Alley') topped the opening bill, assisted at the piano by her husband Fred J. Titus. In support were Beatty and Bentley, the 'niggers'; Rose Elliott, the comedienne, and other first-class acts. Manager for Messrs. Moss and 'Stoll was James Wynes, who came from Stoll's Newport Empire, and the 'Two Houses Nightly' system was adopted. This was the first time this system had been used in connection with a Moss Empires' house and it was a conspicuous success from the start. In connection with the opening of the Nottingham Empire Palace, a joint statement was issued, which ran as follows:

'Messrs. Moss and Stoll control Theatres at Edinburgh, Glasgow, Newcastle, Sheffield, Liverpool, Hull, Birmingham, Cardiff, Swansea and Newport, thus being in a position to offer a separate engagement for each of so many halls in the Tour, the Management have unusual facilities for procuring those artistes whose services Managers, unable to make very tempting offers, ARE COMPELLED TO DO WITHOUT.'

This attitude was, of course, in time to lead to the 'closed shop' or 'barring clauses' in regard to the booking of artistes by the big combines (said to be the 'brain-child' of Frank Allen) and was one of the major factors in bringing about the Variety Artistes Strike of 1907. One of the effects of the 'barring clauses' was to bring about the closure of many small music halls, run by independent proprietors, and thus reduce competition.

Another motto which took its place in the Nottingham Empire programmes of those early days ran as follows:

' 'Tis not in Mortals to command success—but we will do more—deserve it.'

One result of the joint venture at Nottingham between Moss and

Stoll, was that it led directly to the incorporation of all the Moss Empire companies (ten in all) in 1899, and Oswald Stoll became managing director of the lot, a position he held until 1910. Edward Moss occupied the position of Chairman of the new company, which had a combined capital of well over a million pounds.

The three Stoll theatres in South Wales were incorporated in the new set up, but Stoll insisted upon a clause which left him free to build and operate music halls of his own, providing that his own interests did not clash with the Moss Syndicate. His early theatres, the Empires at Cardiff, Swansea and Newport, were all rebuilt on the same sites by Moss Empires in the early years of the century.

*   *   *   *

In 1899 Oswald Stoll bought the Floral Hall Theatre of Varieties in the Belgrave Gate, Leicester, and very soon he decided to build a new music hall on this same site. The new hall could not be called an 'Empire' because there was one already in Leicester. This was 'Sweeney's Empire' in Wharf Street, which had been erected in 1894. (Sweeney had been Chairman at the tiny Argyle in Birkenhead many years before, and had settled down as a music hall proprietor in Leicester after experience in management at Liverpool and Rotherham. After his death, the Leicester Empire was carried on for a time by his widow.)

The only other 'opposition' to Stoll's new venture in Leicester came from Captain Orr Gray's Tivoli Theatre of Varieties, also in the Belgrave Gate, which was built on the site of the famous 'Paul's Concert Hall' of 1865.

The Leicester Palace of Varieties (as Stoll's new music hall was named) was built round the Floral Hall, which was incorporated in the enlarged structure. (In later years the Floral Hall flourished as a cinema.) The Palace was designed by Frank Matcham and again the Moorish style of architecture was employed. The stage dimensions were 58-ft. wide by 40-ft. deep, the proscenium opening being 32-ft. across.

Opening on Monday 17th June, 1901 the first bill at the Palace was topped by that 'Monarch of Muscle' The Great Sandow, with his usual feats of strength. Also on the bill was that well-known comedian from Leeds, J. W. Rowley ('Over' Rowley) together with Ella Dean, the singer. Bottom of the bill was another favourite in Charles Coburn, the 'Man Who Broke the Bank at Monte Carlo'.

The Leicester Palace got away to a good start and put Captain Orr Gray out of business at the Tivoli. This hall was taken over by Frank MacNaghten, then expanding his 'MacNaghten Vaudeville Circuit', who called the hall 'The Tivoli Palace'. Stoll objected, and MacNaghten had to change the title to 'The Pavilion Music Hall'. MacNaghten brought American acts to the Pavilion in an attempt to counter the first-class bills (complete with 'barring clauses') put on by Stoll at the Palace.

*   *   *   *

With the Leicester Palace venture under way, Stoll gave his attention to the Metropolis. In December 1901, he opened the first of several Stoll Empires in London. The hall opened in December 1901 was the Hackney Empire, situated in Mare Street, which immediately put the old and infamous Sebright's Hall of Varieties, run by George Belmont, out of business. Three years later, Stoll built another London suburban hall at Bush Green—his favourite hall—and a separate holding company was formed, known as 'The Hackney and Shepherds Bush Empires, Ltd.'.

About this time Stoll's wife, Harriet, died suddenly, in her mid-twenties following a short illness. Within a year Stoll had married again. His second wife was Millicent Shaw, a Nottingham girl whom he met at a dance when visiting the Midlands on business. The second Mrs. Stoll—later Lady Stoll—bore him three sons, and after his second marriage the Cardiff interests were disposed of, and the Stoll family took up residence in Putney.

The conspicuous success which attended the erection of the London Hippodrome by the Moss Empires' concern gave Stoll the idea that a circus-cum-music hall on these lines would do well in Manchester. In 1903 he negotiated for a site in Manchester's Oxford Street and got Frank Matcham to prepare plans for a monster circus to be erected on this site. Stoll also fancied the idea of a suburban 'Empire' in Manchester, and so was conceived the Ardwick Empire, which was erected first, on orthodox lines.

Situated at Ardwick Green the Empire was a large hall accommodating 3,000 and it opened on the 18th July, 1904 with Fred Karno's famous company of 'speechless comedians' topping the bill with a sketch called 'Saturday to Monday'. In support were Ardell and his Company in 'A Zoological Comedy'; Norah Emerald (of the famous Emerald Sisters); Belle Davis, the comedienne; Hart and Leo, and others, together with the Bioscope. Walter Collins was the manager and prices ranged from 3d. to 2/-.

Large crowds attended the opening of the Empire, which was run on the now famous 'Two Houses Nightly' system and, notwithstanding the large capacity of the hall, many people were turned away on opening night. Plenty of publicity attended the inauguration of the Ardwick hall and Oswald Stoll was very pleased with the results. On the bills it said: 'Empire—at Ardwick Green—always ask for the Tram Junction' so there could be no doubt where the Empire was. Stoll was using methods similar to his early tactics in Cardiff.

The other Manchester theatre, the Hippodrome in Oxford Street, opened on Boxing Night, 1904 only two days after Stoll's huge Coliseum was opened in London. Like the London Coliseum, the Manchester Hippodrome was designed by Frank Matcham. Not only was it as ornate as only Matcham could make it, but it also embodied several features and improvements gained by experience at the London Hippodrome. More than a third of the area of the arena was behind the proscenium arch, which was adjustable, so it could be used either as a circus or an orthodox music hall. There were hydraulic power lifts for the stage bays, and 24 concealed jets to provide water for the aquatic displays. 'A Foot to a Fathom of Water at a touch of a Lever' was the proud caption ·in the programmes and both Matcham and Stoll were delighted with the erection of the new hall.

At the back of the Hippodrome was a spacious stable for the circus horses and other animals, while the adjustable proscenium enabled boats to sail into the arena tank from back-stage, to the amazement of patrons. But Matcham's great innovation was the patent 'automatic mat remover'. This was used to obviate the nuisance caused by the usual clouds of dust raised by men man-handling mats in and out of the sawdust ring. The interior of the hall was tastefully decorated in red, cream and gold, and every seat was described as 'an arm-chair'. Patrons were admitted to sample this luxury at the very modest prices of 6d. to 2/-.

The Manchester Hippodrome opened with a big bill of circus acts, including The Moissetts, on the whirling table; The McConnell Trio of acrobats; Max Gruber's Miniature Circus of Horses and Elephants; Professor Rayfayette's Dogs; Elsie Clair on the high wire; Winona, Winter and Banks, and Post Mason. The resident clowns were 'Jack in the Green'; 'Sir Tommy Fool'; 'Sleepy Sammy' and 'Sergeant Ginger'. Manager of the Hippodrome for Stoll was Mr. E. P. Morgan, from Cardiff.

Mancunians flocked to the new Hippodrome, which did wonder-ful business, and the next news was that Edward Moss was going to follow Stoll's example by erecting a circus on similar lines in Liverpool. Everyone was amazed at the wonderful innovations in the circus ring at the Manchester Hippodrome, and these fitments were widely advertised: 'Come and See the Rising and Sinking

Arena, the Sliding Stage, the Mechanical Mat and the Kaleido-
scopic Fountains' ran the bills.

Like the London Coliseum, Stoll started the Manchester Hippodrome with the idea of running as many performances as possible.
There were two performances daily on four days of the week, and
three shows on Saturday and early closing day.

This prompted the *Manchester Evening News* to comment:

'With the multiplication of places of entertainment in Manchester it seems a great deal for the promoters to expect to fill
this commodious building twice daily and three times on two
days of the week.'

Nevertheless, the Hippodrome did very well indeed at the start,
and certainly put Barrasford out of action at the nearby Grand
Theatre. Jasper Redfern, the Sheffield optician turned film showman, then took over the Grand and ran pictures there very successfully (interspersed with variety acts) for a number of years.

*   *   *   *

Stoll got his idea for putting on several shows a day from a visit
to America, where he went with Frank Matcham to get new ideas
to incorporate in the building of the new London Coliseum. This
building was to be the last word in music hall design, and certainly
everybody was astonished by its proportions when erected.

The London Coliseum cost £300,000 in all to build—a colossal
sum in 1904—and many people prophesied immediate ruin for
Stoll. At one time it certainly looked as if that prophecy might be
fulfilled, but he was not beaten so easily.

What prompted Stoll to build the mammoth Coliseum music
hall was rivalry more than anything else. The big American firm
of Keith had taken an option on the old Princess' Theatre in Oxford
Street, London, which had closed down in 1902 and they proposed
re-modelling it and running it on the American system of continuous variety. Another factor was that Tom Barrasford, whom
Stoll actively disliked, had acquired the old Lyceum Theatre in
the Strand, with the idea of converting that hall into a Palace of
Variety.

The site chosen for the new Coliseum was at the bottom of
St. Martins Lane, and it developed into a race between Stoll and
Barrasford to have their respective music halls open first. Stoll won
by a very short head. He intended to open on 19th December, 1904
but a dense fog settled on London, disrupting everything, and the
opening had to be postponed. The Coliseum opened on 24th
December (Christmas Eve) and Barrasford's Lyceum (as planned)

on Boxing Day, the 26th December. There was no competition from the Princess' Theatre, chiefly because of licensing and other difficulties, and the decision of Stoll to build the huge Coliseum also influenced the firm of Keith not to proceed further with the project.

Matcham had produced some ornate edifices in his time, but the London Coliseum was surely his *piece de resistance*. It was carried out in the Italian Renaissance style, complete with roof garden. The tower, or rotunda, was stiff with pilasters, and there were figures representing Art, Music, Literature and Science at each corner. The enormous tower was topped by the famous globe—a revolving globe with the letters 'Coliseum' inscribed thereon—but. the London County Council objected to this moving sign, most strongly. After some discussion, the letters (instead of the globe) were made to revolve—or appear to do so—and all was well, the bye-laws were not being broken!

The auditorium of the Coliseum held 2,558 people, and every seat was bookable. The interior was carried out in Matcham's usual ornate style of decoration, and incorporated in the building were several new innovations which caused something of a stir in theatrical circles, being regarded as something akin to a 'Nine days wonder' at the time. There were several Tea Rooms, at various parts of the building; an immense 'Baronial Smoking Hall' complete with first-class bars; several so-called 'Retiring Rooms' and even a Post Office where telegrams and telephone messages could be left or dispatched. There was the usual conservatory and somewhat unnecessary fernery.

Back-stage things were just as revolutionary. There was the first moving stage to be seen in this country. This alone cost Stoll £70,000 to install. The idea was to 'speed up' the acts on the American 'quick-fire' principle. Several of the acts could have their settings prepared in advance. There would be no time wasted on scene changes. The stage itself was built up on three concentric rings, and people were invited back-stage to see how it worked.

But surely the greatest of all the 'wonders' to be seen at the huge Coliseum was the unique 'King's Car' which let the side down badly on the one and only occasion it was required for service. The description of the Car in the programme read as follows:

'Immediately upon entering the Theatre, the Royal Party will step into a richly furnished lounge, which, at a signal, will move softly along a track formed in the floor, through a salon into a large foyer, which contains the entrance to the Royal Box. The Lounge-Car remains in position at the entrance to the Box and serves as an ante-room during the performance.'

King Edward VII, who was interested in music halls, paid a visit to the wonderful Coliseum, and the 'King's Car' was there in readiness for him at the entrance. He got in, amid some ceremony, but instead of wafting him to the Royal Box, the car promptly blew a fuse, thereby 'refusing' to budge! The King, roaring with laughter, made his way there on foot. The little car was never used again for its intended purpose, but stored away. Years later it was removed to the Stoll Theatre in Kingsway and used there as a booking office for a time.

There was a huge number of staff employed at the Coliseum when it first opened—360 in all—on the shift system. This figure included 26 lime-light boys! The booking system (every seat in the house was bookable, even the 'Gods') caused chaos at first when shoals of applications came in by post, but all was sorted out eventually.

The opening bill at the London Coliseum was topped by the great Eugene Stratton, the Coon singer, and supporting acts included the Three Pattinsons, on the trampoline; Decima Moore doing Irish jigs; Tina Clementina with her Dogs; the Cycling Cookes; the Juggling Debrauns, and many others. Also on the bill was a scene representing 'Derby Day at Epsom'. This fantastic scene, designed to show off the prowess of the moving stage, employed real race horses, and not long after the opening, tragedy attended. A horse fell off the moving portion of the stage, during the 'race', with the result that the jockey was killed.

It was estimated that 67,000 people saw the first week's performances, at the four shows each day, put on at noon, 3, 6 and 9 p.m. However, the artistes could not stand up to the strain and attendances fell away as the novelty wore off. It seemed that ordinary folk did not take kindly to the idea of sitting in a music hall during the day time. It meant a change of habit, and it did not 'catch on'.

In June, 1906 the Coliseum company failed, and the theatre closed down abruptly. Poor Dundas Slater, the manager, took things to heart and shot himself in a cab whilst leaving the theatre. Stoll, however, was quite undaunted by the failure. He promptly formed a new company called 'The Coliseum Syndicate' to run the building on more orthodox lines. With capital provided by the new company, he re-opened the Coliseum with two shows a day in December 1907. Stoll's rival, Tom Barrasford also failed with Variety at the Lyceum, but for different reasons. This theatre was also re-opened, but by a new management who put in melodrama.

Stoll's 'new policy' at the Coliseum was to put on 'respectable'

Variety, where the family man could take his wife and daughters without fear of blushes. Marie Lloyd never played the Coliseum, great performer though she was, for obvious reasons, but most of the other 'greats' of music hall appeared there.

An innovation prompted by the 'new policy' which proved very popular was the introduction of artistes from the legitimate stage to play in sketches. Seymour Hicks and Ellaline Terris led the way, and they were followed by Sarah Bernhardt and others. It was Stoll's great wish that Sir Henry Irving appear, but he never did, even though Walter de Frece was instructed by Oswald Stoll to approach the great man and ask him to 'name his own price'. With the new policy success came, and Stoll was able to consolidate his own position in the world of music hall.

*   *   *   *   ●

Stoll hankered to be his own master, and in December 1910 resigned his position as managing director of the Moss Empires' syndicate, much to the disappointment of Sir Edward Moss, who was in failing health. The year 1910 was a year of great change in the music hall world. Stoll's old adversary, Tom Barrasford, died following illness, in February, and this factor would no doubt influence Stoll in his decision to break with Moss Empires. Another reason was the formation of another formidable combine— the mighty Variety Theatres Controlling Company—which was a combination of several 'Tours', including the larger Barrasford halls. Walter de Frece, who had previously worked in conjunction with the Moss Empires (particularly in regard to the Manchester Palace), had broken away, and was the managing director of the new combine, under the Chairmanship of Alfred Butt.

The new headquarters of the 'Stoll Tour' were in the Coliseum buildings, and a financial genius named W. S. Gordon Michie was· appointed to run Stoll's complicated affairs. Not long after the breakaway from Moss's, several new additional music halls were built, which ran in conjunction with the existing halls at Leicester, Ardwick, Manchester, Hackney and Shepherds Bush.

First, in 1911 came the Bedminster Hippodrome, a Bristol sub-urban house, opened at Bank Holiday; then came the New Middle-sex Theatre of Varieties in Drury Lane, London, opened in October. The Bedminster Hippodrome was so successful that Stoll erected the Bristol Hippodrome in 1912 (known by its full title as the St. Augustines Parade Hippodrome (Bristol) Ltd.), and also in 1912 were built the Chatham Empire, and two London halls, the Wood Green Empire and the Chiswick Empire.

The New Middlesex Theatre of Varieties was built on the site of the 'Old Mo'' or Old Mogul Music Hall of 1847. It had been re-built as the Middlesex Music Hall in 1875 by a former bar-man there called J. Laurie Graydon who had risen to become its manager. In 1891 Graydon had enlarged the hall again, and claimed to have originated the 'quick-fire' style of variety. Many famous acts of the time had played 'The Old Mo'' (as it was still affectionately called) and Graydon himself was very popular. He had other interests besides the Middlesex, being a director of the Hastings Palace of Varieties and the Middlesbrough Empire. Frank Matcham designed the New Middlesex Theatre of Varieties, and Graydon was joint managing director with Stoll.

Another partnership which Stoll entered into was with Alderman H. E. Davis, J.P. of Chatham, as joint managing director of the New Empire Theatre in that town, erected and opened in 1912. The Empire was built on the site of the Gaiety Music Hall run by Alderman Davis for some years. Prior to this, Alderman Davis (who lived to be 92) had been a captain in the Islington Fire Brigade, and had at one time been proprietor of Deacon's Music Hall, situated not far from Sadler's Wells Theatre in Islington. 'Deacon's' had been swept away in a road widening scheme for trams.

In connection with the London suburban halls, the Wood Green Empire, sited in the High Road, was in direct opposition to the new Finsbury Park Empire of Moss', erected in 1910 to replace the Holloway Empire, which was disposed of. The Chiswick Empire brought first class Variety to a new part of the London fringe. This hall was damaged by fire only a few months after opening in 1912, but was soon restored and in use again.

In 1916 Stoll took over the London Opera House in Kingsway, erected and opened by Oscar Hammerstein in 1911 with the mammoth production of 'Quo Vadis.' The London Opera House had failed as a theatre, and Stoll turned it into a cinema, but gave it his own name—The Stoll Theatre.

Not long after this, Stoll took over the old Alhambra in London's famous Leicester Square. This was the place notorious for its 'Promenade' in former years—a frequent haunt of the so-called 'Ladies of the Town'—but during the First War the London County Council had stepped in and made things here (and at the rival Empire across the way) all very respectable. The Alhambra had been kept going with difficulty (since the departure of the Ladies and their particular clientele) with rag-time and revue, but Stoll turned it back into a music hall—a very respectable music hall . . .

With the acquisition of the Alhambra the New Middlesex

Theatre of Varieties was disposed of. It was sold to George Grossmith who re-opened the place as the Winter Garden Theatre in May 1919, with a lavish production of 'Kissing Time', an extravaganza, which was transferred there following a long run at the Gaiety Theatre in the Strand.

* * * *

After the First War, music hall began to wane in popularity, in face of increased competition from cinemas, and the new revue style of entertainment. The whole pattern of public taste was changing and Stoll—now Sir Oswald Stoll, for he was knighted in 1919—decided to move with the times.

Always interested in 'moving pictures', he had expressed great interest in some early experiments carried out with synchronised talking films by the Gaumont company at the Fulham Grand Theatre in 1904. At that time he expressed the opinion that the film industry, with proper development, might go forward to a great future. In 1919 he decided to enter the film industry himself. Not only did he acquire and open several cinemas, but invested money in film studios in the London area.

The first Stoll cinema to open was the Stoll Picture Theatre in Newcastle. This was the old Tyne Theatre of 1868 in the Westgate Road, run for a time by the Howard and Wyndham concern, and it made a good cinema. Other Stoll Picture Theatres subsequently opened (with vocal, instrumental music and variety acts in support) were the Bedminster Hippodrome at Bristol; The Picture House, Chatham; and the Floral Hall Cinema in Leicester, which formed part of the Palace Theatre buildings, together with the Stoll Picture Theatre in London's Kingsway.

In the 1930's, when Variety as a whole was in the doldrums, Stoll turned several of his music halls over to the new 'Talkies'. These included the Palace Theatre in Leicester (in addition to the adjoining Floral Hall), the Ardwick Empire, and (for a time) even the mighty Coliseum, where the weird film 'King Kong' drew the crowds while the novelty lasted.

In 1935 the Hippodrome in Oxford Road, Manchester, was sold to a big syndicate for conversion into a 'super' cinema. At the same time, the Ardwick Empire, which had been running as a cinema for a few years, was given a 'face-lift' and re-opened as the New Manchester Hippodrome Theatre of Varieties. This hall became a very successful music hall and, particularly in the 'boom' period following the Second War, formed an important part of the re-constituted Stoll Tour.

In 1936 the Alhambra in London was closed and demolished, the new Odeon Cinema being erected on the same site. Stoll had certainly made the Alhambra 'respectable' during his term of office. One of the successes of the Alhambra's music hall period under Stoll had been the show 'Veterans of Variety' which was put on in 1924 for the first time, but often revived. Many old time 'stars' of the music hall firmament had shone again for a brief while on the old Alhambra stage, and how the Londoners flocked to see them. However, some critics said that it would have been kinder for some of these old-timers to have remained just a memory, in retirement, but Stoll did not agree. In 1936 Variety was at a low ebb, and the time had come for films to oust the living entertainers from the stage in Leicester Square.

The huge Coliseum had more or less to abandon Variety also. Films like 'King Kong' and similar epics were shown for extended seasons. Then came ballets and musical plays like 'White Horse Inn'. There were several ice shows, some successful, others not so, but the doors of the Coliseum were kept open.

Came the Second War, and a consequent 'boom' in Variety, but Sir Oswald Stoll did not live to see it. On 9th January, 1942 Sir Oswald Stoll passed quietly away at his Putney home, at the age of 75. And so passed from the scene one of the most remarkable men in the annals of music hall history. A man who, with his top hat and frock coat, his quiet voice and pince-nez, neither looked nor acted like a music hall magnate, and yet he was a great one. He always said he owed his success to his mother. His actual words were: 'It was her courage made my opportunity.'

Mrs. Adelaide Stoll (Sir Oswald's mother) had died in 1924 at the age of 80 and had left £54,000 in her will. Within the entrance of the London Coliseum Theatre, at the back of the foyer, is a bust of her, which her son had erected. It is still there—a tribute to a great mother from a famous son.

*   *   *   *

At the time of Stoll's death, Francis Laidler's comedy panto-mime, 'Jack and the Beanstalk' was playing to full houses at the Coliseum. It had Jean Colin as Principal Boy and Norman Evans, the Rochdale comedian, as 'Dame'. It was one of the best and most successful of the many pantomimes ever produced there, and it was perhaps fitting that a North Country production should bring down the curtain on the career of a Northern music hall magnate.

Some months later, Prince Littler bought the Coliseum, and the other theatres in the Stoll Tour, and formed the new 'Stoll Theatres

Corporation'. These properties were purchased at the bargain figure of £160,000 but this sum included outstanding debts. In point of fact, the Littler family had wanted to buy out the Coliseum Syndicate in 1937 but Stoll had refused to sell.

The Littler family, Prince Littler with his brother Emile and sister Blanche, had started in management at the Royal Artillery Theatre, Woolwich (where their father was lessee) in 1927. Since that time they had progressively added to their control a number of theatres, including the New Theatre, Cambridge; the Opera House, Leicester, and the New Theatre, Cardiff. They had also done very well with touring productions, including the famous 'White Horse Inn' which, as already mentioned, had played at the London Coliseum.

The Littlers carried on the existing Stoll Theatres with their own, and in 1944 added to the number by the acquisition of the Derby Grand Theatre, later disposed of and replaced by the Hippodrome (erected 1914) which had been running as a cinema for some years. With the coming of the Television era, several halls have been converted into television studios, and others closed down.

Prince Littler joined the Board of Moss Empires in 1945 and became Chairman in 1947 in addition to being Chairman of the Stoll Theatres Corporation. With his brother he has been responsible for the production of a large number of pantomimes both in the West End and in the Provinces. He has been described as a 'shy, retiring man' and is concerned with the welfare of variety artistes to no small extent, being President of the V.A.F. Benevolent Fund, and the Denville Home for Aged Actors.

His interest lies in the preservation of the 'live' theatre, and has successfully opposed various 'take-over' bids for some of his theatrical properties by business tycoons anxious to develop the sites for commercial use.

Several attempts have been made to merge the Stoll Theatres Corporation with the Moss Empires' concern, but each time the shareholders have resisted the move. However, as Prince Littler is Chairman of both concerns, the two are united in all but name.

8

The Barrasford Halls

ONE NORTHERN entrepreneur who challenged the supremacy of the Moss and Stoll Empires was Tom Barrasford, who hailed from Tyneside. Pioneer of the 'Two Houses a Night' system, champion of rock-bottom prices, and early advocate of the cinema, to him goes the distinction of creating a 'tour' of 14 halls in four years—truly an astonishing feat of enterprise.

The son of a Newcastle publican, Barrasford was quick to note the success of the Moss and Thornton venture at the Royal Scotch Arms in Newcastle. Those gentlemen transformed the singing room of the old coaching inn into the Empire Music Hall during the winter of 1890. Five years later, Barrasford, in partnership with a man named Varah, took over a wooden circus on the Ormond Street pit-heap in Jarrow, and turned it into a music hall, known as the Jarrow Palace of Varieties. Dick Thornton, the bluff Tyne-sider, who also began as a publican, is credited with coining the phrase 'From Pot-House to Palace' in describing his own rise to fame, but Tom Barrasford could have said 'From Pit-Heap to Palace' and been near the truth, except that most of his music halls were known as 'Hippodromes' and not 'Empire Palaces'.

Expansion of Barrasford's interests began early in 1899 when he acquired the Leeds Tivoli. The Tivoli had grown from a small beginning as Billy Thorne's Portable Theatre, but in 1898 something of a crisis had arisen in Leeds' theatrical affairs. The Moss and Stoll combine had erected and opened the Empire in Briggate, what was described as 'The latest and most up-to-date Empire Palace in the country' and this hall was attracting all the business. Both the Varieties and the former Princess' Palace were in the market, and even the Theatre Royal was feeling the pinch somewhat, for a new dramatic house (the Queens' Theatre in Holbeck) had opened and Messrs. Dotteridge and Longden, the lessees, were having great success there with what was described as 'popular melodrama of the Surrey Theatre type'. The Princess Palace, after standing empty for a time, was taken over in November 1898, by the Leeds and Hanley Theatres Company (proprietors of the

157

Gaiety, Hanley) and the name changed to the Tivoli. The infamous Promenade was done away with, and gold leaf applied to the interior of the hall with a lavish hand, but still the place did not pay. The Company then went into voluntary liquidation. It was to this hall, losing money in spite of every effort, that Barrasford came, in March 1899.

A very similar state of affairs had arisen in nearby Bradford, only a few weeks previously. The Moss and Stoll combine had erected the Bradford Empire in January, 1899 and Frank MacNaghten, the new lessee of the Peoples' Palace Music Hall in Bradford, had countered the inevitable nose-dive in attendance figures at his house by staging his performances twice-nightly (as had been established by him at his Sheffield hall in 1896) with considerable success.

Barrasford decided that such measures were called for in Leeds. The twice-nightly system was almost unknown then, although Harry de Frece claimed to be the originator in Liverpool at his Alhambra in the 1860's and it had been tried at the Wear Music Hall at Sunderland in the 1870's. MacNaghten obligingly lent Barrasford his manager and right-hand man in Fred Baugh (who had been with him since his arrival in this country in 1895) to initiate the 'Two Houses a Night' system in Leeds. But Baugh did not stay with Barrasford very long. He left after only a few months and went back to MacNaghten, who immediately put him in charge of the Oddfellows' Hall in Halifax. Charlie Weldon, the former manager for the Leeds and Hanley Company, and the brother of George Weldon who ran the Dewsbury Hippodrome, was re-instated to manage the Leeds Tivoli.

The Tivoli Music Hall, Leeds, under Barrasford's control, re-opened on the 20th March, 1899 with the great serio-comedienne Florrie Gallimore topping a big bill of artistes. Prices were reduced to 2d., 6d. and 1/-. The performers did not like the 'Two Houses a Night' system and there was a great outcry. Barrasford's attitude was 'Like it, or lump it, it pays and it continues'. In later years he was to admit that the Leeds Tivoli proved 'a little gold-mine' and he had no hesitation in making his home in Leeds. The Jarrow Palace was kept going, however, and this house also went over to the twice-nightly system.

Nothing succeeds like success, and it was not long before further expansion took place. By the end of 1900 Barrasford had a Tivoli Music Hall in Edinburgh under his control, formerly known as the Grand. In 1901 there was added the Tivoli, Birmingham, formerly the Tower Theatre, so called because it had a large tower which dominated adjacent properties in Hurst Street—including the Moss' Empire! Also in this year was added the Alhambra, Hull (which remained the Alhambra, at least for a time, until it became the Hippodrome.) The Alhambra was the former dissenting chapel in Porter Street which many lessees had given up in disgust, but with Barrasford's shrewd bookings and 'Two Houses a Night' it blossomed anew. At Whitsuntide, 1902, the Glasgow Hippodrome was added, a huge place attached to Bostock's Zoo in the New City Road, which did well for a time.

But the real 'Barrasford Tour' got under way after the 'showdown' with that great figure of music hall—Oswald Stoll—later Sir Oswald Stoll. Stoll, who looked more like a Sunday School superintendent than a music hall proprietor—and often acted like one, for he had no sense of humour whatever—was noted for his terse statements and uncompromising attitude. It was then that Barrasford decided to build his own music halls instead of (as hitherto) taking them over, or converting them piecemeal.

Let Councillor Tom Barrasford of Llandudno, grandson of the founder of the Tour, tell the story:

'My grandfather, Tom Barrasford, was involved in a personal vendetta with Sir Oswald Stoll, then Chairman of a vast syndicate of music halls known as Moss Empires. In addition, Sir Oswald ran a Tour of his own.

'Stoll, with his usual cautious nature, would bring over foreign acts and engage them on a weekly basis only. Then, if they showed promise, he would engage them for the Tour at the end of the week. Noting this, my grandfather made it his business to be present on the Monday evening when these trial turns were held, and would rush round to the dressing room with a contract, if he thought they were any good. This aroused Stoll's ire, and he had Barrasford or his representatives barred from attending his halls.

'The direct result of this was that my grandfather resolved to build a bigger and better music hall in every town and city in direct opposition to the existing Moss and Stoll Empires.

'At the time of his death in 1910 he had gone a long way towards achieving this aim. In addition, he had built two large music halls on the Continent—the Alhambras at Brussels and Paris—with the object of engaging there the cream of foreign talent, and so booking them for his Tour, which by that time had reached sizeable proportions.'

The first music hall built by Barrasford was in Liverpool, a city which has long been noted for its partiality towards good music hall entertainment. The site chosen was the populous West Derby Road, where Hengler's Circus had been established for many years. The Circus closed down in 1901 and work began immediately upon clearing the site for the erection of a large hall to be known as 'The Royal Hippodrome'.

Barrasford chose for his architect a man of wide experience in designing music halls—Bertie Crewe. Crewe, who had been responsible for the adaptation of the Bostock hall in Glasgow for Barrasford, subsequently built most of the theatres for Barrasford, but one notable exception was the Newcastle Pavilion, which was erected to the design of Messrs. Wilson and Long, the architects for the edifice known as the Palace buildings, Blackpool. Just as Frank Matcham designed most of the Moss and Stoll Empires, so Bertie Crewe designed the Barrasford Hippodromes, but whereas Matcham favoured the ornate Moorish style, Crewe favoured the more flowing lines of Louis Quinze.

The Liverpool Royal Hippodrome was an enormous house. The circle alone held well over 1,000 persons. The great stage was 80-ft. wide and 40-ft deep, with the proscenium opening 40-ft. across. The ceiling was truly a work of art, being painted by the famous artist Secard, who depicted flying ormorini (or cupids) resplendent upon beds of clouds. A tessellated pavement, the pride and joy of old Hengler, was incorporated in the plans at Barrasford's request. Externally, the Royal Hippodrome was a most imposing edifice. The frontage into West Derby Road contained a line of shops, while the entrance way itself was surmounted by a huge clock.

The Liverpool Royal Hippodrome opened at Bank Holiday, 1902 with a large bill headed by Charles T. Crawford, then a noted comedian. Kelly and Gillette, with their 'Human Billiard Table' speciality, who had appeared with such success at the opening of the Glasgow Zoo-Hippodrome, were also prominent on the bill. Prices were really rock-bottom, at 2d. to 1/-. Mr. E. Walker conducted the large pit orchestra and Mr. Walter Hassan was the house manager.

This, the first of the Barrasford-built halls, was an unqualified success, and big business was done there. In fact, so powerful did this hall become, that the Moss–Stoll combine decided to open up in opposition, in the West Derby Road district, notwithstanding the fact that they already had a large Empire flourishing in Liverpool already.

In 1905 they built and opened the Olympia, another enormous house, on an island site in Boaler Street, only a few hundred yards

SIR OSWALD STOLL, of Liverpool, the founder of Stoll Theatres Corporation.

BUILDER OF EMPIRES

One of J. B. Priestley's "Lost Empires". The derelict interior of the BRADFORD EMPIRE after a fire at the stage end of the building.

THE PARTHENON MUSIC HALL in Liverpool where Sir Oswald was manager at 14.

ROY LEO as "The New Warder" in Will Murray's "Casey's Court" which toured the Empires of Moss and Stoll.

Photo: Telegraph & Argus

Plate 21

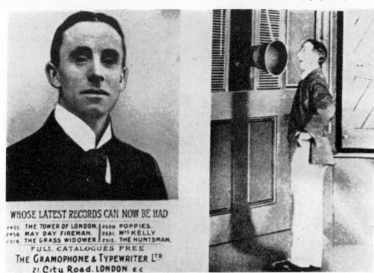

WHOSE LATEST RECORDS CAN NOW BE HAD

2455 THE TOWER OF LONDON. | 2530 POPPIES.
2456 MAY DAY FIREMAN. | 2531. MrS KELLY
2516 THE GRASS WIDOWER | 2515. THE HUNTSMAN.
FULL CATALOGUES FREE
THE GRAMOPHONE & TYPEWRITER LTD
21.Citu Road. LONDON e.c

(Above) THE GREAT DAN LENO making a recording at the old
Gramophone and Typewriter Company studios in 1902.

HISTORY IS MADE!

(Below) THE ORIGINAL MANCHESTER HIPPODROME CIRCUS as
it was in 1904. (It later became a music hall and was demolished in 1935).

THE MANCHESTER HIPPODROME, OXFORD STREET.

TWO PERFORMANCES NIGHTLY. Matinees Tuesday & Saturday

Plate 22

FRED WOOD—Who saved the Leeds City Varieties from becoming a warehouse in 1898.

GEORGE MORTON — The North's "Grand Old Man of Music Hall"—who was 100 years old when he died at Hull in 1938.

MAGNATES AND MANAGERS

ALD. W. H. BROADHEAD, J.P. who ran 16 music halls in the Lancashire area.

JAMES LAURIE GRAYDON, of London, who built the Middlesborough Empire in 1899.

JAMES L. GRAYDON

Plate 23

MUSIC HALL "GREATS"

BUSTER KEATON and members of the "Do You Remember?" Company at the Leeds Empire in 1951. Shown are George Robey, Hetty King, Jack Edge, Dolly Harmer and Peter Bernard. (Below) Signatures of Vic Oliver, Norman Evans and George Formby Jnr. (Right) A Famous Bill.

Plate 24

The **BRIGHTON HIPPODROME** where Tom Barrasford died in February 1910.

TOM BARRASFORD "The Born Hustler" and Champion of "Two Houses Nightly".

TWO FAMOUS MUSIC HALL ACTS OF THE PRE-FIRST WAR ERA

(Below) CHUNG LING SOO, Chinese Magician Extra-ordinary who was accidentally shot dead at Wood Green Empire in 1918. His real name was Will Robinson.

(Right) CORAM and "JERRY". A well-known "Vent" act for many years. Coram was the father of Billy Whitaker who partners Mimi Law.

Plate 25

SIR WALTER DE FRECE

SIR WALTER DE FRECE who formed the Variety Theatres Controlling Company.
(Below) VESTA TILLEY as she performed at the age of four.

VESTA TILLEY (LADY DE FRECE) the Male Impersonator, and "Idol of the Halls".

Two NORTH STARS of yesteryear.

(Below) WEE GEORGIE WOOD impersonating Vesta Tilley in 1909.

Photo: Courtesy of F. Bryson

Plate 26

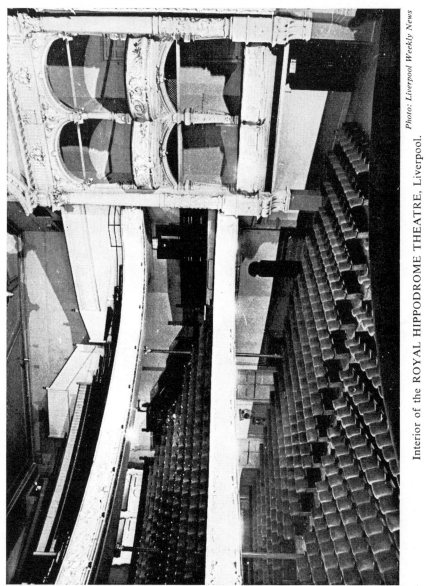

Interior of the ROYAL HIPPODROME THEATRE, Liverpool.

Plate 27

FLORRIE FORDE "The Famous
Principal Boy".

MARIE LLOYD "Queen of the
Music Halls".

EDWARDIAN FAVOURITES
(Left) Eugene Stratton, the great Coon Singer. (Right) Maud Allen, the dancer who
caused a sensation with her interpretation of "Salome".

Plate 28

from the Barrasford Hippodrome. The site of the Olympia was previously occupied by an asylum, and the wags of the district said that Moss was 'barmy' himself to build a music hall there. Designed by Matcham, the Olympia looked like a huge Moorish temple, externally. Within, it was convertible either as a circus or music hall, and was fitted with an enormous tank, capacity 80,000-gallons, for the aquatic displays. The vast hall held 3,750 people comfortably, and Matcham had provided no less than 36 separate exits, but the problem turned out to be how to get people into the place, not out of it.

The Olympia opened with the famous hunting extravaganza 'Tally Ho!', direct from the London Hippodrome, but apart from this one real attraction, the place never really paid its way. Moss Empires put in Pierre Cohen, one of their most astute managers, to try and improve matters, but still the Olympia did not prosper. Finally, there came a compromise with cine-Variety, and during this period an unknown Liverpool performer appeared as Nedlo, the Gypsy violinist. In later years he became Ted Ray, famous as a comedian. Nowadays, the Liverpool Olympia has been adapted as a centre for Mecca Dancing.

*   *   *   *

In 1903 another two halls in the Merseyside area were added to the Barrasford Tour. The first was the Lyric Theatre, in Everton Valley, then a well-known dramatic house, run by H. C. Arnold. The Lyric, which had opened at Christmas, 1897 with the panto-mime 'Bluebeard', was opened by Barrasford as a music hall on Easter Monday, 1903 and even Barrasford was surprised at the results, which exceeded all expectations.

The other hall taken into the circuit in 1903 was the St. Helens Empire, which brought Barrasford into contact with Billy Board-man, always known as the 'Beau Brummel of Managers' for he was never seen at the front of the house without his frock coat and immaculate dress. Sporting a fine waxed moustache, Billy Boardman was to play an important part in the Barrasford Tour.

The position at St. Helens was that Tom Boardman, the father of Billy, had run a public-house singing-room at the George Hotel for some years with great success. This had led to the acquisition of what was always known in St. Helens as 'The Tin and Tinder Palace', in reality an old circus in Corporation Street, not far from the Theatre Royal.

After a few years successful trading, the Boardmans decided to re-build the old Palace, and on 1st June, 1903 the new Empire

F

Music Hall was opened on the same site. Performances were once-nightly and prices were 4d. to 3/-. There was spacious and comfortable accommodation for 1,200 persons at the hall, but the trouble was that patrons who had rolled up in large numbers to the old 'Tin and Tinder Palace' shied away from the beautiful new Empire. It was said in the town 'It was too posh'. Even an attractive opening bill, headed by the local Male Voice Choir, not to mention the sagacious tricks of Harry Edson's Performing Dogs, failed to attract. Subsequent bookings fared no better and soon the Boardmans were in financial difficulties.

After only three months, the St. Helens Empire passed into the hands of Tom Barrasford, who rapidly took stock of the situation. Prices were slashed to 2d. to 1/- and the now inevitable 'Two Houses a Night' system introduced. The name, in common with most of the Barrasford halls, was changed to the 'Hippodrome' and Ernest Walker, the popular musical director from Liverpool, was brought in to 'ginger up' the pit orchestra.

The reconstituted St. Helens Hippodrome re-opened on 12th October, 1903 with Fred Karno's comedy company in 'Jail Birds' and variety support. Success was immediate, but while Barrasford retained booking control in connection with his circuit, he allowed local managers Fred Willmott and Will Sley to take charge. Willmott was well-known for his association with the Roscommon Music Hall in Liverpool, while Sley had connections with an agency. Boardman was moved by Barrasford to Newcastle when the new Pavilion Theatre opened in that city in December 1903.

Two Manchester music halls were added to the Tour in 1903. They were the Grand Theatre in Peter Street and the Regent Theatre in Salford, neither of which proved very valuable to the circuit, and did not last very long. Two further halls added in the South of England were the Bristol Empire and the Brighton Hippodrome, and for a few months the old Britannia Theatre at Hoxton ran variety under the Barrasford banner, not very successfully, until the lease was handed over to Frank MacNaghten after nine months.

The St. Helens Hippodrome was the fourteenth music hall added to the Barrasford Tour in four years, an astounding achievement, and expansion was still going ahead. The halls controlled at the end of 1903 comprised the following:

Palace, Jarrow; Tivoli, Leeds; Tivoli, Edinburgh and Tivoli, Birmingham; Alhambra, Hull; Empire, Bristol; Lyric, Everton; Grand, Manchester, and Regent, Salford. The Britannia Theatre, Hoxton, together with the Hippodromes at Liverpool, Glasgow, Brighton and St. Helens.

In December, 1903 the Newcastle Pavilion, a large building in Westgate Road, was added, the hall opening with a big bill topped by Madame Belle Cole, the noted Tyneside contralto. The naming of this hall 'The Pavilion' coincided with the registration of the Barrasford Circuit as a limited company in London, with Hugh Astley, of the London Pavilion, as Chairman, and Tom Barrasford as Managing Director. The registered office address of the company was in Leicester Place, off Leicester Square, London, W.C.2.

*   *   *   *

Like other magnates from the North, Tom Barrasford had made London his Mecca. The great trek to the Metropolis was on, although Barrasford was unlucky with both his ventures in the capital city. The first venture at Hoxton lasted only nine months, and the West End enterprise only a little longer, but the Circuit flourished in spite of these setbacks.

The Britannia Theatre, Hoxton—or 'The Old Brit' as it was affectionately called—had been made famous by Mrs. Sarah Lane, who had run melodrama and pantomime there for many years. With her death, the fortunes of the theatre declined and it came into the market.

The *Hackney Gazette* sadly commented:

'The popularity of melodrama is steadily on the wane. At the Britannia Theatre, Hoxton, which for over two generations has been the home of popular melodrama, it does not seem to pay.

'This famous old theatre is to become a music hall. It has been acquired by Mr. T. Barrasford, who controls a dozen or so pleasure palaces in the greater provincial cities and he proposes to bring the Britannia into line with them.'

And so at Easter, 1903 the music hall regime was launched at the Hoxton Britannia. But the great days of the Britannia were definitely over. Apart from the weeks when the great Doctor Walford Bodie packed the place with his 'Electric Wizardry' and hypnotic experiments, the music hall era at the 'Old Brit' was a complete flop. The outcome was that Barrasford turned the lease over to his old friend MacNaghten, who ran it for a few years in conjunction with his London halls—known as the Music Halls Proprietary Corporation—until finally it became a cinema. 'Penny Picture Matinees' made their debut at the Britannia as early as 1908, but a place less suited for adaptation as a cinema would be hard to find. Today the 'Old Brit' is no more. It was damaged during the air raids on London in the Second War and afterwards pulled down.

No sooner had Barrasford launched music hall at the Britannia, than he heard the astounding news that his old antagonist, Sir Oswald Stoll, was drawing up plans for the erection of a huge music hall in the heart of London, to be run on 'continuous' lines, as in America. Barrasford had more or less led the way with the 'Two Houses a Night' System, and now here was Stoll coming up with 'Four Houses a Day'!

The site chosen by Stoll for the erection of this massive hall— to be called the Coliseum—was at the bottom of St. Martins Lane, and Frank Matcham had orders to produce an architectural master-piece, which he certainly did. It was in full Italian Renaissance design, with a huge tower, and the so-called 'Grand Salon' had a mosaic floor, while tea could be taken in the 'Conservatory' between performances. There was even an electric car to take Royalty from the entrance hall to the Royal Box on State occasions.

Barrasford, hearing all this, was not to be outdone. Immediately he entered into negotiations for the old Lyceum Theatre, just off the Strand, which was then coming on to the market. The Lyceum was a very old house, and had been run by Sir Henry Irving as a home of legitimate drama for many years. But now the London County Council were insisting on so many alterations to bring the structure into line with safety requirements that the Company, of which Sir Henry was a principal shareholder, had to relinquish possession. After a sale of effects in March 1904, the place was standing empty.

Purchased by Barrasford, architect Bertie Crewe was told to do his best with the building, to turn it into a music hall, but quickly. Crewe promptly demolished it in its entirety apart from the famous portico into Wellington Street, and the back wall. In its place, he proceeded to have erected a comfortable, roomy theatre, resplendent in gilt and plush.

It was a race between Barrasford and Stoll to have their respec-tive music halls open, but Stoll won by a short head. The Coliseum opened on Christmas Eve (24th December) 1904 and Barrasford's new Lyceum on Boxing Day—the 26th!

While the great Eugene Stratton—then at the height of his fame —was the top of the bill attraction at Stoll's Coliseum, the first bill at Tom Barrasford's Lyceum included excerpts from 'Rigoletto' by a company billed as the Lyceum Operatic Company; Captain Taylor's elephants doing the Cake-Walk and riding bicycles; the lightning juggling of Purrocupis; the bird noises of the Permaine Brothers, and the dancing of La Wilma—'Lady artiste in Sand and Smoke'. It was, of course, 'Two Houses a Night' at 6.30 and 9 p.m.

Sir Henry Irving, on his 'Farewell Tour' of the Provinces, was appalled when he heard the news. He could not bear to think of those hallowed boards, where he had played 'Hamlet' so often, and the scene of his great triumph in 'The Bells', echoing to bird noises and the tramp of educated elephants! The very mention of 'Music Hall' became an absolute anathema to him after that.

The Lyceum music hall enterprise did not meet with the success it deserved, or Barrasford hoped for, and again it was the same 'Mrs. Grundy-like' attitude on the part of the L.C.C. (which had caused Sir Henry to give up) that brought about its closure a second time. On this occasion it was an obstinate refusal to grant a liquor licence that caused all the trouble. In June 1905, Barrasford's Lyceum Company was in financial difficulties.

A well-known theatrical journal commented:

'Here we have a magnificent building, with a beautiful auditorium fitted-out in the very best style, and with every up-to-date device to make its patrons comfortable . . . But the great draw-back is the absence of a drinking licence, and on that account will never appeal to the 'young man about town' or to the man who is fond of a glass with his smoke. A man cannot sit through an entertainment where he is allowed to smoke without feeling the desire for something a little stronger than lime juice and soda . . .'

And so, through no fault of his own, Barrasford had to reluctantly bring the Lyceum variety season to a close. During that season famous Continental artistes had made their appearance, for Barrasford had brought them over from his famous Paris Alhambra 'nursery' which at this time had been established. (He also had the Brussels Alhambra for a time, until it met an untimely end by fire.)

Two British music hall acts, which later became very famous, also made their debut at the Lyceum. They were Gertie Gitana, who hailed from the Potteries, and an unknown ventriloquist who came for a week's engagement at a 'Trial Turn' salary, and stayed a month—his salary increasing every week! He was Coram, said to be the first 'vent' to use a military dummy. Coram (real name Tommy Whitaker) began his career on Morecambe sands.

But the Lyceum venture was not entirely in vain. The triumph came in September 1905, when Tom Barrasford was honoured by a Royal Visit to his theatre. The first production of the spectacular ballet 'Excelsior' was seen by Their Royal Highnesses, the Prince and Princess of Wales, afterwards King George V and Queen Mary.

At the end of that year, the L.C.C. still being adamant in their refusal to grant a drink licence for variety performances, Barrasford abandoned the Lyceum for good. It was subsequently purchased by the Melville family for £240,000.

After this, Barrasford made Brighton the centre of his operations. The ice rink of 1897 in Middle Street, in which he had acquired an interest in 1902 and turned into the Hippodrome music hall, was reconstructed. Barrasford himself occupied premises adjoining, known as 'Hippodrome House', and about the same time took over an old music hall in New Road, next door to Brighton's historic Theatre Royal, and turned this into the Coliseum. Prior to this, it had been known as 'Wright's Oxford Music Hall', the New Oxford, the Empire, and other names. In 1909 Barrasford turned it into a cinema.

*   *   *   *

Some re-organisation of the Barrasford Tour was carried out in 1906. The original Tivoli in Leeds was enlarged and improved at a cost of £5,000 and re-named the New Hippodrome. Tip-up seats were installed in all parts of the hall, rich tapestry curtains made their appearance, and students at the Leeds School of Art designed the cherubs in plaster, which adorned the enlarged proscenium arch. Seating was increased and the hall was now capable of accommodating 3,000 persons.

Barrasford's New Leeds Hippodrome opened at Bank Holiday, 1906 with Joe Petersen's musical extravaganza 'King Ikey' with Harry Brown, the local comedian, and full houses were invariably the rule, in spite of the Moss Empires house in nearby Briggate. The reason for the transformation of the Tivoli into the New Hippodrome was because word had got round that Frank MacNaghten, disgruntled at losing a court case about the finances of the Theatre Royal (next door to the Tivoli) had decided to turn it in to a music hall. Also, that Walter de Frece, another music hall magnate, was interested in the Coliseum, and was making a bid for possession. As it happened, neither of these proposals came to anything. MacNaghten turned the Theatre Royal over to Francis Laidler, of Bradford, who was happy to continue with dramatic fare, while Sydney Carter, with his New Century Pictures, obtained the lease of the Coliseum, and turned it into a full-time cinema.

In regard to the Hull Alhambra, a converted chapel, Barrasford had this place renovated as a 'New Hippodrome', but upon completion handed control over to his manager there, Alfred Graham, who ran it in conjunction with the Middlesbrough Oxford Palace, which he had re-opened.

On 31st December, 1906 a new Barrasford hall opened. It was the Hippodrome at Coventry, and a very valuable addition to the circuit. On the other hand several halls which had proved something of liabilities were disposed of. They were all in the Manchester district.

This part of Lancashire never proved very successful for Barrasford. Ted Garcia's old circus in Peter Street, which had run as the Grand Theatre under Barrasford, did quite well for a time (in spite of the Tivoli opposite) but when Stoll's big guns opened up in nearby Oxford Road and again at Ardwick, the Grand was let to Jasper Redfern and his pictures. Likewise, at Salford, business fell away at the Regent Theatre and Assembly Rooms when Broadhead's new Hippodrome opened at the other end of Cross Lane. This too, was disposed of. It was obvious that saturation point had been reached for music hall in Manchester.

Also in this area, a small hall in Oldham, once the Adelphi, which had again been turned into a 'Hippodrome' by Barrasford, was relinquished because the seating capacity was negligible. It was immediately taken over by the Empire Syndicate of Oldham (controlled by Ernest Dotteridge, formerly a touring manager). This Syndicate aimed at securing a monopoly of entertainment in Oldham, and came very near to doing so.

In 1907 another massive hall was built by Barrasford to oppose the mighty Moss Empires. This was the Sheffield Hippodrome, situated in Cambridge Street, which was reputed to hold 4,000 but this figure probably included standees. In its construction it was said to embody the longest circle girder ever put into a theatre. The Hippodrome, which was built to the design of Bertie Crewe, embodied the cantilever style of construction (i.e. no supporting pillars) and was declared open by Miss Elsie Savage, daughter of one of the directors. Also a director was Fred Willmott, the Liverpool agent, and previously an associate of George Belmont, the London entrepreneur.

The Harmony Four, noted vocalists, topped the bill at the opening of the Sheffield Hippodrome on the 23rd of December, 1907. In support were the Davis and Gledhill cycling troupes and the famous Sisters Sprightly, the girls from Wigan, who were always in demand for pantomime. In addition was the famous 'Barrascope' interlude of topical films. The orchestra came in for serious criticism at the opening, but this was soon remedied.

The Hippodrome did not get away to a particularly good start,

but it did much better when it became established and the quality
of its programmes better known. There was great competition in
Sheffield in those days, for the Grand, the Alhambra and the
Empire were all playing Variety, in addition to the new Hippodrome.

That same year saw some activity among the Scottish halls. The
Glasgow Pavilion had been opened, and Barrasford had a hand in
this, together with Hugh Astley, of the London Pavilion. Barrasford
was also associated with Rich Waldron in the running of the
Gorbals Palace, which was erected next door to the Princess'
Theatre. Some time later, the Glasgow Hippodrome passed into the
control of Moss Empires, but by 1914, when the Empress Variety
Theatre at nearby St. Georges' Cross had opened, it was known as
'Joy-Town'. (Later still, it became an exhibition hall and finally a
garage.) The Edinburgh Tivoli also passed into other hands,
becoming the Grand Picture and Variety Theatre.

* * * *

The next year, 1908, saw the last Hippodrome to be erected by
Tom Barrasford opened. This was the Nottingham Hippodrome—
also designed by Bertie Crewe—and sited not a stone's throw from
the Moss Empires' hall. The Hippodrome opened on 28th September, 1908 with R. G. Knowles, the famous comedian, topping a big
bill which included Gladys Huxley, the noted contralto.

Not long after this came the melancholy news that, owing to
persistent ill-health, Tom Barrasford was to make arrangements
with Walter de Frece to assume control of the Tour. De Frece was
a well-known entrepreneur, being at the time the managing director
of a syndicate known as 'The South of England Hippodromes, Ltd.'
and the husband of Vesta Tilley. He was also a song-writer of some
merit, having written 'Following Father's Footsteps' for his wife,
who featured the number in her repertoire with great success. The
De Frece Circuit at this time included such halls as the Hippodromes at Boscombe, Margate, Colchester, Southampton and
elsewhere.

It was hardly surprising Barrasford had broken down under the
great strain of personally supervising his large circuit of music
halls. He was always referred to in the Profession as 'The Born
Hustler' and without doubt he had impaired his health in trying
to do too much. It was stated that he was suffering from the effects
of Bright's Disease and had been ordered to rest at his Brighton
home.

In addition to his music hall activities—and he would think

nothing about dashing to the Continent and back to catch a new act—he was a well-known figure in the racing world, and owned several race horses.

Before he moved to Brighton for health reasons, his horses were trained at Malton, and his two favourites at that time were Little Grafter and Fancy Man, which Fred Finlay invariably rode. Once, when one of his horses was running at Pontefract, Tom Barrasford placed a five-shilling bet on behalf of every member of his staff at the Leeds Tivoli upon the horse, so confident was he of victory. It won, and there were great rejoicings in Leeds that night.

Another of his horses once won the Silver Bell Handicap at Paisley, to his great delight. His racing colours were the red and black of the MacGregor Tartan and when one of his horses was running he wore a tie of these colours—usually a signal for the staff to place bets—as it was sure to be carrying 'stable money'.

He was the inventor of the 'Barrasford Gate', a starting gate device manufactured by the Leeds firm of Borland and Wareham, which was later taken up by the Jockey Club. Billy Boardman, his manager and right-hand man, used to say that it was well-known in the Profession that where there was racing there was always Tom Barrasford. For example, a meeting at Haydock Park would surely call for an inspection of the Liverpool Hippodrome, while a Gosforth Park meeting augured a look-in at the Newcastle Pavilion, and so forth. According to Boardman, he was lavish with his bets, and was consequently well-thought of by the bookmaking fraternity.

He also had a hand in the patenting of an apparatus known as the 'Barrascope'. This was an early form of the cinematograph, and an idea of a Leeds photographer named Owen Brooks, who, with assistance from engineer Borland, put the machine on the market. The first one was installed in the Leeds Tivoli as early as 1902 and topical events were screened there as part of the programme. It proved very popular and all the music halls were eventually equipped with Barrascopes. As early as 1909 Variety was superseded by film shows at the Brighton Coliseum, so convinced was he of the future for 'pictures'.

On 1st February, 1910 Tom Barrasford passed quietly away at Hippodrome House, Brighton, aged 50 years. He left a widow (his second wife, Maud D'Almayne, a former music hall singer) and three sons. Tom, the eldest, was manager at the time of the Keighley Hippodrome, while George was a well-known agent. The youngest son was touring America, partner in a music hall act known as Lake and Barrasford (songs at the piano).

The funeral, one of the largest ever held in Brighton, was very well attended by all ranks of the Profession. They came to pay tribute to a man who did much for the British music hall and was very well respected in all circles.

A colleague of his said in tribute:

'Tom Barrasford was a man of remarkable generosity. He did many charitable deeds in secret.'

And so the last curtain fell on one of Music Hall's most remarkable personalities.

*   *   *   *

Walter de Frece, who took over most of the Barrasford halls, merged them with his own circuit (The South of England Hippodromes, Ltd.) to form a great new combine known as 'The Variety Theatres Controlling Company' (or more frequently 'The Controlling Company'). The ex-Barrasford halls in the new Tour included the Hippodromes at Liverpool, Leeds, Sheffield, Birmingham and Brighton, together with the Paris Alhambra. The Newsome family acquired the new Coventry Hippodrome, later to be known as 'The Coventry Theatre'.

Messrs. Sley and Willmott incorporated the Lyric at Everton into their Circuit, together with the St. Helens Hippodrome, while the Bristol Empire and the Newcastle Pavilion were disposed of as cinemas.

The old original wooden Jarrow Palace was continued for a time after Barrasford's death by the manager, Charlie Lamb, but early in 1911 it was completely destroyed by fire and never rebuilt. It was the quickest and fiercest fire ever seen in Jarrow, according to accounts, and could be seen for miles. Every brigade in the area attended but nothing could be done to save the wooden building.

Walter de Frece, who merged the larger Barrasford halls with his own 'Tour', was born in 1870, the son of Henry (Harry) de Frece, of the Gaiety Music Hall in Camden Street, Liverpool and a prosperous agent in the Roscoe Arcade.

Walter's early life was styled by the music hall world, for the de Frece clan were well established in Liverpool. Jack, of that ilk, had the wooden theatre in Manchester Street called the Alhambra, while Isaac had the old Theatre Royal in Clayton Square. Educated at the Liverpool Institute and in Brussels, Harry was determined that his son should not follow him into music hall management. Walter, his education completed, was articled to a prominent Merseyside architect, but in 1889 something happened to change all that.

In that year the De Frece Agency engaged an attractive 25-year-old to play Principal Boy in Pantomime at the Gaiety Theatre, in Liverpool. She was Tilly Ball, professionally known as Vesta Tilley (the 'Matchless' little Tilly), and the daughter of Harry Ball, a former music hall Chairman. Vesta had been on the stage since the age of four, performing then on the boards of her father's hall, the St. George's Hall in Nottingham. In 1889 she was well-known on the 'halls' as a Male Impersonator.

Nineteen-year-old Walter was immediately 'smitten' by the charms of the attractive Vesta and sat in the front stalls every night of the pantomime and sent flowers round to her dressing room. There were many suitors for the hand of Vesta Tilley at that time—including Oswald Stoll, proprietor of the rival Parthenon Music Hall—and Vesta did not take Walter seriously at first. Later on in the run of pantomime however, she allowed the handsome young Jew to take her to a dance, and rewarded him with a kiss.

That kiss inspired Walter. Against his father's wishes, he broke his terms of office with the architect, made his way to London and found himself a job in the office of Warner's Theatrical Agency. In 1890 Vesta and he were married.

Some years afterwards, Walter de Frece broke away from Warner's Agency and founded one of his own. Then, noting the decline in melodrama, and the consequent rise to popularity of the music hall, he seized opportunity by taking control of several legitimate theatres which had fallen on evil days and converted them into music halls with conspicuous success.

First there came the huge Metropole Theatre at Camberwell, which he turned into an Empire; then he bought up a number of halls scattered about the South Coast area which he turned into 'Hippodromes'. By 1905 Walter de Frece was managing director of an impressive 'Tour' aptly named 'The South of England Hippodromes, Ltd.' Among others, these comprised the former Grand Theatre at Margate; the Grand Theatre at Colchester; the Prince of Wales' at Southampton and a theatre at Boscombe managed by his brother-in-law, Harry Ball, junior. All these halls were renamed 'Hippodromes'. In addition there was the Empire Palace at Wolverhampton (later known also as the Hippodrome) and other Hippodromes were later built at Portsmouth and Southend.

In 1906 Walter de Frece gave his attention to the North of England. First he joined the Board of Directors at the Manchester Palace; then in December of that year he opened his first hall in the North, in his native Liverpool. This was the New Tivoli Theatre of Varieties in Lime Street, built on the site of the St. James's Hall, the former home of Sam Hague's Minstrels. His wife, Vesta Tilley, topped the bill opening the New Tivoli, but the hall was too near the Empire Palace of Moss and Stoll and did not prosper. In 1908 Walter crossed the Mersey and revived the fortunes of the old Metropole at Birkenhead, as 'The New Birkenhead Hippodrome'. Vesta gave this hall a good send-off also.

Another old theatre revived as a music hall was the Blackburn Theatre Royal; closely followed by the Bolton Empire (re-named Hippodrome) and the Oldham Palace, which Walter de Frece built himself. Walter dearly wanted to call this hall 'The Hippodrome' but there already was one—opposite! Many famous acts played the Oldham Palace down the years; Gracie Fields made her one and only appearance in pantomime there in 1915 and the ill-fated Lafayette fulfilled his last full week's booking on its boards. Vesta Tilley made many appearances at the Palace (the last being in 1914) and a full-length picture of her in the uniform of a 'Middy' hung in the foyer for many years.

In 1914 the Variety Theatres Controlling Company was at its height in numbers, for since its formation by de Frece in 1910 other halls had been incorporated, including the Edinburgh Theatre Royal, the Glasgow Alhambra and the Newcastle Hippodrome, which was converted out of Ginnett's Circus. These places, together with the larger Barrasford halls; the South of England Hippo-dromes and the old de Frece Tour comprised the Controlling Company, totalling 18 properties.

During the First War the public taste veered away from music hall entertainment, with the result that many of the halls were closed or sold as cinemas. In 1919 Walter de Frece was knighted for his services to British entertainment and thus joined the select Arthurian circle of music hall Knights which included Sir Oswald Stoll, Sir Alfred Butt and the late Edward Moss.

Sir Walter immediately resigned his position as managing director of the Variety Theatres Controlling Company to take up politics. His place was taken by Charles Gulliver who had suc-ceeded Sir Walter Gibbons as the head of the London Theatres of Variety.

There were many who said that the Knighthood went to Sir Walter's head in more ways than one, as was evinced by his changed manner. He had a way of avoiding his former music hall associates which earned him the nick-name of 'Sir Altered de Frece'. Vesta Tilley, his wife, was made to 'retire' from the halls upon his entry into politics.

Vesta chose Stoll's Alhambra as the venue for this occasion, which took place in June 1920. This was a gesture towards Stoll in memory of the early days at the Liverpool Parthenon and the wonderful songs he had written for her. At the Alhambra Ellen Terry presented Vesta with a large floral bouquet amid scenes of great emotion.

In 1924 Sir Walter de Frece was elected Conservative M.P. for Ashton-under-Lyne in Lancashire and a few years later he stood and was again elected, this time as M.P. for Blackpool. Some time later, his wife's health caused concern, and they made their home on the French Riviera, Sir Walter joining her whenever his Parliamentary duties permitted.

In this connection there is a well-known story about the Commissionaire at the Casino in Monte Carlo who would not admit Sir Walter because he had forgotten his membership card. The Commissionaire knew perfectly well that Sir Walter was a member, but due to the latter's lofty manner decided not to admit him without it.

Sir Walter raged and fumed, but the man was adamant—no card —no admittance! To save further indignity Sir Walter paid another 400 francs for an admission card 'under protest'. Immediately he went to the Chemin-de-Fer table to make an astonishing 'break' of several hours' duration, in which he won himself a tidy 136,000 francs (then £1,500)!

Vesta Tilley passed away at her Monte Carlo home in 1952 after a period of illness, while three years later Sir Walter, who was never the same without her, followed her to the grave.

And so passed from the scene one of the great partnerships and love stories of the Golden Era of Music Hall.

9

The MacNaghten Vaudeville Circuit

ANOTHER FAMOUS entrepeneur with roots in the North, who, while not challenging the supremacy of the Moss and Stoll combines in quite the same way as Barrasford, was successful in establishing a twenty-strong 'chain' of 'Number-Two' halls at a time when competition was fierce, was Francis William MacNaghten.

Frank MacNaghten, as he was known, was born of distinguished parentage during 1870 in India, but was educated in this country at Haileybury, the noted public school. He was related to General MacNaghten, who had a military career of distinction, and to Sir Deighton Probyn, once Keeper of the Privy Purse. After schooling at Haileybury, Frank MacNaghten returned to India to assist his uncle in the running of an indigo plantation at Karachi.

Following a recession in the indigo trade, he returned to this country in 1895 and in Northampton in that year became associated with several gentlemen in the running of the Empire Music Hall in that town. The Empire stood in Goldsmith Street, at the corner with Horseshoe Street, and had been established in 1872 as 'Higgetts' Alhambra', being attached to licensed premises. Later, for some time, Gus Levaine had run it as the Grand Music Hall, and it had also been known by other names.

It was from this small beginning that MacNaghten was eventually to become the managing director of three compaïies: The MacNaghten Vaudeville Circuit, the main holding company, controlling a dozen or so provincial music halls; the North of England Theatres Corporation, which was responsible for a number of dramatic houses, and the Music Hall Proprietary Corporation, which embodied the administration of five London music halls and had an interest in another.

Frank MacNaghten, who always said he was too busy building music halls to marry, was known as 'The Bachelor Entrepreneur'.

According to his secretary, he was:

> ' . . . A tall, handsome man, and in the early days of the Circuit was an impressive figure in his silk hat and frock coat, which he invariably wore at that period.

174

'Although something of a martinet, he took a personal interest in all his employees, particularly those who had been in his service for a long time. He travelled extensively, at one time making a voyage round the world.'

When he had made his mark in the entertainment sphere, Frank MacNaghten had a town house in style at Bedford Court Mansions, London, but he liked Sheffield and preferred to administer his affairs from there.

Northampton Empire did not offer much by way of prospects, in fact it was a small building and could hardly be made to pay, so MacNaghten, with his two henchmen, Fred Baugh and Sidney Arthur, travelled to Sheffield to inspect the Grand Music Hall at West Bar, which, in 1896, was standing empty.

Like the Northampton hall, the Sheffield Grand had had a small beginning. At one time it was known as the Bijou, and was attached to a public house in Snig Hill. 'Mine Host' of those days, one 'Squint' Milner, or Alfred Milner, to give him his real name, had rebuilt the Bijou apart from the public house, as 'The Star Music Hall'. It was rather a low class place, but in 1893 Edward Welding had taken it over, added a plaster front, and carried out interior alterations, turning it into quite a cosy little music hall. It had re-opened as the Grand Theatre at Easter, 1893, and had done quite well for a time. Many top-line 'stars' of the period had appeared there, Charles Coburn among them, and the place was equipped with electric light. Then, in 1895, the Moss Empire Palace had opened in Sheffield, and forced the little Grand out of business. Frank MacNaghten took one look at the Grand, liked what he saw, and moved in, 'determined to succeed'.

With Fred Baugh as house manager and Sidney Arthur as booker, MacNaghten re-opened the 'Grand Theatre and Music Hall' as he billed the place, at Bank Holiday, 1896, on the then almost unknown 'Two Houses a Night' system. It was an emergency measure to combat the big bills put on by Moss and Stoll at the Empire, with which MacNaghten could not hope to compete. On that first bill was Fred Newby, then a well-known comedian; Naomi Ethardo, from a long line of acrobats of that name, who contorted herself whilst perched upon a pyramid of bottles; Daisy le Roy, a serio-comedienne, and others. Success was instantaneous. The cosy little house at the West Bar tram junction was once again in business.

* * * *

Following this success, MacNaghten got the idea that a suburban music hall would do well in Sheffield. With this idea in mind he floated a company in 1897 with a capital of £10,000 to build a hall in the populous suburb of Attercliffe. One of the directors was Fred Lawton, of a firm of solicitors, Hardy, Lawton and Company, of Sheffield.

The Attercliffe Alhambra, as the house was to be called, was a fair sized structure designed by A. Blomfield Jackson, once a partner with the well-known Bath architect C. J. Phipps, and it held 1,600 people. It was carried out in that Moorish style of architecture then so popular, and the interior was very well fitted out. There was a superb act-drop of the Alhambra Court at the Crystal Palace, London, carried out by Mr. McCullock, who was appointed scenic artist. Mr. Arthur was put in to manage, and Mr. Chizdey was also brought from the Grand to conduct the pit orchestra. The electric light was used to advantage and the hall was, of course, to be run on the 'Two Houses a Night' system.

Opening on the 3rd January, 1898 the Alhambra presented Professor Leslie's Leaping Dog act, with full support, but the attendance during the opening weeks was very poor. It could be that Attercliffians had 'spent up' (as the Yorkshire saying goes) after Christmas, or perhaps leaping dogs did not appeal to them, but it was hopefully expected that attendances would improve when the theatre got firmly established.

The Alhambra was not the success hoped for, however, although it did improve as time went on. In 1907 it was sold to T. Allan Edwardes of Derby, who changed its name to the Palace. Edwardes ran it as a music hall until 1913, then disposed of it as a cinema, with which the Roberto Brothers were connected for some time. Years later it was to make a return to greatness as a music hall in the boom period following the Second War.

Just around the corner from the Alhambra, in Pinfold Lane (now known as Staniforth Road) was the Peoples' Theatre, run by Edward Darbey, with dramatic fare. The Peoples', a very plain-looking brick building, had opened on 26th July, 1897 with Mr. Gifford's 'No. 1 Touring Company' in 'No Cross, No Crown'. In addition to the Peoples' Theatre, Mr. Darbey also ran several others, including the Theatre Royal, Rotherham, which had opened in 1894; the New Theatre Royal, Chesterfield, erected on the site of Boswell's Circus in that town in 1896, and the very old Queens' Theatre at Keighley. All these halls were putting on melodrama under Mr. Darbey's management.

In 1898 Frank MacNaghten formed a company to take over all these theatres, known as the North of England Theatres Corporation, and dramatic fare was to be continued. There would be no change over to music hall. The Queens' Theatre, Keighley, a very old building, was not incorporated in the Circuit, but was subsequently rebuilt by another concern altogether. A few years later, however, MacNaghten added another two theatres to the dramatic productions tour: they were the Nottingham Kings' Theatre (formerly the Gaiety Palace music hall) and the Leeds Theatre Royal, acquired in 1902.

In connection with the Vaudeville Circuit, MacNaghten in 1898 entered into an agreement with the Livermore Brothers to take over the Bradford Peoples' Palace as a going concern. The reason being that work had then begun in that city upon the erection of a large .Moss Empires' Theatre, and the Livermore Bros. were anxious to dispose of their interests forthwith. The hall in question had opened originally as the Star Music Hall in 1875 and was built beneath the Princes' Theatre, an arrangement believed to be unique in theatrical architecture. Messrs. Roberton and Holmes had changed the name to the Peoples' Palace in 1894 when they had acquired the building, at the same time carrying out alterations and improvements designed to dissociate the Peoples' Palace with the rather dubious reputation acquired by the former Star Music Hall.

Accordingly, the Bradford Peoples' Palace was leased to MacNaghten from the 2nd January, 1899, and on the 30th of that month the huge Empire Theatre of Varieties opened in Great Horton Road, just around the corner. The Bradford Empire at that time was to be run by a concern known as the 'Liverpool, Leeds and Hull Empire Palaces, Ltd.' as the unification of the Moss Empires group had not at that time taken place. Frank Allen, of Moss Empires, speaking from the stage of the Bradford Empire on opening night, said: 'Moss Empires are the largest syndicate of variety theatres in the world. Nothing will be seen or heard here that will raise a blush or put modesty to shame' (great applause). The Empire opened as a once-nightly hall.

MacNaghten's reply to this broadside was to change the Palace over to 'Twice Nightly' ('Seven and Nine' ran the advertisements) and engage the Great Chirgwin to top the bill 'at Enormous Expense!' Chirgwin did a bit of novelty business with clay pipes in addition to singing his usual lachrymose ballads, 'The Blind Boy' and 'My Fiddle is My Sweetheart'.

The Peoples' Palace more or less held its own with the twice-nightly system—in fact it was not very long before the Empire had to follow suit—and Tom Barrasford who had opened up in nearby Leeds 'borrowed' the idea from MacNaghten, who very kindly lent him his most experienced manager in Fred Baugh, to instruct him in the new principle. Mr. Schuberth, who had been managing the Bradford Palace for the Livermore Bros. was then reinstated in his former position. The musical director at the Palace, one Tommy Murgatroyd, impressed MacNaghten immensely, and was called upon to form pit orchestras at all the subsequent Circuit halls, as and when they opened.

The next hall to be opened by MacNaghten was the Oddfellows' Hall at Halifax, which dated from 1840. The building, from the outside, with its immense Corinthian pillars, looked big enough, but actually only a small concert room within was fitted up for entertainments. Liszt had given a pianoforte recital there in 1841 and in 1858 Dickens had given a reading. In 1888 Joe Helliwell had turned the place into a music hall with Frank Harcourt wielding the gavel as Chairman. In 1897 Harcourt returned to Halifax to re-open the place himself as a music hall, at the same time securing a drink licence, and MacNaghten took it over from him in 1900 as the Halifax Peoples' Palace, with Fred Baugh (now back from Barrasford) as the manager. It did very good business indeed until 1903 when the new Halifax Palace Theatre opened. Even then it continued to run for a time as a music hall until the lease ran out. In later years, from 1920, for a period of nearly forty years, the Oddfellows' ran as the Alhambra Cinema.

*   *   *   *

Over the border into Lancashire, at Blackburn, the Livermore Brothers were managing a music hall named the Palace erected on the site of the old Wesley Mission in Jubilee Street, by the London and Lancashire Theatres Company. The Palace, opened on the 11th December, 1899 with a first-class variety bill topped by Wal Pink in his famous sketch 'The Q.C.', got away to a good start as a once-nightly hall, but business had fallen away badly. The Company was in difficulties and had to go into liquidation in June, 1900. The case was complicated by a pending lawsuit about some scaffolding, and another factor in the closure was that the contractors had exceeded their estimated cost in the actual erection of the building.

An auction of the theatre and its contents was held at the Bull Hotel, Blackburn, and here a curious incident occurred. A local man named Walsh made an immediate bid for the property of £20,000 and, there being no further bids, the property was knocked down to him for that sum. It very soon transpired, however, that Mr. Walsh was in no position to produce the sum of £20,000 or anything like it. It seems likely that he had been used as a 'stooge' to start the bidding at a higher figure than may well have otherwise been the case. The upshot of all this was that the theatre had to be auctioned again, and on this occasion the auctioneers made sure that Mr. Walsh was not on the premises. After some very low bids, the Blackburn Palace was sold to Mr. Barry of Bradford, acting on behalf of Frank MacNaghten, for £12,500.

The Blackburn Palace re-opened as part of the MacNaghten Vaudeville Circuit on 10th September, 1900 as a twice-nightly hall and with new lower prices, ranging from 2d. to 2/–. The gallery, the largest of any theatre in Lancashire, bore the sign: '1,000 seats at 2d.' Charlie Tempest, the comedian, topped the bill for the re-opening under the new regime.

The Palace became the 'Premier Variety Theatre' in the newly-formed MacNaghten Vaudeville Circuit and did consistently good business for many years. Ramsay Macdonald spoke from its stage in 1926 in an election campaign, and top-line music'hall 'stars' who appeared there down the years, before the temporary closure in 1932, included G. H. Elliott, the Chocolate Coloured Coon; Eugene Stratton; Sir Harry Lauder; Wee Georgie Wood; Houdini; the great Walford Bodie; the ill-fated Lafayette; and Lancashire's very own Gracie Fields on more than one occasion.

Now, in 1900, MacNaghten had three 'Palaces' under his control, and it was then decided to name any further theatres which might be acquired 'Palaces' (or rather 'Vaudeville Palaces') wherever possible. His rivals Moss and Stoll had their 'Empires' and Barrasford and De Frece had their 'Hippodromes'.

The year 1901 saw three halls in the Midlands added to the Circuit. They were the Lincoln Empire, purchased from Councillor Beagle and part of the former Masonic Hall, which immediately became the Lincoln Palace; the Gaiety Palace in Market Street, Nottingham, then being run by a nephew of C. B. Cox, the original proprietor, and the Tivoli in Leicester.

Councillor George Beagle, from whom MacNaghten acquired the Lincoln Empire, was a man of enterprise. Sadly, he knew nothing about music halls, for his venture in this field lasted barely three months. Possibly he was unlucky, or tried to do too much. Beagle ran the city's first cut-price grocery store, in the High Street, but lost his seat on the Lincoln City Council when the Carholme Ward went out of existence. He also entered a horse in the Lincolnshire Handicap one year—called Barbetty. It ran, but not fast enough . . . However, his expensive red velvet tableaux curtains—with his initials 'G.H.B.' worked in gold—lasted the life of the theatre, which went under to Hitler's bombs in 1943.

MacNaghten decided to turn the Nottingham Gaiety over to melodrama, so it was re-named the King's Theatre (Edward VII having ascended to the throne) and became part of the North of England Theatres Corporation. The Leicester hall, in the Belgrave Gate, was built on the site of a very famous old music hall known as 'Paul's' which had been run by a man of that name as early as 1865. In 1890 it had been completely rebuilt as the Prince of Wales' Theatre, but this had failed, and in 1894 Captain Orr Gray had turned it into the Tivoli Theatre of Varieties. MacNaghten's intention was to call this hall 'The Tivoli Palace' and indeed did so for a time, until the Stoll Palace opened on a nearby site in Belgrave Gate. (There already was an 'Empire' in Wharf Street run by the Sweeney family.) Finally, MacNaghten called it the Pavilion Music Hall, and so it remained until it was swept away in a road-widening scheme in 1929.

Acquired in 1902 was another dramatic house which became part of the North of England Theatres Corporation. This was the 26-year-old Theatre Royal in Leeds, which had been run for some years by Walter Reynolds, and who retired when MacNaghten took it over. It was next door to the Tivoli Music Hall run by Tom Barrasford, the Jarrow entrepreneur.

MacNaghten lost a lot of money on the Theatre Royal deal at Leeds. In 1904 he brought an action against Reynolds at Leeds Crown Court for alleged fraudulent representation. This alluded to the profits made and lost at the theatre over a period. It was stated that MacNaghten signed to take over the existing lease from Reynolds at the agreed figure of £2,500 per annum rental, but when he took possession found the theatre in a dirty condition and losing money steadily.

It was held that Reynolds could not be responsible for the competition arising from the rival dramatic theatres in Leeds—the Grand Theatre in Briggate and the Queens' Theatre in Holbeck—and in view of his advanced age and pending retirement could not reasonably be expected to spend money on improving the building. MacNaghten lost the case, and then began to consider the possibility of converting the Theatre Royal into a music hall. Barrasford anticipating this, spent £5,000 on improving the Tivoli next door, turning it into the new Leeds Hippodrome. Eventually MacNaghten disposed of the lease to Francis Laidler of Bradford.

*   *   *   *

With a 'tour' well established in the North of England,

MacNaghten, like his contemporaries, Moss, Stoll and Barrasford, had designs on the Metropolis. The first London hall to be acquired was the Foresters Music Hall in Cambridge Road, Mile End. This had been originally one of the old 'singing-rooms' attached to a tavern, but in 1893 it had been completely rebuilt as a well-fit up music hall by William Lusby. It boasted one of the finest stages in London and the capacity of the building was in the region of 3,000. It entered a new era of prosperity under the MacNaghten regime at the turn of the century.

In September, 1902 in partnership with George Belmont, MacNaghten assumed control of the old Surrey Theatre in Black-friars, which had an illustrious history as a home of melodrama under the Conquest family. Upon the death of George Conquest it was turned into a music hall. At the Surrey was a very famous scenic artist in Francis Bull, and Mr. Bull immediately became scenic artist for the entire MacNaghten Circuit.

Another hall running as a variety theatre by George Belmont was the Sadlers Wells Theatre, which had been re-opened by him in 1893. Sadlers Wells was another historic house, whose history could be traced back to 1683, the time of Mr. Sadler. Various theatres had been built on the site in Islington, but the one extant in 1878 was condemned as unsafe. A Mrs. Bateman had rebuilt it in 1880 as a home of melodrama but it had failed. Belmont had surprised everybody by making it pay as a music hall. Now, in 1902, he was anxious to dispose of his interests, to become 'Mine Host' of a public house in the Cambridge Circus area of the West End.

Accordingly, these halls, together with the Eastern Empire at Bow (which became the Bow Palace) were formed into a separate concern under the MacNaghten banner, known as the Music Hall Proprietary Corporation, but working in conjunction with the main MacNaghten Vaudeville Circuit.

The Eastern Empire had grown out of the Three Crowns Tavern, and it stood nearly opposite Bow Church. That fine old Protean actor Bransby Williams had given recitals and dramatic mono-logues there in the days before he became famous. In 1893 it was rebuilt as a music hall by the Marlowe family. In later years Fred Marlowe was to become famous for his active association with the Variety Artists Federation (The V.A.F.). MacNaghten turned the Eastern Empire into the Bow Palace and ran it very successfully.

In 1903 the Britannia Theatre at Hoxton was added to the tour. This was the house of melodrama with which the famous Mrs. Lane was connected, but after her death it entered a lean spell, for melodrama was then on the wane. Tom Barrasford re-opened the old Britannia as a music hall at Easter, 1903, but soon after this he decided to devote all his energies to reviving the Lyceum Theatre in the Strand as a music hall to spite his adversary, Oswald Stoll, who was formulating his plans for the huge Coliseum in St. Martins Lane. Therefore the variety bookings at the Britannia were transferred to the Proprietary Corporation. Actually, the variety period at the Britannia was hardly a success, for apart from the great Doctor Walford Bodie, who packed the place on several occasions, support was thin, and by 1908 'Penny Picture Matinees' were tried in an endeavour to attract more patrons.

While Mr. MacNaghten maintained a London residence at Bedford Court Mansions, he preferred to spend most of his time in Sheffield and so Fred Baugh, his old henchman from the early days, was put in charge of the London halls, with Sidney Arthur as booker. Trial Matinees (to discover new talent) were a feature at the Foresters Music Hall during this period. In February, 1908, a further hall in the Battersea Empire was added, to become the Battersea Palace. In later years Fred Baugh ran this hall himself with a fair measure of success.

*   *   *   *

Prior to 1903 all the halls forming part of the MacNaghten Vaudeville Circuit or its subsidiary companies had been taken over from other concerns. Now in this year the first hall actually to be built by the Circuit was opened. This was the Halifax Palace and, rather strangely, this was the last surviving theatre in 1959 when the Circuit was finally wound up.

The Halifax Palace, situated at a corner site with Horton Street, cost £40,000 to build, and the foundation stone was laid by Alderman Brear the previous year, the 4th of October, 1902. The architects were Messrs. Runtz and Company (builders of the Euston Music Hall and other famous properties) and the new Halifax Palace was to hold 2,500. The hall was built on the cantilever principle (i.e. no pillars in the auditorium) and was well fitted out. There was a beautifully painted sliding roof, and the rich, red tableaux curtains cost £300 the pair. The stage dimensions were: 60 ft. wide, by 32 ft. deep, with a proscenium opening of 30 ft. The Directors of the Halifax Palace Theatre Company, Ltd., were Messrs. T. R. Sanders (Chairman), Edgar Horsfall, C. F. Lawton and H. Birkenshaw, with Frank MacNaghten as Managing Director. Messrs. Sanders and Birkenshaw were local men; Mr. Horsfall an architect and Mr. Lawton a solicitor.

There was a private ceremony the Wednesday before the theatre opened to the public. This was attended by the Mayor of Halifax, Alderman Josiah Wade; Sir Alfred and Lady Arnold, and Archdeacon and Mrs. Brooke of Halifax. At this function a well-known local tenor, Mr. W. F. Fleming, sang the National Anthem and Tosti's 'My Dream'. Mr. Lawton spoke on behalf of the Directors and Archdeacon Brooke remarked: 'I never saw a building go up quicker.' Mr. Runtz, the architect, suitably responded, and the Mayor commented: 'This building is as good as anything they have in Blackpool—All success to the Palace Theatre.'

Mr. MacNaghten, who had just returned from attending the King's Levee in Dublin, in company with Sir Arthur E. Vicars, one of his titled relations, replied, saying:

'The Circuit now controls sixteen theatres and music halls and has met with success everywhere.

'The old "music hall" is in the transition stage from the singing-room to the new vaudeville variety theatre. The MacNaghten Vaudeville Circuit will provide theatres to which a man may bring his wife. I will cater for the ladies. To compete with the big syndicates I intend to import the cream of American and Continental talent.'

The Halifax Palace opened at Bank Holiday, the 3rd of August, 1903 with a big bill topped by Miss Julie Mackay, the American comedienne. Prices were 3d. to 1/- with 'Early Doors' extra. The manager was Mr. W. J. Murray, who came from Blackburn, and Tommy Murgatroyd from Bradford led the pit orchestra.

The new Palace did not meet with the success it deserved at first. MacNaghten had to buy out some of the shareholders, who were somewhat disgruntled. One reason for the meagre returns was that the Grand Theatre at North Bridge, the property of the Northern Theatres Company, changed over from melodrama to variety during 1903, thus causing acute competition. The old Peoples' Palace at the Oddfellows' Hall was re-opened for a time as a music hall, until the lease ran out, whereupon the bookings were transferred to the new Palace.

Later on, things picked up, and many famous personalities played the Halifax Palace down the years. In the wake of Julie Mackay came such 'stars' as George Robey, Gertie Gitana, Florrie Forde, Little Tich, Hettie King, Eugene Stratton, Charlie Chaplin (1906 in 'Casey's Court Nibbs') and Sir Harry Lauder.

Once, in 1920, an unknown Henry Hall (later leader of the B.B.C. Dance Orchestra), playing a concertina as a member of The Harmony Three, over-balanced and fell among the pit musicians.

This, fortunately without sustaining serious injury, but the foot-lights at that side of the stage were broken. Lily Morris, who was the following act, objected strongly to playing to indifferent light-ing, but all was put right in time for the second house.

In a broadcast in 1939 Mr. R. E. Horsfall, one of the original directors, speaking in the series 'Famous Music Halls', revealed that the winter of 1902 when the Palace was built was so severe that the mortar kept freezing. To prevent this, someone suggested that sugar should be mixed with it. This was done, and work was then able to continue. After this secret was revealed in the broadcast, the Palace became known to the Profession as 'Britain's Sweetest Theatre'. Mr. Horsfall was himself an architect, and it was prob-ably he that made the suggestion in the first place. He later designed several of the halls built by the Circuit.

*   *   *   *

Two further halls were added to the Circuit in 1904, at West Hartlepool and Grimsby, and neither proved advantageous acquisi-tions. The old Gaiety in Mainsforth Terrace, West Hartlepool, was built in 1869 as the New Theatre Royal, but confusion with another building in Whitby Street known as the Victoria Theatre Royal, had led to a change of name. At the turn of the century the Gaiety was in the hands of Carlton St. Aubyn, a former actor turned manager. He had turned the Gaiety over to variety in 1902 but after en-countering difficulties had vacated the hall at Easter, 1904.

MacNaghten's agents secured the lease on his behalf, changed the name to the Palace, as was now the usual procedure in suitable cases, and spared no expense in fitting-out the old hall in style. A lounge and smoke room was created, with moving palms, and there was an air of opulence about the theatre never before seen in the Hartlepools district. All was set for a Gala Bank Holiday opening.

Frank MacNaghten returned from America just in time to attend the opening ceremony, and brought with him Celina Bobe, the famous American dancing xylophonist to top the opening bill at the Palace. (The public house adjoining changed its name to the Palace Hotel at the same time.)

The West Hartlepool Palace was truly launched with *eclat* and did very good business as a twice-nightly hall for the next five years—until Dick Thornton erected the new Empire Theatre in Lynn Street—then MacNaghten handed over the Palace to old George Black, who was anxious to find a larger home for his mov-ing picture shows, the tiny chapel in John Street having outlived its usefulness. And so the Palace entered a new era as a cinema. Many years later it was to revert to its old name of 'The Gaiety' under Solly Sheckman, the Blyth cinema showman.

The Grimsby venture was the shortest on record. MacNaghten agreed to run the Palace Theatre on behalf of Messrs. Hewitts, the brewers, who had built the hall on the site of the old Theatre Royal, near their brewery at Corporation Bridge. With a fully-licensed buffet adjoining, the Palace was a fair-sized hall seating 1,500 and it opened on 12th December, 1904 with Harry Tate and Company topping the bill with their famous sketch 'Motoring'.

However, there was severe competition from T. Allan Edwardes, the Derby entrepreneur, who was running the old tin Hippodrome in Railway Street very successfully as a music hall. Also, the Curry family; who ran the Prince of Wales' Theatre, were planning a music hall to be erected in Duncombe Street, to be called the Tivoli. The Brewery Company were not satisfied with the results at the new Palace and Mr. MacNaghten's contract to run it on their behalf was cancelled after six months. Mr. Edwardes then assumed control, on the understanding that the Hippodrome was closed down. This was done and the Hippodrome bookings transferred to the new Palace. In later years the Hippodrome re-opened for a time as a cinema, but it was completely destroyed by fire in 1920.

During the next year or two the Circuit was strengthened by the incorporation of music halls in various parts of the country. Added were the Bath Pavilion (which became the Palace); Gordon's Palace of Varieties at Southampton, and the Grand Theatre, Cardiff, which became the Cardiff Palace.

The year 1907 saw two handsome halls built by the Circuit in the North. They were the Palace-Hippodromes at Warrington and Burnley. Why double-barrelled names were chosen is not quite clear, unless it was a precaution against future opposition. As it was, they were both known as 'Palace Theatres'.

The Warrington Palace was built in six months. Alderman Smethurst of that town laid the foundation stone on May Day, and the opening ceremony was performed on the 23rd of October 1907. The opening attraction was John Tiller's 'High Jinks' Company, a revue with music hall acts, and this was very well received. Tommy Murgatroyd (as usual) officiated in the pit, leading the newly-formed pit orchestra, but on this occasion he had some opposition, for with the 'High Jinks' Company was Kurkamp, the 'singing conductor', whose speciality was singing whilst conducting his own accompaniment by the orchestra. Kurkamp was a great personality, and fairly brought the house down with his rendering of 'Dixie' and other favourites in his rich, full baritone voice. Loud applause also greeted the appearance of the act-drop, painted by Mr. F. Bull of the Surrey Theatre, London. This showed a scene in Rylands Street, Warrington, complete with new electric tramcar!

Similar scenes took place a few months later at the opening of the new Burnley Palace on the 2nd December, 1907. This hall, a large one, holding 2,300 persons, was designed by Messrs. Richard Horsfall and Sons, of Halifax, now appointed architects for the Circuit.

According to the Prospectus issued for the erection of the Burnley Palace, the Limited Company to be formed would have £15,000 subscribed in £1 shares. Several local men became Directors, and Mr. Lawton, of Messrs. Hardy, Lawton and Co. of Sheffield, was the Secretary. Land had to be purchased at a cost of £7,600 before work on erection could begin. Shareholders were told: 'With Mr. MacNaghten as Managing Director, there is every prospect of success.' The only opposition in the town at that time came from W. C. Horner's Empire in Cow Lane, a converted spinning mill. Mr. MacNaghten was to receive a salary of £300 per annum for his services and Mr. Lawton £100 to act as Secretary.

The 'High Jinks' Company opened the Burnley Palace, as had been the case at Warrington. Mr. MacNaghten was present at the opening and made a speech, revealing that Burnley Palace was the twentieth hall to be added to the Circuit, as it then stood. Mr. MacNaghten went on to say that the halls owned or controlled at December, 1907, comprised the Palaces at Bath, Blackburn, Bradford, Cardiff, Lincoln, Southampton, Warrington and West Hartlepool. There was the King's Theatre at Nottingham, the Leicester Pavilion, and the Theatre Royals at Attercliffe, Chesterfield, Rotherham and Leeds. The London halls comprised the Bow Palace, Foresters Music Hall, Sadlers Wells Theatre, the Surrey Theatre, and an interest in the Britannia Theatre, Hoxton.

Continuing, Mr. MacNaghten went on:

'I am often asked why I call my halls "Palaces" and "Hippodromes". This is to draw a distinction between the old "musichall" of the past, frequented by men only, and the new Vaudeville entertainment of the present day, to be patronised by women and children.

'Anything noticed of an objectionable nature should be reported immediately to the manager. It will receive my immediate attention in Sheffield.'

The Burnley Palace did quite well as a music hall, in spite of opposition from Mr. Horner. The Palace was a large, most comfortable hall, well situated in 'The Centre'. The outlay on land purchase for this most central site had been money well spent.

*   *   *   *

February, 1908 saw the Battersea Empire taken over and added to the London Circuit, run by Fred Baugh. The Empire was in York Road, Battersea, and had originated in the Magpie, an old song-tavern attached to a public house. In 1875 it was known as 'The Battersea Music Hall' and a decade later it was flourishing under the control of G. W. 'Pony' Moore, as 'The Washington Music Hall'. The name was changed to the Empire at the turn of the century, and with the MacNaghten regime came another change of name—this time to the Palace.

At Whitsuntide Mr. MacNaghten took over the Pier Pavilion, Southport, on a seasonal basis. This hall had been erected in 1902 when the Pier was reconstructed, and had previously been run with Variety entertainment by a Mr. Bury. Mr. Ernest Longden, late of the Surrey Theatre, was put in to manage, and the Southport Pavilion opened on the 11th May, 1908 with the Bensons, direct from their success at the Palace Theatre, London, in a comedy scena entitled 'The Page and the Maid', with a strong supporting company.

The Pier Pavilion ran as a once-nightly hall only, and Raymond's Bio-Tableaux (an early form of the cinema) formed an important part of the programme. It was at this hall that 'Trial Matinees' to discover new talent were put on, and any act showing promise was given a tour of the Circuit.

Bank Holiday Monday, 1909 was a red-letter day for the MacNaghten Vaudeville Circuit, for on that day two new halls were added to the tour, and both proved very successful. One of them was the Huddersfield Palace, built by Richard Horsfall and Sons, and erected at the corner of Venn Street and Kirkgate. It was a stylish house, with a cupola, and the interior was very spacious, holding 1,600 comfortably. Charles T. Aldrich (the quick-change artist who later appeared at the first Royal Command Performance in 1912) topped the opening bill, which was very well received. The Palace was in direct opposition to the Hippodrome run by the Northern Theatres Company, but after some two years or so, the Palace proved the most popular Variety house of the two, and the Hippodrome became a Playhouse in all but name.

The other MacNaghten hall opened on that auspicious day was

the Carlisle Palace, in Botchergate. This had been erected by a company of local business men in 1906 and Signor Pepi, the Barrow entrepreneur, ran the Palace in conjunction with his halls at Barrow, Blackpool, Middlesbrough and other places.

The Carlisle Palace was losing money steadily, in spite of the fact that there was no opposition in the city, and at Easter, 1909, Pepi's services were dispensed with and the hall closed down. It was then leased to Frank MacNaghten who immediately spent a considerable sum of money in alterations and decorations. It re-opened with a large bill, topped by Will Douglas's Troupe of Five Jolly Bakers, on the 'Two-houses Nightly' system, and a special late tram was arranged to take passengers and patrons to Newtown after the last show. Mr. Julius Simpson, from West Hartlepool, was the new manager, and an arrangement was made with the Gaumont Company for the regular supply of 'Palace Pictures' which became an important part of the programme.

Under MacNaghten's energetic control, the Palace began to flourish, and ten years later, in 1919 he took over the lease from the Company and the Carlisle Palace passed into the control of the MacNaghten Vaudeville Circuit.

The year 1910 saw Variety discontinued at the Surrey Theatre, London, the hall reverting to melodrama. In 1911 Fred Baugh took over the lease of the Battersea Palace himself and ran it for a few years. On the other hand the Gordon Theatre at Stoke-on-Trent and the Grand at Stalybridge were added to the Circuit, both changing their names to 'Hippodromes' in the process.

*   *   *   *

The First War saw many changes, including the waning popularity of music hall. Many of the MacNaghten halls were disposed of at this time and the Music Hall Proprietary Corporation wound up. The North of England Theatres Corporation lasted until 1929 when the last of the halls playing melodrama (the Rotherham Theatre Royal) was disposed of as a cinema. Rather curiously, this hall made a striking 'come-back' a few years later as the Regent Theatre of Varieties, under new management.

In the 1930's came a further slump in music hall fortunes, consequent upon competition with new 'Talkie' cinemas and to some extent radio and dog racing. In 1932 the Blackburn Palace, with its huge capacity, was closed down by the Circuit as uneconomic. In 1934 Frank MacNaghten decided to convert some of the remaining halls into cinemas and so a separate film section of the Circuit was formed. The eight remaining halls of the Circuit at that time comprised the Palaces at Blackburn, Bradford, Burnley, Carlisle, Halifax, Huddersfield, Southampton and Warrington.

The Blackburn Palace re-opened in 1936 after alterations as a cinema, and the following year the Watch Committee of Bradford Corporation were concerned about the safety aspect of the Palace Theatre, Bradford, which was built beneath the Princes' Theatre. The renewal of the licence was refused and the Palace closed its doors for good in May, 1938. It was the Circuit's intention to build another variety theatre in Bradford, but the war clouds were gathering, and also in that year Mr. Frank MacNaghten passed away, aged 68 years.

A big fire destroyed the Huddersfield Palace in 1936 and a fine, modern theatre was built on the same site and opened the following year. The New Palace was built on cinema lines, complete with operating box, but it continued to be used as a variety theatre and at no time showed films. During the Second War it did very good business indeed, as did the Halifax Palace, eight miles distant.

During that War, in 1942, the only other Palace operating as a music hall, the Southampton Palace in Above Bar Street, was completely destroyed by enemy action. Mr. Jack Frettingham, the manager, then came to Halifax to take over the Palace in that town, a position he was to retain until the end.

While the two Palaces did good business in the 'boom period' which followed the Second War, in the 1950's the advent of television caused another slump and the Huddersfield Palace closed for a time in 1954. It re-opened after alterations but closed again in 1957. It was later re-opened as a Continental Theatre under new control.

At the end of 1957 the Circuit's three cinemas (at Blackburn, Carlisle and Warrington) closed down, but have since been re-opened by other concerns. The Halifax Palace attempted a revival by becoming a repertory theatre, but this was a failure. In 1959 that closed too, and the Circuit was wound up by the then Chairman, Mr. K. C. Meneer.

And so closed a notable chapter in music hall history.

10

Full Circle

IN THE 1950's television had been added to compete with the theatres and cinemas. Few would have thought it possible that the appeal of the cinema could rise and fall in a lifetime, but it did in no uncertain fashion. The rising popularity of television also killed the 'Post-War Boom' in Music Hall (or Variety as it had become).

But the proprietors of theatres and cinemas are showmen and do not give up easily. They fight back. The cinemas went in for wider screens, three-dimensional films, Cinerama and Cinema-Scope in an attempt to win back declining audiences. They had some success as far as the city-centre cinemas were concerned, in the larger towns, but the tiny street-corner 'movie house' in the suburbs was doomed. Hundreds of these closed down in the 1950's. Only the city cinemas allied to the big circuits were able to survive.

One result of the television competition on Music Hall proprietors was to stimulate them to present shows in the theatres which could not be shown on the tiny screen—in other words 'Girlie Shows'—and also to present the Continental style of entertainment. 'Continental' style means that eating and drinking are permitted in the auditorium whilst the stage show is taking place. This was, in effect, a reversion to the very earliest days of Music Hall in which entertainments took place in the supper rooms and song taverns. Music Hall had truly gone 'Full Circle'.

*   *   *   *

But to go back to the 'Thirties': The music hall magnates did not give up without a fight—even though it did seem the taste in public entertainment was changing. In the years of the all-conquering 'Talkies' several new variety theatres were built—and rebuilt—in an attempt to recapture lost business.

In some quarters the belief was held that, given a brand new theatre and bright surroundings, business would soon pick up again, when the novelty of talking films had worn off.

One praise-worthy attempt to cater for Variety lovers on these

190

lines—which unfortunately failed—was made at Stockton-on-Tees. Here, the position in brief was that the Hippodrome, for long the home of the town's music hall entertainment, was burned down in 1932. This was run by the Metcalfe family (trading as 'North Eastern Entertainments') and they decided to restore the Hippodrome as a 'Talkie' cinema, in view of the rather parlous state of the music hall at that time.

This decision left Stockton without Variety entertainment, the only 'live' hall in the town being the small Grand Theatre in Bishop Street, where repertory was then the bill of fare.

And so two Stockton brothers—Charles and Alfred Lewis—who professed to have 'great faith in the living theatre', decided to build the finest Variety theatre in the North East on the site of the Globe Cinema, at the top end of the High Street. Alfred, who was a Town Councillor at the time, said he earnestly believed that 'the tide of prosperity was returning to Teesside' and that the new theatre would be proof to all of that new prosperity.

The architects for the New Globe Theatre of Varieties were Messrs. Percy L. Brown and Sons, Ltd., of Newcastle upon Tyne, who were instructed to prepare plans for a building to hold 2,400 persons. The local firm of McLeod and Co. Ltd., of Thornaby-on-Tees were the general contractors, and the fibrous plaster work (considered an essential part of Variety theatres) was entrusted to Messrs. Webster, Davidson and Co. Ltd., of Sheffield.

The new building was ready for opening on the 18th December, 1935. The Globe was a fine structure, with a very wide frontage onto the High Street. It was sunk well below the ground; in fact, the balcony line was only twenty feet above street level. Green and gold was the interior colour *motif,* and a notable feature was the Pierrot and Pierrette style of decoration.

The then Mayor of Stockton, Alderman W. Newton, performed the opening ceremony, supported by Councillor Lewis and his brother, amid scenes of great enthusiasm. The opening attraction was the revue 'Why be Serious?' starring Will Mahoney, the comedian who had appeared that year in the Royal Variety Performance. Also in the revue were the famous Tiller Girls; Joe Griffin, a singer; Eric Hayes (described as a 'crooner'); Ernest Shannon doing 'impressions'; Bob Gant, an entertainer, and dancers Lennox and Powell. Prices were very modest at 6d. to 2/-.

Unfortunately, after a good start, the optimism of the Lewis brothers was not fulfilled. Either the tide of prosperity had not turned far enough, or Teessiders did not want Variety and revue. First-class bills, such as the then very famous Henry Hall and his

Orchestra (supported by well-known acts) were playing to half-empty houses, and it was not long before the new Globe Theatre of Variety was compelled to close its doors through lack of support.

It would seem that the populace of Stockton-on-Tees at that time did not want 'live' entertainment at all, for the little Grand Theatre in Bishop Street (the old Star Music Hall of 1883) fared no better. This also closed down in 1936, to re-open later in the year as the Plaza Cinema. Connected with the Grand Theatre for many years (before the change-over) was Mr. J. G. Curry, who managed the hall on behalf of the Grantham Theatre Circuit, of Newcastle upon Tyne.

The fate of the Globe was that when the doors did open again, this was also as a cinema—or rather, a super-cinema—for the A.B.C. circuit took over Globe in 1937. Devotees of the 'live' theatre had then to travel to Middlesborough, five miles away, where Variety still flourished at the Empire (erected in 1899 by J. Laurie Graydon, of the Middlesex Music Hall in London and later carried on by the Bastiman family of Middlesborough.)

However, the 'live' theatre was not entirely lost to Stockton for, in the rebuilding of the Hippodrome in 1933, the stage and equipment for a theatre had been retained. The Metcalfe family who controlled it reverted back to Variety for some years during and shortly after the Second War. Then came a spell of repertory before it was sold to Essoldo Cinemas in 1958. There are still occasional 'live' shows there and an annual pantomime at the A.B.C.-controlled Globe.

*   *   *   *

The Huddersfield Palace, opened on 1st March, 1937 (on the site of an earlier Palace destroyed by fire) has the reputation of being 'the last music hall to be built in the North of England', but the last *variety theatre* to be built was the New Blackpool Opera House in 1939. (Since that time the old Hippodrome in Church Street, Blackpool, has also been rebuilt as the A.B.C. cinema and theatre).

The New Blackpool Opera House was actually the *third* building of that name to occupy the site adjoining the Winter Gardens. The redoubtable William Holland, the self-styled 'Peoples' Caterer', who in his early days had been connected with the North Woolwich Gardens and the Albert Palace at Battersea, was responsible for the erection of the first Blackpool Opera House in 1889. This was destroyed by fire and a second Opera House opened on the same site in 1911. This also fell a victim to flames and a third building —the present New Opera House—was erected by the Blackpool Tower Company and completed in 1939.

FRANK MACNAGHTEN—Founder of the MacNaghten Vaudeville Circuit and other combines.

THE BACHELOR
ENTREPRENEUR

LEEDS THEATRE ROYAL — A MacNaghten Theatre from 1902–1909 when it was disposed of to Francis Laidler, Yorkshire's "King of Pantomime.

NOTTINGHAM GAIETY PALACE —Which MacNaghten acquired in 1901 and turned into the Kings' Theatre.

SCOTT BARRIE—"Dame" Comedian and favourite Northern "Drag" artist of the pre-1914 era.

Photo: Yorkshire Post

Plate 29

BILLS and BILLS!

Bills of the pre-1914 era contrasted with gaudy "Girlie" day-bills of the 1950's.

Plate 30

THE NYMPHS LOOK DOWN on a scene of desolation. The derelict Bedford Palace at Camden Town. Not even "F.J.B." could save this one . . .

(Below left) "AFTER THE FIRE": The fire-blackened "Two Performances Nightly" sign— All that remained of the old Argyle Theatre at Birkenhead after the "Blitz".

FORGOTTEN THEATRES

(Below) THE LAST ACT: Bulldozers play the last scene at the old Victoria, Burnley.

Plate 31

Sir LAURENCE OLIVIER as Archie Rice, the music hall comic in John Osborne's "THE ENTERTAINER". This picture, made by Woodfall Films, was shot on location in the Alhambra, Morecambe.

ENTERTAINERS ALL

PUB-LAND
KIM LESLIE singing with Tommy Fisher's "Mis-Fits" in the Dolphin Hotel at Wakefield.
(A scene from the film "THIS SPORTING LIFE").

CABARET — Theatre Club entertainer and TV personality BOB MONKHOUSE, who also controls the CHANGE IS CLUB in Bath Lane, Newcastle upon Tyne.

CLUB-LAND—"Mansfield's Entertainment Personality" JOHNNIE SINGLETON, a favourite Midlands Club Compere, and frequent broadcaster from "Radio Nottingham".

Plate 32

This opened for the season in style on the 15th July of that year with the Jack Taylor revue 'Turned Out Nice Again' starring George Formby and his wife, Beryl. Without doubt, the New Opera House is one of the finest theatre buildings in the country. Designed by C. H. McKeith (of Derham, McKeith and Partners) the hall seats 3,000. The massive stage, 100ft wide and 60ft deep, with a height to the grid of 110ft, is believed to be the largest in the country. Designed on the cantilever principle—that is, no pillars in the auditorium to obstruct the view—there is dressing room accommodation for upwards of 100 performers, while as many settings can be flown into the huge grid above the stage. The operator's box is also equipped with the latest cinematographic projection equipment for the showing of films 'off-season'.

The New Opera House at Blackpool is truly a magnificent structure and made a fitting venue for the first Royal Variety Performance to be held in the North (in 1955) in the presence of H.M. Queen Elizabeth and H.R.H. the Duke of Edinburgh.

Not far from the New Opera House in Blackpool is the Queens' Theatre, which is today also very successful, and upon which stage in the summer season is to seen and heard a galaxy of talent, the wage bill for same running into almost astronomical figures.

The Queens' Theatre started modestly enough in 1877 as the Borough Bazaar, but was always known in its early days as 'Bannister's' after its proprietor. Soon after the First War, Bert Feldman, the song publisher, took over the ground floor of the premises for song-plugging, and it was not long before entertainments were also being held in the large hall above.

In 1928 the upper hall blossomed out as a Variety theatre in the season, and 'off-season' there were films and repertory. About 1930 Bert Feldman gained control of the whole building and decided to re-build the entire structure as a moern Variety theatre. The old 'Feldman's' closed down after the 1937 season and in that winter considerable structural alterations were effected.

The architects for the rebuilding were Messrs. Derham, McKeith and Partners, of Blackpool, and the alterations cost £10,000. The old Bazaar of 1877 became unrecognisable. A new stage and scene dock were built on at the rear of the premises, the two floors being merged into a single building, with a circle. The new stage was now 19ft high, 21ft deep and the proscenium opening 25ft wide. Interior decorations were very pleasing and were carried out in eau-de-nil, russet and gold style. Many ideas incorporated in the re-modelling were put forward by Bob Johnson, Mr. Feldman's manager for many years.

G

The Blackpool Feldman's Theatre in its new guise opened with Burton Lester's Cowboy comedy show 'The Round-Up' on Easter Monday, 1938. It was a huge success, as was the first seasonal show 'Rockin' the Town', a revue starring comedian Reg. Bolton.

Jimmy Brennan, the Northern theatrical magnate, who bought Feldman's Theatre for £82,000 at an auction in 1952 and turned it into the highly successful Queens' Theatre, was a former Barrow scrap metal dealer. During the First War, at the age of 26, he bought the Tivoli Music Hall in that town (the old Star Palace, converted into the Tivoli by Rino Pepi) on the advice of Bert Aza, the agent, and made money running it. Later on, he bought several cinemas, including the Gaiety and Coliseum in Barrow, from the widow of Captain Calvert Routledge who was killed in action during 1917.

From this beginning Jimmy Brennan branched out as a theatre and cinema magnate and at one period had 28 cinemas and several theatres under his control. The latter included the Liverpool Pavilion and the Hulme Hippodrome. In 1935 Mr. Brennan acquired an active interest in the Wigan Hippodrome, a prosperous Variety theatre, previously run by the Worswick family. This was extensively modernised but in 1956 it was completely destroyed in a disastrous fire.

*   *   *   *

Another Northern music hall magnate with Blackpool connections was Alderman William Henry Broadhead, who died in 1930 at the age of 83, but his 'Tour', much reduced, lasted until 1955, being carried on by his grandchildren—Percy Baynham and Avril Broadhead.

Broadhead was a native of Mansfield (Notts.) who became a builder's apprentice at the age of fifteen. Later he was sent to Manchester on building work and there met and married Lottie Birch of Longsight, also opening a painting and decorating business in the city. In 1883 his health gave concern and he was ordered to live by the sea. He chose Blackpool and in 1889 began to organise 'swimming entertainments' at the old Prince of Wales' Baths on the sea front. Without doubt, these were the first organised 'aqua shows' in the country.

1893 saw Broadhead an Alderman, and also actively connected with the directorate of the Victoria Pier (now known as the South Pier) and a director of the Blackpool Tower Company. He became an advocate of temperance (when he came to run theatres, many of them never had a liquor licence) and was twice Mayor of Blackpool.

The first theatre he built was the Osborne in Manchester, opened

13th April, 1896, followed by the Metropole. Both these halls were erected in poor districts of the city and the idea was to bring dramatic productions 'of an uplifting moral nature' to a working-class public at prices they could afford. Then came the Grand Junction in 1901 followed by the Floral Hall and Hippodrome adjoining, making 'A vast Palace of Amusements for Hulme patrons'.

Not long after this interest in melodrama waned and the position arose that people were being turned away from the Hulme Hippodrome (showing music hall) with a capacity of 1,500 while the Grand Junction, which held 3,000 was playing to half empty houses. In 1905 the names of these halls were interchanged—the original Hippodrome became the Grand Junction (later the Playhouse) whilst the larger hall became the Hippodrome—and so Music Hall patrons were adequately catered for.

Rapid expansion of the Music Hall circuit took place after this, and at its height 'The Bread and Butter Tour' (as it became known) reached a maximum of fifteen properties, all within a few miles of Manchester. For some years, following 1909, the huge Winter Gardens at Morecambe came under Broadhead's control and in 1912 Richard Flanagan's Lyceum at Eccles was acquired—to become the Crown Theatre. The last Broadhead hall to be built was the Kings' Palace at Preston, opened in 1913.

Doubts were openly expressed at that time about the wisdom of building yet another palace of amusement in the town, as there were already two theatres and two music halls (the Theatre Royal and the Princes' Theatre, and the Empire and the Hippodrome, respectively). Incidentally, the Hippodrome in Preston was already a Broadhead house. With this multiplicity in the places of entertainment, the Princes' had had to go over to films, due to poor business, and yet here was Broadhead erecting yet another theatre in the town! It was suggested that 'saturation point' had already been reached in the number of halls open, with regard to the size of the population.

Broadhead's rejoinder to this criticism was to state that the new Kings' Palace would be the 'Most up-to-date Dramatic Theatre in Lancashire' and that he intended to bring to Preston, operas from the Grand Junction Theatre in Manchester, and pantomimes from the Pavilion Theatre, Liverpool. There would be no drink licence at the Kings' Palace, nor 'Promenade', but instead there would be two large lounges where tea and other light refreshments would be served.

The Kings' Palace Theatre, Preston, opened 6th February, 1913 with Charles Barnold's dog and monkey troupe in a scena entitled 'A Hot Time in Dogville' supported by Star Variety! The reason given for this extra-ordinary change in policy was (it was stated) that the Hippodrome (the other Broadhead theatre in Preston) was playing pantomime, and that the Circuit was anxious to keep up the big following for Variety, and its tradition, for which they were famous. Some weeks later, when pantomime at the Hippodrome was finished and Variety resumed, the stage of the Kings' Palace was occupied by Frank Adams' Dramatic Repertoire Company, giving a series of plays 'of an uplifting moral nature'—according to the bill matter.

The Preston Kings' Palace Theatre was different from most of the other Broadhead Theatres in its design and decoration, both internally and externally. Whereas the other Broadhead halls had a very set 'square' look about them—there was a rumour in the Profession that Broadhead had built them with the idea of turning them into factories if they failed as music halls—the new Preston theatre had a glazed terra-cotta exterior and looked very clean and smart from the outside, in fact upholding the best traditions of the Broadhead Motto: 'Quick, Clean, Smart and Bright'.

Inside, the Kings' Palace had a three-domed ceiling with a proscenium arch supported by colonnades of rouge-et-noir marble. The decorations of the hall were carried out by Mr. Bartlett, who had been responsible for the interior work at the Hammerstein Opera House in Kingsway, London (later the Stoll Theatre). These decorations were in the style of Louis XV, the motif being an attractive rose-de-barri pink. Seating capacity was for 2,600 (with standees 3,000) while the stage was 75ft wide by 35ft deep. Applegreen curtains added to the very pleasing general effect.

Manager at the Kings' Palace was Harry Winstanley who later became responsible (as general manager) for the whole Broadhead Tour, working from the Hulme Hippodrome. Mr. Edward Leigh (pupil of Heckover) was employed as the scenic artist. Topping the bill at the Preston Empire, the same week the Kings' Palace opened, was Jack Pleasants, the Bradford-born comedian; there was pantomime at the Hippodrome; films at the Princes' and Mr. George Alexander's Company in 'Bella Donna' at the Theatre Royal in Fishergate.

. In later years the Preston Kings' Palace became a 'Talkie' cinema for a time, but its final phase was as a Variety theatre again. When it closed down in 1955 it was the last of the Broadhead halls, apart from the Royal Hippodrome in Salford which outlived it by a few months.

The huge Morecambe Winter Gardens, reconstructed by the Broadhead Circuit in 1909, dated from 1878 when the site was originally occupied by 'The Palace, Baths and Aquarium'. Under Broadhead's control the former Aquarium became the Empress Ballroom; the baths became refreshment bars and billiard rooms, and the Palace was greatly enlarged to become the King's Pavilion music hall, capable of accommodating 3,000.

When many of the Broadhead halls were disposed of (in the 1930's) the Morecambe buildings (which had become the Winter Gardens) passed into the hands of the Obank Syndicate, who turned the huge theatre over to talking films. However, some years later, 'live' shows returned and the building passed into the control of Moss Empires in 1956.

Another Morecambe building which returned to use as a music hall after many years as a cinema, was the Alhambra, situated on the West End Promenade.

Dating from 1901, the Alhambra Palace (as it was originally named) was erected above the Alhambra Market and in its early years boasted a roof garden, from which wonderful views of Morecambe Bay and the Lake District could be obtained. Alderman John Gardner was responsible for its erection and the hall opened with the great Chung Ling Soo ('Chinese Magician Extra-Ordinary') topping a big bill of artistes. However, following the Broadhead enterprise at the Winter Gardens, the Alhambra became a cinema and continued as such until 1946 when Terence Byron revived the 'live' tradition there with a seasonal summer show.

In 1959 the Alhambra gained great notoriety when it was occupied by a film company making a picture of John Osborne's successful play 'The Entertainer'. Taking the part of Archie Rice—a broken-down music hall comic—was Sir Laurence Olivier. The theatre's interior made a fine setting for the film.

*   *   *   *

Several old music halls sprang to life again during the Second War and for a time afterwards, under the control of the Essoldo Cinema Circuit, of Newcastle upon Tyne.

The originator of the circuit was Solly Sheckman who, in 1925, re-opened the old wooden building known as 'Will Tudor's Circus' at Blyth as a boxing stadium. The place prospered and Mr. Sheckman extended his activities to the St. James' Hall in Newcastle, promoting there both boxing and wrestling tournaments. Then in 1930 two cinemas were acquired from Messrs. Blacks, of Sunderland. These were the Gaiety at West Hartlepool and the

Blyth Theatre Royal; other halls were progressively added and in 1939 there were about a dozen cinemas in the Sheckman Circuit, then known as 'North East Coast Cinemas, Ltd.'.

During the War the cinema combine expanded rapidly and by the 1950's there were over 200 'Essoldo' cinemas. The name 'Essoldo' was adopted as it was a transposition of Esther, Solly and Dorothy, the names of Mrs. Sheckman, Solly and their daughter.

The first Essoldo cinema to go 'live' was the Queens' at South Shields, but unfortunately the venture lasted only a few months. During the night of 9th April, 1941 Hitler's bombs destroyed the place, which was not restored. The show playing there at the time (to capacity business) was Lucan and McShane with their road show 'Old Mother Riley', and most of the properties were lost.

The South Shields Queens' was a notable building. It was built as 'The Borough Theatre' but due to a change in policy opened in 1913 as a 'Pictures and Variety' hall, as the Queens'. Built in Classical style, and occupying a corner site in Mile End Road, the Queens' held 2,000 and had a 40-ft. square stage, capable of taking large touring shows. It was designed by Messrs. Gibson and Steinlet, of North Shields, who were architects for twenty other theatres and cinemas in the North East.

During the War both the Blyth Royal and the Bishop Auckland Eden went 'live' again, after years as cinemas. Firstly it was repertory, by Frank H. Fortesque and his company, but later on Variety and revue were put on, playing to good business. In 1942 the Middlesbrough Royal was taken over and live entertainment put on, even though the Empire there was going strong with Variety under the energetic control of William Bastiman, J.P.

In other parts of the country the Variety revival continued under the Sheckman banner (with bookings by the Mannie Jay Agency) at the Doncaster Grand; the Barrow Coliseum; Penge Empire; Sheerness Hippodrome; Wakefield Opera House and the Southport Garrick. The latter is a very beautiful theatre, built in 1932, on the site of the burnt out Opera House.

*   *   *   *

A short lived venture was at Darlington, where the Premier Variety Agency rather optimistically tried to revive the old Livingstone Hall (a cinema for many years) as a Variety theatre in 1952. This was launched with a flourish as 'The New Astoria Theatre' but the enterprise lasted only a matter of months, principally because there was another Variety theatre in the town—the Hippodrome—run by 'Teddy' Hinge.

A very popular figure at the New Astoria during its short life was the musical director, Felix McCoy. An immaculate figure in full evening dress, he always received an ovation as he walked through the auditorium (followed by the spotlight and impressive 'drum roll') to take his place on the conductor's rostrum.

In another part of Darlington was the New Hippodrome, which was much more successful. This dated from 1907, having been erected in that year by the renowned Signor Pepi, who ran it in conjunction with other halls at Carlisle, Barrow, Bishop Auckland and Middlesbrough. Marie Loftus, the comedienne from Stockwell, Glasgow, topped the opening bill of 2nd September, 1907. Many famous stars of the music hall stage appeared there, including the great Walford Bodie, Florrie Forde (a great favourite) and Wee Georgie Wood made an early appearance. In 1927 the great ballerina Anna Pavlova packed the place.

The New Hippodrome ran for some years as a cinema after Pepi's death, and came under the control of E. J. Hinge, the Newcastle cinema magnate. In its latter years it reverted to Variety and revue and as such a place of entertainment it survived until June, 1956 when it closed down. (It has since been re-opened as a Civic Theatre.)

'Teddy' Hinge, who was responsible for the New Hippodrome's re-opening as a Variety theatre in the 'Post-War Boom' years, died in July, 1961. He was a native of Kent, and in his early years was an actor in touring productions. He toured for a long time with the 'Jollity Boys' and in 1910 was in stock company in Newcastle. There he met Stanley Rogers who owned a chain of cinemas in the North East. Mr. Rogers offered him the management of the Blaydon Palace—silent films and Variety—and Teddy accepted. When Mr. Rogers died, Hinge became managing director of Stanley Rogers Cinemas, Ltd. which was later re-named Hinge Circuit Cinemas, Ltd. and other properties acquired.

In 1946 Hinge's Productions, Ltd. was formed, with offices in Newcastle, to produce variety shows at Byker Grand and Gateshead Empire, as well as at the Darlington Hippodrome. Both these halls had run as cinemas for a long time—Byker Grand since 1910—and both made a successful return to 'live' entertainment. In 1954, however, with the 'Boom' period over, they were relinquished.

* * * *

The first indication of a 'Post-War Boom' in Variety came early in 1945 when Harry Buxton, of the Gaiety Theatre, Manchester, announced that he was prepared to change over his entire cinema

'empire' (comprising 23 halls) to live entertainment! What had
prompted this astonishing announcement from the head of the
Buxton Cinema Circuit was the impressive support received when
a pantomime was put on at the Pilot Cinema, Kings Lynn at
Christmas, 1944. This pantomime ran much longer than anticipated
and led Mr. Buxton to believe that there was a big potential following for music hall in the Provinces.

Among cinemas controlled at that time by the Buxton Circuit, in
addition to the Gaiety Theatre, Manchester and Kings Lynn Pilot,
were the Bradford Empire; Burnley Palace; Riviera, Teignmouth;
Regal, Blackburn; Regal, Bolton; Queens' Theatre, Ashton-under-
Lyne; Central Hall, Grantham; and the Colne Hippodrome.

This announcement upset Francis Laidler, of the Yorkshire
Theatres Co. Ltd., very much. Mr. Laidler issued a statement to the
effect that the terms of the lease under which the Buxton Circuit ran
the Bradford Empire precluded live entertainment in any form, and
that he could not permit any relaxation in this respect. Another
blow to Mr. Buxton's aspirations came at Manchester, where the
Watch Committee categorically refused to grant a theatrical licence
in respect of the old Gaiety Theatre, which had run as a cinema
since 1921.

In fact there was considerable opposition from many sources to
Mr. Buxton's schemes, and at Colne, where he did succeed in
restoring Variety, expectations were not realised. At Burnley, where
live entertainment was revived at the Palace (a cinema since 1934),
Mr. Buxton compromised by turning the lease over to Freddy
Butterworth, who ran the Burnley Palace for a few years as a music
hall in conjunction with his highly successful 'F.J.B. Circuit'.

*   *   *   *

One of the outstanding figures of the 'Post-War Boom' in Variety
was Freddy Butterworth—or 'F.J.B.' as he was known to the
Profession.

In fact it might be said that Mr. Butterworth did the near-
impossible.

The year 1935 was a year when the cinema-going craze was at its
height. All over the country hundreds of theatres and music halls
had been wired up for sound films. Shadows and canned nasal
accents reverberated across the footlights: people said Variety was
dead and it certainly seemed so. And yet, Mr. Butterworth—a
cinema manager himself—calmly got financial backing and set
about creating an entirely new 'Tour' of 'Number Two' variety
theatres by turning cinemas back into music halls!

It was an astonishing feat—on a par with that of Barrasford of years before—for the Tour consisted of a dozen or so halls when the 'boom' was at its height around 1950.

The first cinema to engage F.J.B.'s attention was the Scunthorpe Palace. In November 1935 comedian Joe Adams topped the first Variety bill in some 20 years. Scunthorpe was a rapidly growing steel town and soon the Palace was rebuilt as the Savoy, 'The Showplace of Lincolnshire', according to the bills. Latest type bucket seats were installed; a new colour motif in rose-de-barri pink and apple green graced the re-styled interior, and perhaps prophetically, the new building incorporated a Western Electric sound system and television box! Pianists Ivor Moreton and Dave Kaye (from Harry Roy's Band) topped the bill under the new order of things.

Mr. Butterworth then turned his attention to Lincoln and Grimsby, and both these places had music halls when the Second War broke out in 1939. An early casualty was the Grimsby Tivoli, for on 16th July, 1943 Nazi bombs wiped it out. Undeterred, F.J.B. promptly negotiated for the Palace Cinema, and moved in when the film booking programme was completed, with Variety, Talbot O'Farrell topping the first bill.

Promoted to manager at the Grimsby Palace was A. J. Mathews, who was to remain with the F.J.B. Circuit throughout its reign. Musical Director at the Palace was Ralph Powell, a musician of repute, and quite definitely the only 'M.D.' in the business with a genuine Stradivarius violin!

The War brought prosperity to the rapidly expanding F.J.B. Circuit, for the light-hearted Variety and revue bills put on at that time contrasted greatly with the grim realities and austerity then prevalent. In 1945 the Burnley Palace re-opened its doors as a 'live' hall; then came York Empire and a most notable acquisition in the transfer of Wolverhampton Hippodrome from the mighty Moss' Empires. (The latter was to remain the most prosperous hall in the Circuit until its destruction by fire in 1956.) A company known as Kilburn Varieties Ltd. was formed to run the Kilburn Empire and the Bedford Palace at Camden Town. Like his predecessors, Freddy Butterworth had reached the Metropolis!

In 1950 the Tour was at its height. Included were the Southampton Grand (restored after bomb damage); Bristol Empire; Aston Hippodrome; Norwich Hippodrome and the Boscombe Hippodrome, in addition to those already mentioned. Then Mr. Butterworth acquired the Chine Hotel at Bournemouth as an investment,

*G

and lived there. Booking control for the dozen or so theatres was in the hands of Frank Pope, the London agent.

The last hall to be acquired was the Northampton New, in 1954, but soon after this, due to the spread of television, the halls fell by the wayside, one by one. In 1959 Aston Hippodrome, the last of them, passed into other hands.

One, reason for the decline was that fewer and fewer of the touring revues took the road (the mainstay of 'Number Two' halls) providing booking difficulties. However, 'F.J.B.' made a notable contribution to Variety while it lasted.

*   *   *   *

Taking the 'Girlie' shows firstly: one of the curious and interesting facets of the 'Post-War Boom' in Variety had been the rise of what came to be known as 'touring revues'. As the popularity of television became more widespread—as more and more stations opened—the producers of these revues introduced 'posers' into their shows to attract business. The posers were, of course, chorus girls chosen for their Junoesque proportions, who bared their charms (or most of them) twice-nightly for the pleasure of patrons.

But, just as there had been eating and drinking in auditoriums before, there had been undressed females on the stage before. There is nothing new under the sun and certainly not in show business. A hundred years ago there were the 'Poses Plastiques' at the Parthenon, Liverpool, and other halls—which were 'living statuary' —although the models wore pink fleshings, the idea was the same. Also, there were all-female shows at the Whitebait Music Hall in Glasgow, where the performers were 'wired-in' for their own safety!

Fifty years ago, the music hall magnates became more daring. On the halls were touring acts like 'Madame Clasen's Living Art Bronzes'; The Venetians, in their 'Living Statuary' act, and the most famous of all, 'La Milo', billed as 'The Inimitable Breathing Marble'.

'La Milo' was Pansy Montague, an Australian girl, who posed (like so many of her present day counterparts) 'for art's sake'. She was petite, with a buxom figure, and appeared apparently completely nude, her body being covered with an enamel-like substance. Her poses included 'Hebe—the Goddess of Youth'; 'Sappho'; 'Venus de Milo'; 'Maidenhood' and 'Diana'. In between the poses her husband, who travelled with her as manager, did lightning-sketches of popular personalities under the stage name of Cruikshank.

In May 1907 she appeared at the Huddersfield Hippodrome,

and so daring was she that there was talk by the Church authorities in the town of her act being suppressed. This only led to 'House Full' boards being put out at the Hippodrome!

At Lincoln, a year later, it was stated that her rare grace had won the approbation of a very Puritanical critic of that day— W. T. Stead. In 1911 Pansy was mixed up in court proceedings and revealed her real name of Mrs. Eggena, but all came right in the end. She was an Australian girl, born on a ranch near Melbourne.

In 1908 Maud Allen, a classical dancer, caused a sensation at the London Palace Theatre with her dance interpretation of 'Salome'. The story got about that Maud wore nothing whatever beneath her diaphanous draperies, with the result that large crowds beseiged the Palace to see her.

The following year she made a provincial tour, causing controversy wherever she appeared. In February 1909, she was due to appear at Preston, but a meeting of the town clergy at the Guildhall caused the Watch Committee to withdraw their permission. In Manchester, a member of the Watch Committee is said to have been detailed to interview Maud (then appearing in a nearby town) and persuade her to wear panties beneath the draperies; then permission would be given. The story goes that Maud refused entry of the said gentleman to her dressing room, and refused to regard the mission in a serious light. When asked by the Press whether there *was* anything beneath the draperies, her reply was the 'classic' answer: 'No Comment'.

In August 1909, she was appearing at the Tower Theatre, New Brighton, and long before 'curtain up' there was 'standing room only' in all parts of the theatre. Many women attended, and at one performance the ladies very openly expressed their strong disapproval. The manager had to appeal for order before Maud could get on with her *piece de resistance* which was danced to Mendelssohn's 'Spring Song'. A writer on the event in the local Press commented:

'The dancer was visibly affected (by the demonstration) and one was impressed by the fact that she takes her art very seriously indeed.'

Manchester finally compromised in the matter by engaging Miss Mabillia Danielle to dance 'Salome' at the Theatre Royal. Whether Miss Danielle gave an undertaking to wear panties is not recorded in the minutes . . .

The 'Number Two' halls had their own 'Salome' in the person of Helen Roberts. She, too, caused controversy, particularly in

Darlington, but the fashion for 'Salome's' and nude posing died down, as do most crazes, only to be revived again later, to come up 'new' for another generation.

One example of this is the craze tor wrestling, which came strongly into vogue again in the 1950's. This led to many promoters in various towns, and consequently cut-throat competition. The solution was found when the various managers pooled their resources and spheres of influence in a concern known as 'Joint Promotions, Ltd.'.

The craze sixty or so years ago seemed to be sparked off by the Great Sandow, who toured the halls with his feats of strength. Then came Jack Carkeek, the Cornish wrestler, who was given a chance at the City Varieties in Leeds, to show his mettle by proprietor Fred Wood. Other managers got wind of this success, and there followed The Terrible Turk, and Hackenschmidt who drew enormous crowds. In 1908 at Manchester Hackenschmidt was challenging all and sundry from the stage at the Palace Theatre, while in nearby Salford the Sultan of Ranogoo was doing the very same thing. Why they did not simply fight each other and have done with it, is no doubt one of the unfathomable secrets of 'show business' . . .

*   *   *   *

Another facet of show business which changes with the years is the vogue for music. What was called 'Ragtime' was sparked off by a visit to America by Albert de Courville, as an emissary of the Moss Empires, to bring to this country exponents of a new style which was then causing a sensation in the United States.

The very name 'Ragtime' is supposed to have been coined by a negro in Coney Island, New York. When carried away in ecstasy by a pianist's curious habit of missing a beat in the music intentionally, he shouted: 'Man, play that ragged tune again!'

The late Peter Bernard, a French-Canadian whose real name was P. B. Lamorte, and who in later years ran the Huddersfield Theatre Royal, was one of the 'Pioneers of Ragtime'. In an interview with Leslie Baily, of B.B.C. 'Scrapbook' fame, he said:

'It was at a matinee at the London Hippodrome on the 23rd September, 1912 that I first sang 'Ragtime' in Europe.

'In 1912 I was in Coney Island, New York City and Albert de Courville, the famous London producer, came from England and arranged to take a Ragtime troupe there. Al Jolson and "Schnozzle" Durante were there at the time.

'Albert de Courville took seven of us to England and with

Melville Gideon (later famous as the pianist with the "Co-Optimists") we made our debut at the London Hippodrome in Charing Cross Road as the "Original American Ragtime Octette".

'We packed the Hippodrome for 14 weeks, then we made a tour. We were followed by a revue called "Hullo, Ragtime" which filled the vast London Hippodrome and ran up 451 performances there.'

In the foyer of the Theatre Royal, Huddersfield, which Peter Bernard ran from 1955 right up to his death in 1960 (as a repertory theatre in conjunction with his second wife, Nita Valerie), there hung a playbill of which he was very proud, and never neglected an opportunity of drawing anyone's attention to it, if they evinced the slightest interest in show business.

The bill was dated Easter Monday, 24th March, 1913 and related to the Stoll music hall known as 'The St. Augustines' Parade Hippodrome' in Bristol. The top of the bill act was the 'Famous Original American Ragtime Octette' and in support was Lupino Lane, the famous comedian and pantomimist, and Fred Russell, the noted veteran ventriloquist, and father of the great Val Parnell, of London Palladium fame, together with other supporting acts.

The personnel of the American Ragtime Octette on this bill was given as Peter Bernard, George Britt, Harry Bloom, H. Tinner, Jack Butler, N. Coster, William Woods and Charles Reid (pianist). This was the make-up of the Octette for the tour following the season at the London Hippodrome.

In 1952 there was some correspondence in the Profession's own paper *The Performer* about the Octette and its activities, and a letter appeared from Jack Butler, one of the original members, then retired from the Profession, and living in Coventry.

Jack Butler wrote:

'I, like Peter Bernard, was one of the original Octette and am still here. I have retired from show business after being with the late Duggie Wakefield for the last ten years.

'The solos sung by the different members of the Octette were "Hitchy Koo" (Peter Bernard); "Ragging the Baby to Sleep" (George Britt); "Ragtime Jockey" (Peter Bernard); "Ghost of a Violin" (Harry Bloom) and "Waiting for the Robert E. Lee" (Jack Butler and George Britt).'

Peter Bernard continued as a solo turn—songs at the piano—in Variety until 1952 when he married Nita Valerie, the Preston-born soubrette. Then they took over the Winter Gardens Theatre at New Brighton for a season or two, before taking the Winter Gardens Players to Huddersfield.

Peter used to like to reminisce about the old Octette and with very little persuasion, would warble:

> 'Oh! Every evening hear her sing,
>
> It's the cutest little thing,
>
> Got the cutest little swing,
>
> Hitchy-Koo, Hitchy-Koo, Hitchy-Koo'

*   *   *   *

Between the wars the fashion changed from Ragtime to the syncopation of large jazz bands. At several of the larger London hotels there sprang up orchestras like the Savoy Hotel Orpheans, where Carroll Gibbons held sway, and it was not long before these large orchestras took the Variety stage by storm. Broadcasting also helped to make them popular, and bands like those organised by Jack Hylton, the Bolton lad who played the organ at the old Stoke Newington Alexandra in 1913, and Jack Payne, who was co-opted to run the B.B.C.'s own dance band, became famous figures in the dance band world.

Other bands from the larger London hotels included Ambrose and his Orchestra, from the Mayfair Hotel; Harry Roy's Band from the Kit Kat Club; Sydney Lipton's Orchestra from Grosvenor House; Lew Stone from the Monseigneur Restaurant, Charlie Kunz, Billy Cotton and many others.

Many of these large dance bands toured the variety halls and made big money—in particular Ambrose, Harry Roy and Billy Cotton. Two very notable pianists began with Harry Roy and later made a great name for themselves as a double turn in Variety. They were Ivor Moreton and Dave Kaye.

Of these large orchestras, only Billy Cotton and his Band survived the years. They were a big draw with their 'Wakey-Wakey' band show on television and 'Billy Cotton's Music Hall' (in which Guest Artistes were introduced) was also very popular. The rest of them had fallen by the wayside, being unable to adapt themselves to the new medium and changed conditions.

Nowadays the era of the big stage band is definitely over. The emphasis is upon small groups—about the size of the American Octette—but how far removed from them in style and presentation! Twanging guitars and one-note saxophones have replaced the quaint jazz of the Ragtime bands, not to mention the long-haired, knock-kneed so-called vocalists. However, the small group is now definitely back in favour, but in a new guise.

There was a time when organs were very popular. The era of the cinema organ began about 1920. Then came the portable touring organs of the music halls, such as that large and magnificent instrument (weighing 9 tons in all) travelled around by G. R. Pattman upon which all sorts of effects could be produced. Pattman was a F.R.C.O. and formerly played at St. Mary's Cathedral in Glasgow. Following his tours of the music halls, he ended his career as resident organist at the Astoria Ballroom in Charing Cross Road, London.

In the 1930's no 'super' cinema worthy of the name was complete without its Mighty Wurlitzer, but during the Second War these instruments suddenly lost favour. In 1969 only Reginald Dixon held the fort at Blackpool Tower upon one of these instruments, which he played for dancing. Now he has retired.

*   *   *   *

When television was becoming more widespread in the 1950's, the mainstay of the 'Number Two' theatres was the popular touring revue, in which such figures as Terry ('Toby Jug') Cantor, Curly Jay, Dan Young and Ken Palmer were prominent. In an attempt to make these revues even more popular the proprietors and producers of these delectable delicacies decided that nudity was the answer. One reason being that nudity could not be displayed on television, whereas it could be introduced into the music halls provided that the bounds of propriety were not exceeded and that the Lord Chamberlain was satisfied that the law in this respect was being complied with.

What seemed to be the main essential—or could it be the bare essential?—of these requirements, was that the nude should not move. On occasions when they did, there was trouble and sometimes legal action was invoked, as was the case with Phyllis Dixey. Miss Dixey was a 'stripper' who toured the halls in the 1940's and 1950's accompanied by her husband Jack ('Snuffy') Tracey, who acted as her manager. Usually her show was entitled 'Peek-A-Boo' and this was a legacy of a very successful war-time show she had appeared in at London's Whitehall Theatre, which had run a long time.

Miss Dixey, like most of her contemporaries, posed 'for art's sake', and she became almost an institution at the Leeds City

Varieties, where she paid a return visit every year, usually about
Christmas time, with her 'Peek-A-Boo' show. On at least two
occasions Miss Dixey overstepped the mark and the result was
legal action brought about by 'common informers'. One notable
case was at Scunthorpe, and another was at Northampton, after
an appearance at the New Theatre. In connection with this latter
case, Lou Warwick, in his admirable book 'Death of a Theatre'
has written:

> 'Miss Dixey was a "stripper" with a difference, stripping
> with a dignity almost achieving decorum. She showed no more
> awareness of the entertainment value of her disrobing than
> if she were doing it for the doctor instead of goggle-eyed
> rows of men.

> 'She had toured the country without much objection being
> taken to her act, but when she came to Northampton someone
> in the audience was really startled by what he (or she) saw,
> and chose to become a common informer by complaining to
> the police . . .

> 'Pinning Miss Dixey down to face the summons "that she
> did exhibit an indecent act" proved somewhat difficult, for she
> was still touring. Three times she failed to turn up at the
> Court House . . . When she did finally submit herself, and
> after the police had given some diverting evidence about the
> exact sequence of her movements on stage, and how she came
> down into the auditorium for a gentleman patron in the front
> row to assist her by undoing a button, the case was dismissed,
> and Mrs. Grundy had been defeated.

> 'Also given in evidence was the fact that Phyllis Dixey
> announced as she first appeared: "I expect you are waiting to
> see Phyllis Dixey, the cow. I am Phyllis Dixey. I am just
> 50 and perhaps three" a statement which was received with
> incredulity by all concerned.'

In February, 1959, the newspapers reported that Miss Dixey
was happily working as a cook. She had gone bankrupt in the
intervening years, due to the decline in the number of music halls.

Other 'Stars of Strip' in the 1950's were 'Jane' who appeared
with a little dachshund, 'Fritzi', and who was based on a character
made famous by the *Daily Mirror* cartoonist Ferrier, and Blondie
('Godiva') Haigh, so-called because she had attempted on one
occasion to ride almost naked through Piccadilly Circus in London,
mounted on a bicycle, for a publicity stunt.

A typical 20-week Tour of the 'Number Two' music halls taken by an actual touring 'Girlie' show in the early 1950's, showing the takings:

Theatre	£ Profit	£ Loss
Aston Hippodrome	99	—
Norwich Hippodrome	93	—
Bristol Empire	5	—
Walham Green Granville	—	88
Grimsby Palace	—	35
Bedford Royal County	—	25
Salford Hippodrome	45	—
Preston Hippodrome	—	4
New Brighton Tivoli	43	—
West Bromwich Plaza	28	—
(second week) do.	—	15
Poplar Queens'	—	35
Woolwich Empire	—	64
Keighley Hippodrome	32	—
Islington Collins	23	—
Camberwell Palace	4	—
Chatham Empire	21	—
Chesterfield Hippodrome	—	15
Burnley Palace	—	15
St. Helens Royal	—	53
	£393	£349

Nett Profit on 20-week Tour = £44.

But the mainstay of the 'Number Two' variety theatres in the declining years of the 'fifties was the touring revue, incorporating a Nude Show. A good description of this type of show is given by Lou Warwick.

His apt recollection runs as follows:

'The Nude Show was generally a second class revue—a speciality act or two, a comedian and his feed (that's the man who says the straight lines, leaving the funny ones to his higher-paid partner), a few sketches (often so familiar that one knew the end shortly after the first lines had been said); a musical act, and a team of chorus girls employed especially in "production numbers"—favourite among these was the Can-

Can, which was witnessed week after week, *ad infinitum.*

'And last, but not least, were the Nudes. Most weeks it was in the singular, with just one young woman going through a routine of poses, accompanied by a usually saccharinous commentary, and divided by the curtains swishing to and fro—in order to allow the young miss to move from one pose to another, movement being forbidden in the public gaze. Some weeks however, it was nudes in the plural, and one week saw six feminine chests bared in one eye-taking finale.

The titles of some of these shows made interesting reading. A few that spring to mind in that period include 'Sexciting', 'The Naughtiest Girl of All' (this starred Pauline Penny, assisted in the comedy sphere by her husband and manager, Barry Piddock); 'We Never Clothed' (an ingenious variation of the theme of the London Windmill Theatre production 'We Never Closed'); 'Bare-skins and Blushes'; 'Halt, Who Goes Bare?' and almost inevitably 'Strip, Strip, Hooray!'

The peculiar part about these shows was that the revue itself often contained nothing to connect it with the title, giving one the impression that more thought had often gone into the choice of title than into the actual production itself. In fact one critic said of 'A Night with the Naughtiest Girls' that if that was all they were capable of, then 'sin' was on the way out . . .

*   *   *   *

The position was reached in the late 1950's that so many music halls had closed down that it was not worth a manager's while to put a touring show on the road. While many managers and agents simply went out of business, or rather, went into other lines of business (one Bolton variety agent became a house and property agent) others sought alternative means, particularly those who had done well out of the touring Nude shows.

One of these, Paul Raymond by name, did very well indeed for himself by investing the proceeds of four years 'strip shows' into the Revuebar which he opened in Brewer Street in London's Soho. In 1960 he was reported to be making £2,000 a week out of the business—more than ten times the salary of the British Prime Minister!

Paul Raymond's is quite a success story. Born Geff Quinn in Glossop in 1928, as a young man he used to like to take the train into Stockport or Manchester and spend all his spare time and cash at the music halls there. After the war he opened a second-hand pram business in Manchester, but was always 'show business

crazy' according to one of his associates, and threw up this undertaking to take a chance with Nude show management in London.
There is a legend that when he arrived in London in the early
1950's—upon the back of a lorry—he had only one-and-fourpence
in his pocket!

The Raymond Revuebar opened in 1958 and after two years in
business there Paul Raymond owned a £20,000 house and several
cars. His attractive wife was formerly Jean Bradley, a dancer in
the Ballet Montparnasse that graced one of his early touring
revues. (His first touring revue was 'We Strip Tonight' which ran
from 1953 to 1957 and rather appropriately made its farewell stage
appearance in Manchester.)

The Raymond Revuebar is said to be worth well over £125,000.
It was formerly the Doric Rooms, a dance-hall with a liquor
licence, and made an ideal building for adaptation as an intimate
theatre club. The Revuebar seats 300 and there are three strip
shows a day; 70,000 members are reported to be on its books and
the bar takings 'fantastic'. Small wonder Paul Raymond is reported
to be making £2,000 a week in a world of crazy values.

*   *   *   *

An alternative to the 'Girlie' type of show as a means of keep-
ing the music halls open was the 'Continental' idea first tried out
at Hull in 1958 by Mr. Harold Clarke at the Palace Theatre. This
form of show was subsequently adopted by other managements,
notably at Middlesbrough, Bolton, Chatham and Huddersfield, but
not with the same degree of success. However, the Continental
style was later adopted by the theatre clubs, nowadays so prevalent.

Actually, the Continental idea was simply a reversion to the
very first formula of the old music halls of a century ago of eating
and drinking in the auditorium.

The first of these 'Continental' conversions, the Hull Palace, was
the idea of managing director Harold Clarke, head of Kingston
Varieties, Ltd. The Palace was an old building, dating from 1897,
and for many years part of the Moss Empires' circuit. It was closed
due to bomb damage in 1940 and remained closed until 1951 when
it was repaired and sold to Kingston Varieties, Ltd.

This company ran the Tivoli, Hull, also out of action for a time
in the war. For a few years both halls ran as music halls. However,
with the decline in attendances, due to television, it was decided to
close the Tivoli and concentrate activity at the Palace. The Palace
continued as Hull's variety theatre until 1957 when dwindling

audiences caused concern. The outcome was Harold Clarke's idea
to convert the Palace into a Continental-style hall.

The new Continental Palace opened at Easter, 1958 and was a
great success. It was widely advertised as 'Hull's Gay Spot', and
continued to do well for a number of years. This conversion was
closely watched by other managements and no sooner was the Hull
venture under way than the announcement was made that plans
had been passed for the conversion of the Moss Empires' London
Hippodrome into a theatre restaurant, to be known as 'The Talk
of the Town'. This altered building opened later in 1958 and was
also successful.

Mr. Clarke made the following statement at the re-opening of the
Hull Continental Palace:

'The time has come for a change in the formula of Variety.
The people want a new angle and I believe I have found it.

'My wife and I made several trips to the Continent to study
methods of entertainment presented there and this is the result.
The Palace will not be a Club, but a place where the whole
family can go, or the young man take his girl friend. There
will be no Strip-tease.'

'There will be a cover charge at 2/6d. (the Promenade at
the back will cost only 1/-) and for this sum patrons can watch
the show and have a drink, and can go up on the stage to
dance to a resident band which will replace the pit orchestra.

'At 10 p.m. each night a Master of Ceremonies will act as
Host for a spell of Olde-Tyme Music Hall with everyone
joining in the choruses.'

But what gave the Hull Palace its real 'Continental' atmosphere
was the removal of the traditional seating from the auditorium and
the substitution of tables and chairs, at which waitresses served
drinks and food as the show went on. The Hull experiment was
closely followed by other managements in all parts of the country
and it was not long before other similar schemes were under way,
apart from the London Hippodrome venture.

The Middlesbrough Continental Empire opened its doors in
March 1959 and for a time did well. Then business fell away and
after a period of closure was sold as a Bingo hall. Other short-
lived conversions were at Chatham, Bolton and Castleford. Another
Continental Palace to go over finally to Bingo was the Huddersfield
Continental.

However, if the Continental-style music halls failed, they at least
paved the way for the Theatre Clubs, where eating and drinking
is permitted in the auditorium while the show is in progress.

Usually there is gaming of some sort in connection with the building being a Club for members only. One notable exception is the Batley Variety Club opened in March 1967, where so far, at any rate, gaming is not permitted. Theatre Clubs are now 'big business' and the Bailey Organisation likens itself to 'The Moss Empires' of Clubland'. Strangely enough, this concern originated in South Shields and Newcastle.

The popular television show 'Stars and Garters' focused attention on the entertainment in public houses, which is also now enjoying a boom following the demise of the music halls.

* * * *

What killed Variety? Is it in fact dead? Certainly the whole public taste in entertainment has changed. The Nudes killed the family show and the family show died because the novelty had gone from it. The sight of a man standing on his head or a girl trying to make both ends meet had become a novelty no longer. It had all been done before. It is just a matter of how much better one act can perform the feat than another. There was nothing new in Variety and Variety died because the very essence of freshness had gone from it.

Although Variety died in the music halls it goes on flourishing in the clubs and pubs—the modern counterpart of the old concert rooms—where in fact it all began. Always, it seems, there will be the urge for self-expression and so there will be some medium for entertainment, be it pub or club, pavilion at the end of the pier, or cabaret. Even radio and television . . .

'There's no Business like Show Business.'

It certainly has magic. There will always be someone somewhere who will take a chance with a new venture. And, who knows? The public taste in entertainment may change again. There's no business like it . . .

Finale ... Curtain Fall ...
By Public Demand

ALTHOUGH HERE and there, at places like the City Varieties in Leeds, the New Metropole in Glasgow, and a few survivors of the Moss Empires' combine Variety struggles on, 'Music Hall' died in the 1950's.

It has been a long time dying. As long ago as 1920 the critics were writing off Music Hall as a back number. It was dead, but it would not lie down. However, the advent of the 'sixties really wrote 'Finis' to it. The taste in entertainment had changed.

Early in 1958 the Woolwich Empire closed down. It was not the last Music Hall in London—for the old Metropolitan struggled on a few more years—but it was the last South of the Thames.

Daily Mail critic Robert Muller wrote its epitaph in telling words. The report was so typical of the demise of many other Empires and Hippodromes throughout the country:

'In a grey side street behind Woolwich Market a theatre is dying. From the grimed walls the posters are gasping their last promise of glamour: "Ecstasie" is the title of the final show.

'The old silver star on the door of No. 1 dressing room is smeared with lipstick. There is a strong aroma of cold tea and cats . . .'

'Come on, girls,' says Les, the stage manager.

'With the house almost empty (the show is continuous) the Four Empire Lovelies come strutting on-stage to proclaim that diamonds are a girl's best friend . . . Fresh and bouncy, they giggle at the men standing in the wings. Understandably. There are more of them there than out front . . .

'From the empty gilt boxes, cherubs are grinning down on another patron (single, male) as he tramps down the creaking centre aisle.

'Hands deep in overcoat pockets, he chooses his seat, slumps down and confronts himself with his own misery. He is still alone. Up there is Experienced Comic . . .

214

' "Do you drink?" Experienced Comic opens his act. "Here, suck this", and he hands a baby's bottle down to the pianist. Not a titter.

' "I know there's somebody out there", he tells the silent witnesses of his despair, "I can hear them breathing". (There are 39 men and 3 women in the stalls). "I never surrender" he says. "What I want to know is, what would happen if I told *old* gags?" Silence . . .

'After fifteen long minutes, Experienced Comic takes his bow. Leaving the stage he glares at his audience. He would consign us to a lingering death, if we were not dead already.

'On with the Show.

'Exotic Model minces about in panties and bra, waving a chiffon square. The patrons keep their hands deep in their pockets. They can't be asleep, because occasionally there is the sound of chocolate breaking.

'The general manager is dapper and busy. He says: "We're closing for lack of biz, see? We go into darkness, tomorrow. Everybody gets the sack. This place will deteriorate and deteriorate, and that will be the end of it. Do you know how many theatres have closed in the last three years (1955–8)? One hundred and fifty-five. So where are you?

"Don't miss this next act . . . Rusty . . . I'm producing her myself. For the West End . . ."

'Rusty (going places) is a sequinned blonde who croons down a microphone.

'In the course of her second song, she unzips her dress down the front and begins to pose . . .

'In the dress circle bar a sleepy patron listens to the voice coming through the loudspeaker. 'Marlene Dietrich' he says to himself.

'Dirt-track' says Emily, and pours herself a small port. Emily has been a bar-maid here for 40 years.

' "We used to have Gracie here", she says. "Marie Lloyd, too. And Nellie Wallace and Charlie Chaplin. These young folk never even heard of the old-timers. Nudes. That's what has killed the business. Who wants to take their children to see girls undressing?"

'Down in the stalls, hooting, gurgling and barking accompany Rusty's last rites. A few pseudo Teddies, armed with chips, field-glasses and their girl friends, are squirming in their seats . . .

'Joe, the tiny-eyed juggler comes on, in a black wig and red bow tie. He is in his seventies. 'Cheer up, cheer up', he admonishes his patrons. 'Who said that lady was a cripple? She had two legs in one knicker!

'That gets a laugh.

'Later, Exotic Model goes on for her fan dance. She grits her teeth bravely at the boys who break the heavy silence with kissing noises and ironic shouts of 'Lo-ver-ley'. Exotic Model ends her act in transparent nightie.

'Empire Lovelies get ready to go on. June, one of them, is 20. "I'll never leave show business" she says, breathlessly, her eyes shining. "It's not work to me, it's pleasure. Doesn't matter how upset you are. You go out there and you're sort of smiling for them, see?

'The Four Empire Lovelies go on to close the show. They sing:

' "There's no business like Show Business . . ." '

Down comes the curtain and its Curtain Fall for another old Music Hall.

Acknowledgments

MANY PEOPLE have assisted the author in the preparation of this book, which has been compiled by reference to cuttings, newspaper files, books, reminiscences and interviews with many people over a period of 20 years.

In this connection journalists have been especially helpful, both by indicating sources of material and the placing of cuttings and other data at the writer's disposal. Their ranks include Emrys Bryson of Nottingham; G. F. Morton of Lincoln; J. W. F. Lyons of Doncaster; Miss Y. N. Evans of Radcliffe; Stanley Chadwick of Huddersfield; Lou Warwick of Northampton and Peter Holdsworth of Bradford, together with his predecessor, the late J. C. Handby ('Mr. Dangle' of the *Telegraph and Argus*).

Theatrical journalists who have assisted, both by providing introductions and data, include James Hartley, Gordon Irving and D. Knox-Crichton (all of *The Stage*) and Messrs. Bruce Benson, Ted Cooper and Alfred J. Leighton of *The World's Fair*.

Others, to whom the author is indebted for research on his behalf, include Ted Bottle of Leicester; Harold Brearley of Manchester; Alex Robertson of Dundee; Harold Manning of Birmingham and Dennis Farquhar of Wallasey, near Liverpool.

Assisting with the illustrations have been Arnold Lever (Larno); Roy Leo; Tommy Graham; Harry Davis and the Exors. of the late H. O. Barry. The *Yorkshire Post, Sunderland Echo, Bradford Pictorial* and the Associated Newspapers group have contributed pictures, together with Press photographers D. Worrall and B. Fearnley. Other photographs have been loaned by private collectors.

Thanks are due to the Dalesman Publishing Company, of Clapham via Lancaster (publishers of 'Poms-Poms and Ruffles') for permission to reproduce certain material and photographs; to the *Daily Mail* for co-operation over Robert Muller's feature; the work of Miss M. Toyer (on Northampton), Miss R. M. Farrell (on Dick Thornton) and Arthur Willcox (Moss' Empires) is acknowledged, while the British Music Hall Society has been helpful.

A 'Stupendiforous Ta' is due to Ken Dodd for his Introduction and interest; a very great 'Thank You' to George Wood, O.B.E. for kindly writing the Foreword, also another one each to Eric Martin and Johnnie Singleton, for, without their constant encouragement, the writer would have downed tools long ago.

217

Personality Index

'Lancashire Lassies', 93
Lashwood, George, 29, 36, 62, 89
Lauder, Harry (Sir), 30, 36, 39, 46, 55, 98, 179, 183
Laurel, Stan, 50, 96, 113, 116
Lea, Lilian, 37, 129
Leglere, George, 143-144
Leno, Dan, 24-26, 38, 46, 77-79
Leo, Roy, 113
Littler, Prince, 135, 155-156
Livermore, Brothers, 28, 177-178
Lloyd, Marie, 26, 28, 46, 61-62
Loftus, Marie, 26, 43, 128
Lucan and McShane, 91-92, 198

MacDermott, The Great, 49, 58-59
MacDonnell, Leslie, 53, 135, 179
MacNaghten, Frank, 75, 127, 143, 146, 147, 158, 162-163, 166, 174-189
MacNaghten Vaudeville Circuit, 174-189
Mackney, E. W., 18, 58
Marriott, R. B. (Critic), 105
Martin, Eric (Agent), 94
Matcham, Frank (Architect), 51, 125-126, 129-130, 131-135, 144-150, 153, 160-161
Milo, La, 202-203
Miller, Max, 76
Modley, Albert, 72, 95
Morecambe and Wise, 90
Morell and Mouillot, 49, 128
Morton, Charles, 17, 19, 20, 58-59, 67
Morton, George, 41, 129
Moss Empires, 121-139
Moss, H. E. (Sir Edward), 29-30, 71-73, 121-136, 144, 148, 152, 157, 161, 172
'Mumming Birds', 96
Murray, Will, 112-113
Music Hall Proprietary Corporation, 21, 181-182

Naughton and Gold, 52
Nervo and Knox, 52
Nicholls, Horatio, 81
Norris, Max and Maisie, 56
North of England Theatres Corporation, 174, 176, 180
Northern Theatres Company, 130, 183, 187

O'Farrell, Talbot, 91, 201
Ohmy, King ('Ohmy the Flier'), 38, 78, 102
Olivier, Sir Laurence, 197
Osborne, John, 197
O'Shea, Tessie, 92

Palmer, Ken, 97, 207
Parnell, Val, 52, 67, 138
Parsons family, 93
Pattman, G. R., 207
'Paul's', 63, 146, 180
Paul, Sam, 84
Payne, George Adney, 19, 51-52
Payne, Jack, 206
Peers, Donald, 37, 42
Pepi, Signor Rino, 74, 188
Pink, Wal, 97, 126, 178
Pitt, Archie, 104

Pleasants, Jack, 46, 88-89, 196
Pope, Frank (Agent), 202
Popplewell family, 53-57, 84
Powell, Sandy, 95
Priestley, J. B., 54
Pryde, Peggy, 61, 123
Randle, Frank, 95-96
Ray, Ted, 86-87, 161
Raymond, Paul, 210-211
Reeve, Ada, 26
Retford, Ella, 51, 92
Robey, George (Sir), 75, 84, 183
Ross, Don, 91-93
Rowley, J. W., 43, 49, 146
Roy, George le, 73, 99
Royal Family, 43, 46, 56, 79, 87, 106, 110, 150, 151, 165, 180, 193
Russell, Fred, 52, 67

Sachs, Leonard, 32
Sandow (Strong Man), 35, 72, 146
Sheckman, Solly, 184, 197-198
Sheridan, Mark, 40, 89
Sherwood, Tom, 77, 86, 91
Shields, Ella, 51, 62, 92
Slater, Jimmy, 97
Slingsby, Harry (Captain), 129
Soo, Chung Ling (Magician), 71-72
South of England Hippodromes, 171-172
Stoll, John G., 141
Stoll, Oswald (Sir), 20-21, 37, 64, 85, 105, 129, 134-136, 140-156, 159, 164, 171-172, 182
Stoll Tour, 84, 89, 100, 140-156
Stratton, Eugene, 36, 73, 80, 115, 151, 179, 183
Stuart, Leslie, 73, 80
Sutton, Randolph, 92
Sweeney, Sam, 31, 38, 146, 180

Tate, Harry, 97, 130
Tate, J. W., 92, 132
Thornton, Charles, 44-45
Thornton, Richard ('Dick'), 33-37, 49, 75, 89, 123-128, 134-138, 157, 184
Tich, Little, 24, 76-77, 183
'Tichborne Claimant', 31-32, 65, 123
Tilley, Vesta, 22, 31, 36-40, 49, 62-63, 135, 142-143, 168, 171, 173
Turner, Clarence ('Tubby'), 87

Valerie, Nita, 205
Vance, The Great, 58-59
Victoria, Vesta, 39, 47, 92

Walford Bodie ('Doctor'), 29, 47, 84, 98-101, 112, 163, 179, 182, 184
Wallace, Nellie, 43, 51, 62
Whelan, Albert, 63-64
Whiteman, John C., 46-47, 85, 88, 93, 130
Whittle, Charlie, 88
Williams, Bransby, 27, 46, 74-75, 181
Wilton, Robb, 42, 86
Wood, Fred, 44, 46, 70, 85, 88, 130
Wood, Wee Georgie (O.B.E.), 89-90, 114, 129
Worth, Harry, 94
Wright, Lawrence, 81

COLNE
Hippodrome, 200
COVENTRY
Coventry Theatre, 170
Hippodrome, 170
DARLINGTON
Astoria, 198
Livingstone Hall, 198
Hippodrome, 198-199
DERBY
Grand Theatre, 156
Hippodrome, 156
Palace, 66
DEWSBURY
Empire, 86, 115
Hippodrome, 158
Theatre Royal, 111
DONCASTER
Grand, 100, 198
Palace, 98
DUBLIN
Empire, 137
Star, 22
DUNDEE
Alhambra, 28
Clarence, 27
Gaiety, 28
Kings', 28
Palace Theatre, 28
Seagate, 27
EDINBURGH
Albert, 29, 124
Alhambra, 29, 124
Ducrow's Circus, 29, 124
Empire, 29, 70-71, 121, 125, 136
Gaiety, 29, 121, 124-125
Grand, 168
Operetta House, 122
Southminster, 29, 124
Theatre Royal, 138, 172
Tivoli, 158, 162, 168
Waverley Market, 29, 122, 124
GATESHEAD
Empire, 36, 62, 135, 137-138, 199
Hippodrome, 26
King's Theatre, 36, 135
Queens' Varieties, 26
Royal Varieties, 26
Theatre Royal, 26
GLASGOW
Alexandra, 30
Alhambra, 122, 138
Argyle Street Varieties, 128
Bostock's Zoo, 136, 159
Britannia, 30
'Campbell's', 29, 49
Coliseum, 89, 137
Collosseum, 48
Empire, 30, 128, 136
Empress, 50, 168
Falcon Theatre, 48-50
Folly, 29, 31, 49

GLASGOW—continued
Gaiety, 19, 27, 30, 124, 128-129
Garden of Eden, 30
Grand Theatre, 136-137
Hippodrome, 52, 136, 159-160, 162
Joytown, 168
Jupiter, 29, 40
'Levy's', 29
Magnet, 48-49
Metropole, 29, 48-50, 136-137
New Gaiety (Cinema), 128
New Metropole, 48, 50
Oddfellows', 29, 31, 48
Oxford, 30
Palace (Gorbals), 50, 168
Palace (Watson Street), 49
Pantoptican, 30
Pavilion, 56, 98, 168
Philharmonic, 29, 49
Princess' Theatre, 168
Queens', 30, 49
Scotia, 19, 29, 48-50, 73, 96, 124, 128
Shakespeare, 29
Star, 27-30, 124
Tivoli, 28, 49, 128
West End Playhouse, 50
Whitebait, 29-30, 49, 202
GOOLE
Coliseum, 55
GREENOCK
Empire, 28
Lorne, 49, 121
GRIMSBY
Empire, 24
Hippodrome, 185
Palace, 185, 201
Prince of Wales' Theatre, 185
Theatre Royal, 185
Tivoli, 185, 201
HALIFAX
Alhambra (Cinema), 178
Gaiety, 130
Grand Theatre, 130, 183
Oddfellows' Hall, 158, 178, 183
Palace, 87, 95, 182-184, 189
Peoples' Palace, 178, 183
Shay Gardens Pavilion, 76
Templeton's Varieties, 77
HANLEY
Empire, 25, 133
Gaiety, 25, 31, 133, 158
Grand (Circus and Music Hall), 25, 133-135
Mitre, 25
Old Vine, 25
Peoples' Music Hall, 25
Pavilion, 25
Theatre Royal, 134
HARROGATE
Opera House, 111
HARTLEPOOL
Alhambra, 36
Empire, 36, 70, 135-138, 184
Gaiety, 184-185, 197